Too many works about spiritual warfare are more about Satan than God, more about anecdote than the Bible, and more about power displays than Christian discipleship. This book, too, will likely stretch you—perhaps even to points of disagreement at times—but it takes you to the bottom line of victory in spiritual warfare: living daily in the power of God. Read this book, and learn from a man who longs for the entire world to know this Christ-centered victory.

—DR. CHUCK LAWLESS,
Dean, Billy Graham School of Missions, Evangelism,
and Church Growth
The Southern Baptist Theological Seminary

Can there be consistent victory against our selfish disposition, our seductive and oppressing environment and the unseen, dark power of our enemy? Jerry Rankin answers these questions with a resounding "yes" in specific, clear, exciting, compelling biblical detail. The book is Scripture saturated, evangelical in orientation, and packed with powerful illustrations from the author's personal experience. It will give the reader guidance, encouragement, conviction, and hope for living a victorious Christian life.

—DR. ROBERTSON MCQUILKIN
President Emeritus, Columbia International University
Author of *Life in the Spirit* and *Living the Life*

If anybody knows that servants of God are in a furious battle with an unseen enemy, my friends Jerry and Bobbye Rankin do. If anybody knows that the enemy will do anything he can to halt kingdom work, Jerry and Bobbye Rankin do. And if any two people know how to brush themselves off after an unexpected assault, then stand back to their feet with twice the power, Jerry and Bobbye Rankin do. As the day-in, day-out leader of an army of several thousand missionaries mobilized around the globe, Dr. Rankin is in a unique position to tell people like you and me what God is doing around the world. From an eyes-on, hands-on perspective, he can also tell us what Satan is doing to try to stop him. As much as anyone I've ever met, Dr. Rankin knows this battle is real and what it takes to be consistently victorious. He is an experienced warrior in this worthy fight. He knows what works. He knows what doesn't. He also knows the roles of love and forgiveness, without which Jesus assured us a kingdom divides and falls. Of all things I love best about the Rankins, this is chief: they are rock solid in doctrine but not stifled or stuffy in how they live it out. They're all about Jesus and how He reaches the hearts, saves and fortifies the lives of real people.

—BETH MOORE, Author and teacher
Founder of Living Proof Ministries

SPIRITUAL
WARFARE

SPIRITUAL
WARFARE

THE BATTLE
FOR GOD'S GLORY

JERRY RANKIN

B&H
PUBLISHING GROUP
NASHVILLE, TENNESSEE

978-0-8054-4880-1

Published by B&H Publishing Group
Nashville, Tennessee

Dewey Decimal Classification: 235.4
Subject Heading: SPIRITUAL WARFARE \
DEVIL \ SPIRITUAL LIFE

7 8 9 10 11 12 • 18 17 16 15 14

DEDICATION

This book is dedicated to the thousands
of missionaries who have ventured into
Satan's territory to claim the kingdoms of
this world as the kingdoms of our Lord.
They have stood firm against religious
opposition, government restrictions,
and even persecution and have not succumbed
to the enemy's subtle efforts to discourage,
distract, and defeat them. With faith in the
Word of God, they have claimed the victory
purchased and assured by our Lord
Jesus Christ. They were driven by a vision
that God would be exalted among
the nations. God was glorified in their
lives because they did not love
their life, even unto death.

CONTENTS

FOREWORD

A theme central to Scripture but largely neglected; a hope that for most has withered—these come alive in the pages of *Spiritual Warfare: the Battle for God's Glory*. This is the life message of Jerry Rankin—lived out before written down, as I can testify from personal observation.

Is there any hope in this life for winning out in the battle against our selfish disposition? Our seductive and oppressing environment? The unseen dark power of our enemy? "Yes! Yes! Yes!" says Jerry Rankin. And he says it most convincingly.

And who can consistently experience this victory? Some spiritually elite among us? "No! No! No!" says Jerry Rankin. It's God's own intended birth gift to every one of His children. But how can this be? The author answers this question in specific, clear, exciting, compelling biblical detail.

The book is Scripture saturated. The author doesn't just cite proof texts for the points he wants to make. The Word comes alive in power as it is constantly woven into the text. The reader may not agree with the interpretation of some passage, given the hundreds that are used; but most are clearly the point of the passage.

The book is packed with powerful illustrations, many astonishingly so. I'm not one easily moved by the printed text, but more than once I found the tears flowing. Or the example so convicting I had to pause and ask God to forgive. Or to empower. Or times the story would evoke a simple, "Thank you, Jesus!"

The book, as one would expect from the author's background, speaks powerfully to the missionary. But the illustrations drawn from around the world are of equal benefit to the nonmissionary, because the biblical truth expounded is universal.

The book is broadly evangelical in orientation. The author demonstrates full confidence in the authority of Scripture but avoids extremes that often characterize teaching on a Spirit-energized life. Perhaps you may discover some disagreement in understanding what the Bible teaches on a particular point, given this large sweep of Bible teaching on the subject. But most surely will find . . .

- Clear guidance on how to live the promised life.
- Deep conviction about falling out of step with the Spirit.
- Strong encouragement to engage the battle.
- Hope surging that victory is indeed the Christian's birthright.

I did!

—Robertson McQuilkin
President Emeritus, Columbia International University
Author of *Life in the Spirit* and *Living the Life*

PREFACE

I'm not sure when I first became aware that the struggle to live a life worthy of my identity as a Christian was spiritual warfare. Becoming a Christian at the age of ten brought a consciousness of a relationship with God that was secure. I knew that trusting Jesus Christ as my personal Savior had resulted in my sins being forgiven. Nevertheless, there was a new sensitivity to wrongdoing and attitudes and behavior that were not appropriate for a Christian. I would like to think it was the conviction of the Holy Spirit, but at that age it was probably just as much the threat of a paddling or the displeasure of my parents that instilled a sense of guilt for frequent failure. I really did want to grow in my faith and live according to God's Word, but victory over my old sin nature continued to be elusive.

By the time I had finished high school and entered college, I was confident God was calling me into the ministry and possibly to missionary service. Someone gave me a book by C. S. Lewis called *The Screwtape Letters*. Reading that book made me aware there is an enemy who is determined to defeat us in our Christian walk. This enemy is intent on rendering us ineffective in our resolve to live for the Lord and serve Him. The book is a series of letters, as Lewis imagined they would be written, by Screwtape, the captain of one of Satan's demonic hosts, to one of his little demon agents, a nephew by the name of Wormwood. Wormwood had been assigned to a young man who had recently come to faith in Christ. I remember the book starting out with something of a reprimand of Wormwood. He had lost the battle for this individual's soul, a battle that could never be regained. But Screwtape proceeds to advise him that if he used appropriate strategies and clever tactics, he could be assured that this man's life would never count for anything as far as the kingdom of God is concerned.

The letters are advice on strategies to defeat a Christian in his daily life. One letter advises Wormwood to influence the young man to neglect his prayer time and devotional life, which would render him absolutely powerless. Another says to persuade him to doubt the truth and authority of God's Word. The result would be no foundation of faith on which to build an effective life in the power of God's Spirit. One of the tactics, with which I readily identified at that time in my vision of someday being a missionary, was particularly relevant. It was to let him have good intentions about serving the Lord and making plans about what he is going to do someday. But get him to procrastinate and keep putting it off, always seeing what he was going to do as something in the future. The letter suggests he'll never reach the point of realizing his only opportunity to have an impact on eternity comes in what he does in the present.

The book gave me valuable insights into the fact that subtly and cleverly Satan is trying to tempt us to sin and render us ineffective in serving God and living for Him. However, with maturity and additional challenges to my aspirations of attaining a Spirit-filled life, I came to realize that this adversary was not simply trying to trip me up by his occasional temptations but to deceive me into embracing a carnal, self-serving lifestyle. I found the struggle to interpret life and reality by my feelings and experiences, rather than the truth of God's Word, to be a continuing struggle. As a growing Christian I was disillusioned by the elusive victory and constant failure.

I understood the distinction between sin and righteousness and fairly successfully learned to appropriate God's grace rather than try to win that battle through my own efforts. As carnal values and immoral lifestyles lessened in their appeal, it was disconcerting to find that doubt and pride were devious ways the enemy continued to afflict me with his fiery darts. Awareness of ungodly attitudes hidden deep in my heart was evidence of a fallen nature not yet fully crucified. The external manifestations of Satan's power and dominion on the mission field through demon possession and the oppressive presence of evil in a world of spiritual darkness only served to enlighten my understanding that the real battle was within.

This book is an attempt to share the insights gained from my own pilgrimage. As a veteran missionary I shared my understanding with new colleagues arriving on the field. I hoped they could avoid my own years of struggle to lay hold to a higher dimension of victory not only in overcoming the cultural barriers used by the enemy but in spiritual equipping for the task. For several years this material has been shared in the orientation of new missionaries being sent out by the Southern Baptist International Mission Board. Many have written on the subject of spiritual warfare, and I have drawn insights from many of those resources, but basically the approach is to focus on what we are told in God's Word. Faith is the victory that overcomes the world. It is our shield of faith that quenches all the fiery darts of the evil one. That faith is not just our faith in Jesus Christ and His death on the cross that procured the victory for us, but it is faith to believe God and all that He says about our enemy and how we are to fight the battle.

The reader will discover that every reference to our enemy and spiritual warfare in the Word of God is in the context of victory. That being the case, I pray that the insights shared in this volume will help the reader grow in faith and claim the victory that we have been given in Jesus Christ, and God will be glorified.

I am indebted to the influence of many friends and colleagues over the years who modeled a life that glorified God. They testified of God's truth and nurtured in me an insatiable desire to live the kind of life of obedience that glorified Him. I have been humbled by the response to my teaching on this subject and the constant encouragement to share these insights in book form. I want to acknowledge the support and assistance of my wife, Bobbye, who was a loving critic of my communication style and helped to shape my words to conform to what she understood I wanted to say. Close friends and colleagues, Chuck Lawless and Clyde and Elaine Meador, patiently and meticulously reviewed the manuscript and helped shape the content and wording. A special word of appreciation is due to Anita Bowden who edited the manuscript and Fonceil Blake, my executive assistant, who provided technical assistance, covered administrative matters, and protected my calendar to allow the personal time needed to complete this project.

Also it has been a joy to work with the staff of B&H Publishing. Writing on such a topic has been a matter of spiritual warfare in itself, but George Williams and

David Shepherd patiently and persistently continued to encourage me in the project year after year, as did John Kramp of LifeWay Christian Resources. Brad Waggoner, Thomas Walters, Kim Stanford, and Jean Eckenrode have made this book a true partnership. Their apparent vision for its impact on the kingdom went beyond just publishing and marketing another book. It has been a blessing and joy to work with them.

—Jerry Rankin

CHAPTER 1

THE REALITY OF SPIRITUAL WARFARE

For our battle is not against flesh and blood,
but against the rulers, against the authorities, against
the world powers of this darkness, against the spiritual
forces of evil in the heavens.
—Ephesians 6:12

We had just arrived for our missionary assignment in Indonesia and were a few months into language study. Enjoying the tropical climate, adjusting to new culinary delights, and feeling welcome among the gracious, hospitable people of our host country, we were beginning to think we would evade the expected cultural shock in our smooth adjustment. One Monday morning our Sundanese household helper arrived for work emotionally distraught. She always went home to her village on weekends, and upon her return on this particular occasion, something was obviously troubling her.

"What's wrong? What happened?" we asked with concern. She explained that her daughter had become demon possessed. Not fully comprehending the situation she described, we were unprepared for her appeal that we go with her to her village and pray for her daughter. We had bonded closely with her; and although she was a Muslim, she respected us as missionaries and recognized that I was kind of like a priest or some kind of spiritual leader. It didn't matter whether we were Muslim or Christian; she just wanted someone with some spiritual authority and power to help her daughter.

We agreed to adjust our schedule to go with her to her village and pray for her daughter later in the week. I wasn't sure what we were going to encounter, so I spent the next couple of days praying and fasting. The serenity of the village, shaded by waving palm trees and surrounded by endless fields of golden rice ready for harvest, was broken only by barking dogs and children playing noisily. Thatched bamboo houses, each with an overhanging grass roof, built closely together, reflected community neighborliness. Friendly greetings belied the serious concern and understanding of why we had come.

As we entered the house and our eyes quickly adjusted from the bright sunlight to the darkened room, we found a beautiful teenager tied to the bamboo bed where she was sitting. Her clothes were torn, her hair disheveled, and she was snarling like an animal. When we walked into the room, she glared at us and said in clear and perfect English, "Jesus Christ is not God; Mohammed is the servant of the most high god." Well, OK; that's an expected Muslim perspective. I didn't think anything about it until her mother told us on the way home that her daughter had lived in this remote village all her life, was uneducated, and didn't speak English!

We prayed for her in the name of Jesus, and there was no visible response or results. I didn't know anything else to do. But it was an alarming experience. I began to think, *Is this what we're going to encounter here in Indonesia? Are we equipped for this?* It wasn't long until we began to learn that where the gospel has not been proclaimed and Jesus is not known, Satan has considerable dominion and power. Demon possession is not uncommon in such places; and we had, indeed, ventured into Satan's territory.

A few months later, when we were becoming involved in our assignment of starting house churches, I was leading a group that was ready to confess Christ as Lord and Savior. I could tell in their personal conversation that they were responding to the Bible studies and the witness I had been presenting. Dark-skinned Javanese were crowded into the dirt-floored house, the light from a dim, flickering lantern reflecting off white pairs of eyes. Each window was filled with the silhouettes of curious neighbors. I felt the moment had come when I could ask them individually, but simultaneously and collectively, to pray and become followers of Christ. Leading them to take this step and make this decision was an auspicious, holy moment.

As we were moving toward that point of invitation and decision, one of the women started screaming and cackling. She had been a part of the group week after week, had always seemed normal and attentive, but suddenly became disruptive. Everyone was clearly embarrassed and tried to hush her, but she just kept screaming. Spontaneously, without any forethought, I said, "In the name of Jesus, be quiet!" She suddenly slumped in her chair as if in a trance. We continued with the service, and in a moment she sat up, appeared to be normal, and, in fact, was one of those who received Christ as Savior that night. It was apparent that Satan was making a last-ditch effort to disrupt the loss of souls in his dominion and prevent these people from becoming followers of Christ.

My sensitivity to the reality of spiritual warfare has grown over the years. I'm not sure what I truly believed about the presence and activity of Satan prior to going to the mission field. My understanding of the struggle with sin, even as expressed in my preaching, had more to do with personal resolve and human effort than a battle that was going on in the spiritual realm of life. However, it did not take me long following my arrival in Indonesia as a missionary to lose all skepticism regarding the reality of the power of Satan as manifested in cultures and places where Christ is not known.

Some years later we were visiting one of our colleagues in Indonesia. While we were in their home, two university students dropped in for a visit. They had been studying English with this missionary couple and were gregarious and fluent. They were always excited about meeting Americans and practicing their English. As we were talking, my wife, Bobbye, moved the conversation to a spiritual focus. Confident that these students had heard a witness from this missionary family, she asked one of the young men about his understanding and impression of the Christian faith. The young man started perspiring and blushing, and it was apparent that he was uncomfortable. Suddenly he jumped up and darted out the door. His friend apologized for his abrupt behavior and, politely asking permission, also left. Our missionary friends explained to us that they had been witnessing to this young man, and according to their understanding he had made a pact with a "dukun," which is a kind of witch doctor that has power to cast spells, in order to get relief from an abusive father. He had had the dukun cast this spell, and as a result he was in spiritual bondage, as we would think of one selling his soul to the devil.

The last time the young man was in the missionary's home, he asked a lot of questions that reflected a spiritual inquisitiveness. The missionary got the Bible for him to read as they did not want their witness to appear to be just their words; they wanted him to read it as the authority of God's Word. They opened the Bible and pointed out the Scripture for him to read, and he said, "But there are no words there. The pages are blank." The print was there on paper, but he kept saying, "The pages are blank. There are no words in this book." The Scripture says the god of this world has blinded their eyes lest they see, hear, and understand (2 Cor. 4:3–4). There are many whose hearts are hardened and are spiritually blind, but it is disturbing to think that Satan could literally blind a person from seeing the Word of God.

A missionary in West Africa related the experience of a man telling him of his son's demon possession.

> For some time now he has had terrible visions
> at night and has fallen ill. After consulting my
> Muslim teacher and our village spirit doctor, we
> decided that we must give Adamou, my son, to the
> evil spirit that has been tormenting him before
> the spirit kills him. We purchased the black goat
> and the three white chickens needed for sacrifices
> to be made on the day of the ceremony. We took
> gifts, the sacrifices, and payment to the spirit
> doctor the day before the ceremony and received
> all the instructions for the coming day.

My son was visited by the spirits that last night before his ceremony. One could hear his cries all over the village. We all agreed it was the will of Allah that he would become one with the spirit the following day. At one point during the ceremony, the chickens were beheaded, and the blood was allowed to flow over my son's body. At that point a powerful spirit by the name of Fonda Beri took control of my son. He began to talk to us and tell us who he was. He told us that he would give us wisdom and guidance when we travel. Each time someone in the village wants to go on a trip, we must speak to him and find out the day we should leave and when we should return.

He threw my son about and rolled him in the sand before he left. At the end of the ceremony, the spirit doctor gave my son an amulet to wear around his neck, identifying him with his spirit. The next day we took my son to our Muslim teacher so we could buy another amulet for him to wear around his arm. This amulet has verses from the Koran in it and will protect my son each time he is possessed. I am now greatly respected in my village because my son is possessed by such a powerful spirit. Our family will receive many gifts in the future as people from my village come to gain wisdom from my son's spirit before they travel.

Well, how do you explain things like this? Are they just coincidences or natural phenomena? Or are they manifestations of a spiritual power? The Bible talks about demons and the spirits, and they clearly recognize Jesus. He conversed with them and attributed cause and effects to demons and their spiritual powers. Was the Bible just conforming to a primitive worldview because this is how people of that day understood it? Was aberrant behavior attributed to demons because they didn't really understand mental illnesses, epileptic seizures, and other psychological phenomena? Or could it be that we're the ones who are naïve in our Western rationalism and have discounted the reality of what goes on in the spiritual world?

Missionaries are aware of manifestations of Satan and demonic activity. Believers in the West also encounter Satan's activity in their lives and society every day. But we seldom recognize it because it is cleverly disguised and is discounted by our rational worldview. That is what this book is about. While there are those who see spiritual warfare in terms of demon possession, territorial spirits, generational bondage, or perceived outward manifestations of Satan's power and dominion in the world, the primary focus is what we encounter within our own lives. We need to recognize Satan's lies and deception and the attacks to which we are subjected daily. We need to understand how Satan defeats us and robs us of the victory and power we've been given. That's where the real battle lies. And only when we resist and walk in victory personally are we equipped to deal with some of the outward manifestations so prevalent in our world.

We are going to attempt to understand the reality of spiritual warfare, the nature and character of our enemy, some of his primary strategies that readily defeat us, and, finally, how we can walk in victory on a daily basis. As we study the truths of God's Word, Satan's lies will be exposed, and we will understand why faith, believing what God says, is the victory.

> *Spiritual warfare is not so much about demon possession, territorial spirits, or generational bondage as it is overcoming Satan's lies and deceits in our own life.*

Spiritual warfare needs to be understood in the context of God's purpose. He has a specific will for each of us, but basically His purpose and desire is to be glorified in our life. The Bible uses various terms to reinforce this. In Romans 8:29 God's purpose is that we be conformed to the image of Christ. "For those He foreknew He also predestined to be conformed to the image of His Son." Why does God predestine us to be conformed to the image of Christ? It is in order to glorify Him. Satan tempts us to sin in order to keep God from being glorified. We have an enemy that is intent on robbing God of His glory in our lives. God is glorified when we are conformed to the image of Christ and live like Him.

That is why He saved us, not just to keep us from going to hell. It was necessary for Jesus to bear the penalty of our sin on the cross so that by our believing in Him we could be restored to the image of Christ that had been lost in the fall and in our sin. God saves us by grace, not just so that we can be assured of eternal life in heaven. That's the bonus of having been restored to the image of Christ.

Paul's prayer in Ephesians 3:16 describes God's desire that we "be strengthened with power through His Spirit in the inner man." Why? Is it just for our blessing and benefit? No, it is for God's glory, and it comes from Christ dwelling in our hearts by faith as explained in verse 17. John 15:4 says we are "to abide in Christ" (NASB). First John 2:6 exhorts us to "walk just as He walked." Ephesians 5:18 describes it as to "be filled with the Spirit." All of this is what God does for us and desires for us because He is glorified when we abide in Him, live the Christlike life, and are filled and controlled by His Holy Spirit. It is not simply for our benefit. He saves us, redeems us, and restores us to a relationship with Himself, gives us a new life in Christ, and fills us with His Spirit not exclusively for our blessing but for His glory. Too often we think of becoming a Christian as just being saved from sin. But God's purpose is to conform us to the image of His Son; He has to redeem us from sin in order for that to happen. God's desire in your life—every day, all the time, in every behavior and attitude—is to be glorified. And that is His purpose in all that He does and allows to happen to us.

If God's purpose for us personally is that He be glorified in our life, what is God's purpose in the world and among the nations? It is also that He be glorified. That is His purpose in redeeming the nations and peoples of the world. It is why He calls us as His people to a mission task. He said in Psalm 46:10, "I am God, exalted among the nations, exalted on the earth." He wants the nations and all the peoples of the earth to praise Him and exalt Him. This is expressed in many references throughout the Bible such as Psalm 96:1–4, "Sing a new song to the LORD; sing to the LORD, all the earth. . . . Declare His glory among the nations, His wonderful works among all peoples. For the LORD is great and is highly praised." Obviously Satan does not want God to be glorified among the nations. Hence, the warfare commences to divert us from fulfilling our mission to declare His salvation among the nations. But neither does he want God to be glorified in our lives, so the warfare rages with him also as he does whatever it takes to deprive God of that which would glorify Him in our lives.

Notice what the Bible says about what God has given us as born-again believers and how Satan has deceived us and lied to us, convincing us to accept that which is contrary to God's truth.

- PEACE—John 14:27, "Peace I leave with you. My peace I give to you. I do not give to you as the world gives. Your heart must not be troubled or fearful."
- JOY—John 15:11, "I have spoken these things to you that My joy may be in you, and your joy may be complete."
- POWER and STRENGTH—Acts 1:8, "But you will receive power when the Holy Spirit has come upon you, and you will be My witnesses." Philippians 4:13, "I am able to do all things through Him who strengthens me."
- VICTORY—Luke 10:19, "Look, I have given you the authority . . . over all the power of the enemy."
- HOLINESS and BLESSING—Philippians 4:19, "My God will supply all your needs according to His riches in glory in Christ Jesus." Second Peter 1:3, "For His divine power has given us everything required for life and godliness."

We have all of these blessings because we are in Christ. This is what accompanies our salvation and what it means to be restored to the image of Christ. We don't struggle and work to have a life characterized by peace, joy, power, and victory over sin; we have already been given all of this because God's Holy Spirit lives within us. This is what God's Word tells us about the reality of our experience and position in Christ. It is all summed up in 2 Corinthians 5:17, "Therefore if anyone is in Christ, there is a new creation; old things have passed away, and look, new things have come."

These verses and promises are not unfamiliar, but are they a reality in your life? Are these characteristics evident in your daily experience? Instead of having abiding peace each day in every situation, do you struggle with anxiety? Do you find yourself worried about finances, security, the welfare of your children, or other concerns? Jesus said we have peace so where is all that worry and anxiety coming from? It is certainly not from God. Is someone robbing you of the peace He has given? In contrast with what God's Word tells us—that we have been given fullness of joy—do you struggle with discouragement, depression, inner turmoil, and conflicts? Could someone be twisting the thoughts and perceptions in our mind, causing us to doubt and disregard what Jesus has given us?

Instead of having power to be His witness, do you find yourself intimidated, hesitant, and shy about sharing your faith? Where is the evidence of the power He said we've been given when we received the Holy Spirit? Instead of walking in victory, do you accept defeat, struggle with temptation, and sin and look on living the Christian life as futile? Why do we spend so much time seeking our own comfort and security, influenced by the values and attractions of the world instead of accepting the sufficiency of blessings assured by God? He said He would give us everything that we need, but we take it upon ourselves to be sure that He doesn't drop the ball or something doesn't fall through the cracks. We are not sure God is going to provide for us adequately so we think we have to pick up that responsibility for Him.

Instead of holiness and godliness that comes from His presence within us, we struggle with temptation, lustful thoughts, and self-gratification as if all that has not really been crucified with Christ. Hebrews 6:9 says, "Dear friends, . . . we are confident of the better things connected with salvation." If this is the pattern of our lives, in contrast with what God said He has given to us, could it be that someone is deceiving us? Is it just our own weakness or lack of resolve, or is there an enemy that wants to defeat us? Is there someone who is striving to deprive us of all that would bring glory to God in our lives?

The reality is that we are in a battle. We see meager evangelistic results in our witness and mission efforts. We concede to obstacles raised by a postmodern world that resists and rejects our Christian message. But is this the way God intends for it to be? I often visit missionaries serving in places that are resistant to the gospel and see their discouragement. I ask, "What do you think God wants to do here?" They often reply, "I don't know. I would like to think He wants to bring these people to faith in Christ, but there is no evidence of that. We are just hoping for some response." Where did that attitude come from? God says, "I am God, exalted among the nations" (Ps. 46:10). Jesus said, "If I am lifted up from the earth I will draw all people to Myself" (John 12:32). Who discourages us to believe contrary to what God has said, accepting obstacles to global evangelization, when that is clearly

God's purpose? Who discourages us from a persistent witness because we are convinced it is futile and people will not respond? And even when we have success, it is often followed by dissension, disrupted by moral failure with our own minds constantly fighting defeatist attitudes.

I once read a newsletter from a missionary couple serving in West Africa. They said, "When we got married, we agreed there was one word we would never use, never even think about—divorce. We just don't allow ourselves to go there, don't even entertain the thought. Murder, perhaps, but we would never discuss or even think about divorce!" They continued, "And when we were appointed missionaries, we made a similar decision that we would never talk about resignation because God had led us here. Whatever the cost, we'll never even entertain the thought of being disobedient to serve God where He has led us." They went on to describe discouragement, a burglary, mugging, and illnesses that everyone seems to be subjected to in West Africa—things that bring a lot of missionaries home. "But we just made the decision, 'We're not going there,'" they said. "We're going to believe God and be obedient to His call."

Why is it that Satan is able to get a foothold in our thoughts and feed discouragement and defeatist attitudes? Why is it so easy for him to get us to focus on our own comforts and needs, nurture a sense of entitlement and turn us away from obedience? It is because of our self-centered nature and what we want and feel we deserve. In the process God is robbed of the glory He desires in our life and ministry. We may not neglect to witness or be disobedient to God's will, but when we act and express attitudes contrary to the nature and character of Christ, God is no longer glorified.

However, we seldom think of this as spiritual warfare. It is so normal that we just brush off as human nature the lack of spiritual maturity, or weakness in our own faith and commitment. After all, this is just the way we live. We accept it as the norm. But we need to understand that the effectiveness of Satan's strategy demands anonymity. Sometimes the evil manifestations of his work are open and blatant. But his deception is most successful because of his ability to work in secrecy and darkness. If his tactics were to be exposed, and we were readily aware of how Satan is distorting the Word of God and deceiving us to embrace defeat, we would readily resist it. We don't realize that it is his deception and lies that cause us to accept less than what Christ has given us and to disregard the promises of God that would enable us to walk in victory.

We need to recognize the reality of spiritual warfare and that we have an enemy robbing us of a victorious life in order to deprive God of His glory in our lives. We may accept it as the normal reality of our day-by-day life, but it is not what God intends for us. Yet that is what Satan wants us to think because he does not want to be exposed. In fact, to expose him and bring his tactics to light is to defeat him because he works most effectively in darkness and deception. John 3:20–21 puts the deeds of Satan in this perspective when it explains, "For everyone who practices wicked things hates the light and avoids it, so that his deeds may not be exposed. But anyone who

> *Satan's primary objective is to rob God of His glory in our lives.*

lives by the truth comes to the light, so that his works may be shown to be accomplished by God."

I have been sharing these studies in each session of our missionary orientation and training for several years. I must confess I really don't like to do these studies because I have learned each time that I will come under attack. Something will happen—a word of criticism, a letter or e-mail that will attack my integrity, misunderstanding with a colleague, something that is totally abnormal. I can feel the anger rising up within me and this voice saying, "Who do you think you are, talking about spiritual warfare and how to claim spiritual victory?" Self-doubts and a sense of unworthiness plague my mind. My notes seem to be just words, lacking conviction and a genuine expression of my life. It invariably happens, and I have often thought it would be easier simply not to teach on spiritual warfare. Others testify about things occurring that are not normal during the sessions. Conflict and distractions interfere with being able to focus on the lessons. Satan will try to distract us, create doubts, and bring personal attacks to try to contradict the truth of God's Word. As you read this book, let me encourage you to pray for God's hedge of protection because Satan does not want you to grasp and apply what His Word clearly tells us about his tactics in our life. He does not want to be exposed, nor does he want us to claim the victory God has given us.

Scripture alerts us over and over to the fact that we are to be sober, serious, vigilant, and alert. It is amazing how we just brush over those warnings and ignore the implications of what God is trying to tell us. Members of an army battalion are most vulnerable when they think enemy troops are nowhere near. If they think the enemy is hundreds of miles away, they can relax and take a little R&R.

That's when they're most vulnerable, when they think an attack is not eminent. But soldiers are most vigilant when they know the enemy is right over the next hill and is going to attack at any time. This is what the Bible tells us about our enemy in the spiritual realm. We are told time and time again that our enemy is like a roaring lion seeking to devour us. He is always there. He is seizing every moment, every opportunity. We are enlightened regarding his tactics. We are told to stand firm, to be alert. Don't give place to the devil. Resist him. But who causes all this to be ignored? Who obscures these warnings in our thinking to keep us from being constantly vigilant? Who keeps us from recognizing what is happening when something in our life is contrary to the Spirit of Christ and to the holiness and faith to which God calls us?

Do you ever find your mind wandering during prayer and Bible study? My wife, Bobbye, and I have our personal devotional time each morning and later usually pray together. Sometimes she will ask, "What are you reading in your devotional time?" And I would reply with reference to the passage, "Well, I'm over in Leviticus, chapters 16, 17, 18." "What did you read?" she would ask. "What did the Lord say to you?" I would often stammer in reply, "Well, you know— Leviticus 16, 17, 18." I had no idea what I had read! I find that happens often while praying in the morning. I have an agenda and prayer concerns a mile long! I never get them covered. I start pouring out my heart in supplication regarding all the things that I'm dealing with and need help with. I'll suddenly realize that I'm not praying at all; I'm fretting. I'm working out all of my plans for the day and what I'm going to do. I'm no longer talking to God and worshipping Him; I'm planning my agenda.

Does that just happen? After all, my intention is to glorify God by coming to Him in fellowship and prayer. Maybe that doesn't happen to anyone else. But could it be that we have an enemy who has access to our mind and is constantly trying to interfere with our communion, disrupting our intimacy with the Father? Is there someone who wants to prevent me from experiencing the fullness of blessing and assurance of what God wants to be revealed in me? Has someone deceived us to think it just happens or that it's hard to concentrate on God in prayer or to understand His Word?

You would think the Scripture says, "Ignore the devil and he will flee from you." That's what we do most of the time. We just ignore him. We don't pay any attention to him. To the contrary, to ignore the devil and fail to heed what the Bible tells us about the reality of our adversary is to become vulnerable to his deceit and lies and give him free access to our heart.

Look at some of those familiar passages of Scripture that tell us about the reality of spiritual warfare. As you read the Bible with the idea of spiritual warfare in mind, it's amazing the volume of Scripture that reinforces this theme.

> Finally, be strengthened by the Lord and by His vast strength. Put on the full armor of God so that you may stand against the tactics of the Devil. For our battle is not against flesh and blood, but against the rulers, against the authorities, against the world powers of this darkness, against the spiritual forces of evil in the heavens. This is why you must take up the full armor of God, so that you may be able to resist in the evil day, and having prepared everything, to take your stand. (Eph. 6:10–13)

Be sober! Be on the alert! Your adversary the Devil is prowling around like a roaring lion, looking for anyone he can devour. Resist him, firm in the faith. (1 Pet. 5:8–9)

We know that we are of God, and the whole world is under the sway of the evil one. (1 John 5:19)

For although we are walking in the flesh, we do not wage war in a fleshly way, since the weapons of our warfare are not fleshly, but are powerful through God for the demolition of strongholds. We demolish arguments and every high-minded thing that is raised up against the knowledge of God, taking every thought captive to the obedience of Christ. (2 Cor. 10:3–5)

In every situation take the shield of faith, and with it you will be able to extinguish the flaming arrows of the evil one. (Eph. 6:16)

Therefore, submit to God. But resist the Devil, and he will flee from you. (James 4:7)

It is obvious that Satan is diametrically opposed to Christ, to the church, to the extension of God's kingdom, and to individual Christians experiencing the God-glorifying power, blessings, victory, and fullness of God's Spirit that He intends. He is behind spiritual failure, discord, dissension, carnal living, and worldliness. He seeks to deprive God of being glorified in our lives by defeating us and robbing us of everything God has given us.

In John 10:10 Jesus alerts us, "A thief comes only to steal and to kill and to destroy. I have come that they may have life and have it in abundance." Christ has given us the victory. He has given us everything we need to fulfill His calling and to live for Him. But Satan robs us of the joy and peace Christ has given. Through doubt he destroys the sense of power that we should have to witness and serve God effectively. He deprives us of the holy life and blessing we have in Christ by deceiving us to embrace that which is contrary to God's will. When we come to Christ and are born again, Satan has lost the battle for our souls. We belong to God, and Satan can never regain ownership. But in vengeance and jealousy of God's glory, he does all he can to defeat us, rob us, and destroy the victory we have in Christ.

He lies; he deceives; he works through our minds to distort God's truth, convincing us to see circumstances from our perspective rather than believing what God tells us. We often wake up in the morning and begin the day by succumbing to Satan's lies. The alarm clock didn't go off. We wake up and are running late, and the kids are already squabbling and fussing; it's raining outside, and we think in exasperation, *It's going to be one of those days!* The day begins with a defeatist attitude. Who plants those thoughts in our mind contrary to what God says? We are told, "This is the day the LORD has made; let us rejoice and be glad in it" (Ps. 118:24). "Because of the LORD's faithful love we do not perish, for His mercies never end. They are new every morning; great is Your faithfulness" (Lam. 3:22–23). Do we think God's thoughts? Do we accept His truth? Do we see reality in terms of what He tells us? Or do we interpret our daily experiences and circumstances by what Satan puts in our minds? We have an enemy who constantly speaks to us, shaping our thoughts in subtle and devious ways to accept attitudes contrary to what God tells us. He causes us to deny the truth of God's Word, yield to our natural tendencies, and forfeit the blessing and victory God has provided and intends for us to have.

Second Corinthians 2:11 says with reference to Satan, "For we are not ignorant of his intentions." To be ignorant of Satan's schemes and devices is to be defeated by the devil, conformed to the world, and defiled by the flesh. In fact, we have a trinitarian enemy. The devil is opposing us. The world around us is distracting us. The flesh—that old, sinful nature—is within us, seeking to defile us. They are all conspiring to defeat us, collaborating and working together to rob God of His glory in our life. The battlefield is our life, our soul. Satan uses our old, sinful nature and convinces us that it has not been crucified and rendered powerless, in spite of what God's Word tells us. Christ is victorious, but we are robbed of His power and the reality of that victory when we allow the values and attractions of this world to permeate our thinking and influence our values rather than living in submission to His lordship. As long as we're in this present world, Satan is using it to pervade our thinking and shape our values. Spiritual warfare is an ongoing, daily reality.

C. S. Lewis said in his introduction to *The Screwtape Letters* that we're often guilty of two equal and opposite

> *The devil is against us, the world is around us, and the flesh is within us, collaborating to defeat us in our Christian walk.*

errors. One is to disbelieve in the existence of Satan. The other is an excessive, unhealthy obsession with him. With either, he is delighted. We need to realize the danger of each of these. If one doesn't believe in the reality of a personal devil and the spiritual powers of darkness that exist in our world, that makes one extremely vulnerable. Not only does it deny the truth of God's Word, but such skepticism gives Satan free reign to influence our thoughts and behavior. But on the other hand, to have an excessive, unhealthy obsession with Satan—the attitude that the devil made me do it or there is a demon behind every bush—attributes to him a power and control that he just does not have. Giving the enemy excessive attention feeds his deceptive lies, and deception and brings our thoughts and attitudes into conformity with his perspective. Rather, in faith we must believe the truth of God's Word and accept that the victory God has given us is reality.

We also make a mistake in how we think of Satan relative to the Holy Spirit, especially in our understanding of the battle between the flesh and the spirit. We often consider them on a par with each other, as if they were two equal combatants seeking to claim our allegiance and control our actions. There is a tension between good and evil; Satan seeks to entice us to choose his way while the Holy Spirit is jealous for us as God's possession. We are often deceived even in our distorted understanding of the warfare. Persuaded that Satan has a power that, in fact, he does not have, we readily give in to our selfish nature, an inclination to sin and embrace carnal, worldly values. That Satan has such a power is an illusion fed by his deception.

Who is the Holy Spirit that lives within us? He is Almighty God—Jesus Christ, to whom all power and authority have been given. But who is Satan? The devil is a created being, a fallen angel. The word *angel* in the Scripture means "messenger." While angels are spiritual, heavenly hosts created to worship God, their assigned role is that of a messenger. As a messenger, Satan primarily speaks to our minds. There are Old Testament passages that speak of disasters and affliction being attributed to Satan. Jesus spoke of the woman bent over as being in bondage to Satan, but Satan does not have power in the physical realm except as it is granted by God. If Satan were given authority and power over the physical domain of life, expressways would be a massive pileup of wrecks, and everybody would be stricken with cancer. But he doesn't have that kind of power or liberty to destroy life. As in the example of Job, he was able to do nothing apart from God's permission, and the only reason God allowed him physically to afflict Job was so that God would be ultimately glorified. God is sovereign over the universe, and Satan is only a messenger, a fallen angel. His only power and authority are in speaking to our minds, hence his strategy is to deceive us that we might embrace something that is not true and contrary to God's Word.

An illustration of this would be our quoting Romans 8:28 in times of hardship, trials, or adversity. "We know that all things work together for the good of those who love God: those who are called according to His purpose." We are not blaming God for what happens to us. But we recognize the providence and sovereignty of God—that He can take any disaster or tragedy, the grief experiences of life, and has the power and ability to bring good out of it. He can use it for our welfare and blessing. In the same way Satan doesn't cause all the trials and adversities in life, but if we believe him rather than God, he can use those same circumstances for evil to defeat us and to rob us of victory. He is a messenger, who distorts God's truth and seeks to change our perspective on our circumstances and daily experiences by his lies and deception.

In 2 Thessalonians Paul commends the believers at Thessalonica for their faithfulness, even in the midst of persecution and affliction. He assures them of his prayers on their behalf, "So that the name of our Lord Jesus will be glorified by you, and you by Him" (2 Thess. 1:12). He acknowledges that they have an adversary but affirms God had given them the victory over him. "But the Lord is faithful; He will strengthen and guard you from the evil one" (2 Thess. 3:3).

In his book *Victory over the Devil,* Jack Taylor writes, "We need to discover there is a battle, decide that we are on the Lord's side, declare that He has won, and determine that we will walk from victory unto victory."[1] A major part of the victory in spiritual warfare is awareness—recognizing and understanding the reality of the battle on a day-by-day basis. Being perceptive and aware of the schemes and strategies of our enemy, we need to decide we belong to the Lord and affirm all that we have in Him. We have everything God's Word tells us has been given to us in Christ. We must not allow Satan to deceive us and convince us otherwise. We declare that Christ has won the battle, and we can walk in that victory.

CHAPTER 2

THE NATURE OF OUR ENEMY, PART I

So the great dragon was thrown out—the ancient serpent who is called the Devil and Satan, the one who deceives the whole world. He was thrown to earth and his angels with him.
—Revelation 12:9

When I became president of the International Mission Board and moved to Richmond, Virginia, my wife and I had been in Asia for twenty-three years. We had lived in some remote places, and I can assure you we didn't have much that was appropriate to bring home to America to set up housekeeping in Richmond. We had to go through the process of buying a house, furnishing it, and decorating it. It was a long, time-consuming process and took a while since we were fully engaged in other responsibilities. As we made decisions about color schemes, window treatments, rugs, furniture, and decor, we found that we didn't necessarily agree, but we eventually made it through those decisions, and our marriage survived! As we were discussing the decor of the house, my wife, Bobbye, said, "I want the Word of God in every room in our house." Like many families we have some cross-stitched Scripture verses and framed plaques, but what she was implying was, "I want the Word of God to be a reminder to us in every room of His presence and that we belong to Him."

During that time I was seeking to develop these studies on spiritual warfare, and I thought, *Satan probably has the Word of God posted in every room and corridor of hell.* The verse that I believe he has posted there is Matthew 24:14, where Jesus said, "This good news of the kingdom will be proclaimed in all the world as a testimony to all nations. And then the end will come." Why would Satan be so obsessed with that verse? He knows that the end will come, and he knows exactly what that implies. All of his wickedness and trickery will be finished. He and all of his demons will be cast into the lake of fire and outer darkness. But Jesus said that won't happen until the gospel has been proclaimed in the whole world to the *pante ta ethne*, all the peoples of the world.

Could Satan have had anything to do with totalitarian governments keeping nations closed to a missionary witness? For seventy years he thought this strategy was working in the Soviet Union and Eastern Europe, as he kept many of the peoples of the world from having access to the gospel. But those barriers have crumbled in God's providence. That strategy is no longer working.

Only in the last twenty years or so, we have come to understand our mission task in terms of the people groups of the world. Our task is not just sending a missionary to a nation, the countries on our map. Jesus has sent us to disciple all the people groups of the world—all the language, ethnic, and cultural groups. That was not understood previously as we saw our mission task in terms of evangelizing each country. Could Satan have had anything to do with distorting and diverting our mission strategy in carrying out the Great Commission so that vast people groups would remain hidden from our awareness, neglected in our witness and still unreached? Perhaps so, but obviously that strategy, which worked so successfully for centuries, is now failing as research has revealed more than eleven hundred people groups in the world, and those groups are systematically being reached with the gospel.

However, it seems that Satan has another strategy to oppose the advancement of God's kingdom and His being glorified among the nations. This may be the most effective of all—convincing Christians that missions is optional. One can choose to be involved or not. My own denomination takes pride in five thousand missionaries, but that's only .03 percent of Southern Baptists who take the Great Commission seriously and personally by going in response to God's call. Our forty-three thousand churches channel only 2.5 percent of their financial resources to international missions. Satan's strategies are apparently effective in keeping those words of Jesus from being fulfilled because he is effectively keeping the good news from being proclaimed to all nations and peoples.

In our own life, when he gets us to live for self rather than in submission to the lordship of Christ, when he influences us to speak and act in ways that do not bless and edify others and to behave contrary to the character and nature of Christ, he has successfully won a victory and deprived God of His glory.

Why are we subjected to spiritual warfare? Isn't God all powerful? Hasn't Jesus already defeated the devil on the cross? Why doesn't He just put a hedge of protection around us? "They belong to Me. You have no business interfering in their lives and robbing them of My blessings. I'm not going to allow you to tempt this brother and deceive him." Why aren't we immune from temptations once we put our faith in Jesus Christ? Can we just say, "Greater is He who is in me than he that is in the world" (1 John 4:4, author's paraphrase) or claim the blood of Jesus, and that will take care of it?

Something is to be said about what we confess and how it is connected to what we believe—what we have faith in. But there must be some substance behind our confession. The words of our mouth must truly reflect the devotion of our heart; otherwise our words are empty confessions and meaningless in terms of empowerment in the spiritual realm.

> Victory in spiritual warfare is not a formula but learning to appropriate by faith the victory Jesus has already given us.

Victory in spiritual warfare is not a simple formula. It is not a matter of instructions on how to do it or what to say in steps 1, 2, and 3. Victory is the fruit of our relationship with the Lord as we walk with Him and learn to appropriate by faith the victory He has already given us. Jesus is our victory. He is the one who has defeated Satan. But victory implies a battle. If we are to be victorious in that battle, we need to understand the nature of our enemy.

Satan is a created being, a fallen angel created by God. Being all-knowing and omniscient, God knew that Satan would rebel and fully understood the ramifications of what his fall would entail. Does this make God responsible for evil? After all we reason that He didn't have to go ahead and create him. He obviously had the power in His providence to keep that from happening. Some rationalize that God created Satan deliberately and allowed evil to come into the world out of the necessity of giving us freedom of choice. To choose, there have to be options. If we cannot choose, we really don't have a free will. We are just a kind of puppet or robot. However, we are created in the image of God with free will and the capacity to choose or reject God and His will. Was creating Satan, knowing he would fall and bring evil into the world, a moral necessity? Answering such questions in the affirmative should bring us to the conclusion that such an explanation is contrary to the nature of God. Yet some theologians and many everyday Christians rationalize and want to blame God for the evil in the world as well as for the dilemma we face in spiritual warfare.

Many Christians have accepted a common perception that is sometimes called "diabolical dualism." They reason that God is not responsible for Satan and evil cannot be attributed to Him. God didn't create evil, and it wasn't an intentional part of God's original plan. But it's like a cancer that has grown out of His control. Evil and injustice are rampant in our world today; carnal values and immorality are pervasive in our own society and throughout the world. Surely God never intended it to be this way and is not pleased, but it has grown beyond His control to do anything about it. However, this is not biblical and clearly demeans who God is and His power. It also dismisses the victory Christ has won on the cross and God's redemptive activity as irrelevant. We cannot simply deny His power, authority, and sovereignty in an effort to understand the current condition of our world, spiritual warfare, and the one behind it.

Following the tragedy of September 11, 2001, in which thousands died in terrorist incidents at the Pentagon and the World Trade Center, the secular media and commentators expressed an interesting perspective. In their typical skepticism they questioned the existence of God. They reasoned that if there was a God, He was not all-powerful or He would have prevented such a tragedy. However, if God is all-powerful, they said that He is not good, or He would not have allowed such a massive loss of life. The same reasoning emerged after a quarter of a million people lost their lives in the Asia tsunami in December 2004. God is either not all-powerful, or He is not good because if He is good He would not have allowed this to happen, so He must not be all-powerful. But if He is all-powerful, He must not be good because He had the power to keep this from happening and didn't do it. It is obvious where such twisted logic leads.

As servants of the one God who is the holy, righteous, all-wise, and all-powerful Creator of the universe, we must reject all explanations of Satan's origin, power, and activity that contradicts God's revelation of Himself in His Word. We must start with a firm understanding of God's perfect moral nature as holy, good, and righteousness, and that He is an omnipotent, all-powerful God, Sovereign over the universe. People have debated the source of sin and evil in our world for centuries and will continue to do so. But we obviously have to start with a foundational, unequivocal understanding of who God is and His nature as we try to understand the one who is opposed to His glory in our lives.

The reality is that creation was a part of God's plan and design. God made man in His own image, which included the capacity of free will. Loving and serving God would be meaningless if it were not a volitional choice and we had no other alternative. Apparently angels, as heavenly, spiritual beings created to serve and worship God, have this same choice. Satan is a fallen angel who coveted God's glory and chose to rebel against God's authority.

The reference in Isaiah 14:12–14 is usually considered an analogy to this event. "Shining morning star, how you have fallen from the heavens! You destroyer of nations, you have been cut down to the ground. You said to yourself: 'I will ascend to the heavens; I will set my throne above the stars of God. I will sit on the mount of the gods assembly, in the remotest parts of the North. I will ascend above the highest clouds; I will make myself like the Most High.'" Ezekiel 28 and Revelation have similar references, but notice the arrogance that characterizes his nature. "I will ascend. I will be exalted. I will be like the Most High."

We need to realize that blatant, immoral evil is no worse than a self-centered life. All rebellion against God and living for self deprives God of His glory and is contrary to His will. The exaltation of self and disobedience characterize Satan. And we are going to see that this is basically the nature of the flesh in the battle between the flesh and the Spirit. The flesh is not just blatant sin and immorality; it's essentially a self-centered life, living for self instead of God.

Because of his rebellion Satan was rejected from heaven, and the warfare commenced. I believe the words of Jesus in Luke 10:18 referenced this event prior to the foundation of the world. The disciples, having returned from their evangelistic tour of proclaiming the gospel of the kingdom and healing the sick, reported they were amazed to find that even the demons were subjected to them. In response to this testimony, Jesus said, in reference to His eternal preexistence as one with the Godhead, "I watched Satan fall from heaven like a lightning flash" (Luke 10:18).

Yes, God knew the consequences that would follow when Satan was cast out of heaven. He knew the temptation that Satan would bring to man, the crown of His creation. He foresaw the evil and conflict that would be fomented in the world. But God's love was so amazing, He went ahead with creation, knowing the battle that would ensue. He was not responsible for Satan's rebellion and self-serving motives that catapulted him from His holy presence, but God was fully aware of the continual warfare to which we would be subjected. But even before the foundation of the world, redemption was planned, and victory was assured—not just ultimately or theoretically but as a daily reality to those who are in Christ. In fact, following that first sin in the garden of Eden, God made clear what the outcome would be. In Genesis 3:14–15 God said Satan, the serpent, would be cursed, and the seed of the woman, the Redeemer who would come, would strike his head.

God allowed evil and suffering to be perpetrated against Job because of the greater glory that would accrue from his faithfulness. In the same way we will bring greater glory to God by our faithfulness in claiming the victory in temptation and trials than if we had never experienced them. Scripture reveals a great deal about the reality of spiritual warfare, but every reference is in the context of victory. However, we are going to see that even Scripture has been distorted to get us to accept defeat, to believe that victory is elusive, and to believe Satan has a power over us contrary to the truth of God's Word.

Satan Is an Adversary

We need to consider what the Scripture reveals about our enemy. Knowing his characteristics helps us understand the nature of his strategy and how he works. Obviously the Bible describes him as an adversary. In fact, the word *devil* comes from the Greek word *diabolos,* which means "to oppose." Satan is antagonistic to God's plans and purposes. He wages continual warfare, seeking to counter everything that would glorify God. But he can't win; he has already been defeated on the cross.

Colossians 2:14–15 says, "He erased the certificate of debt, with its obligations, that was against us and opposed to us, and has taken it out of the way by nailing it to the cross. He disarmed the rulers and authorities and disgraced them publicly; He triumphed over them by Him."

Hebrews 2:14 says, "Now since the children [that's us] have flesh and blood in common, He also shared in these, so that through His death He might destroy the one holding the power of death—that is, the Devil." Jesus became flesh in order to die. God can't die; He's eternal. Yet as the only sinless being qualified to die for our sins, He had to become a man, incarnate in flesh and blood, to identify with us, the children, in order to die. Included in His redemptive purpose of dying was God's provision to defeat the devil and render him powerless.

Why are we subjected to those continual accusations and temptations if Satan has been disarmed and defeated? First John 3:8 says, "The Son of God was revealed for this purpose: to destroy the Devil's works." Has Christ come? Has He been revealed? Has He died? Yes, and this is what He did in His death. Satan was defeated. So what's the explanation of Satan's power and influence being so pervasive in our world and in our lives? Why do we continue to be susceptible to his lies and deception?

Basically it's about vengefulness. Satan has been defeated. He has been thrown out of heaven. One day he will be cast into outer darkness, and all his wickedness and deceit will be finished forever. Revelation 20:2–3 tells us of this future judgment when "He seized the dragon, that ancient serpent who is the Devil and Satan, and bound him for 1,000 years. He threw him into the abyss, closed it, and put a seal on it so that he would no longer deceive the nations."

Meanwhile he is trying to thwart God's purpose to be exalted among the nations and to delay His kingdom being extended to the ends of the earth. He finds delight in getting us to choose sin and self instead of glorifying God by submitting to His will and living a righteous and holy life. Satan is gratified when he can deceive those in the world to embrace the shallow, false riches of worldly values. He is especially elated when he can get those of us who are God's possession, a holy people, to fail to reflect the excellencies of His glory in our lives. In vengefulness he is seeking to deprive God of His glory.

The real battle is Satan's opposition to God. He is jealous of God's power and glory. In vengefulness he seeks to embarrass God through our failure and carnal living. We are constantly under attack. Satan wants to destroy and defeat us, but we are pawns he uses in the conflict against God. He delights in thumbing his nose at God when we act with self-serving motives and indulge in lustful gratification rather than walking in holiness and obedience to God. Even when we try to live the Christian life in our own strength and effort rather than accepting the power of God's Holy Spirit,

Satan is mocking God because of our lack of faith to believe and accept the victory He has given us.

The assurance of victory is especially evident in our mission task to proclaim the gospel to the nations. We are told in Habakkuk 2:14, "The earth will be filled with the knowledge of the LORD's glory, as the waters cover the sea." Psalm 22:27–28 says, "All the ends of the earth will remember and turn to the LORD. All the families of nations will bow down

> *Scripture reveals a great deal about spiritual warfare, but every reference is in the context of victory!*

before You, for kingship belongs to the LORD; He rules over the nations." Now that is reality, albeit in the future. That's what God is in the process of doing in the world. But obviously Satan doesn't want that to happen.

Satan's opposition to God's kingdom purpose was evident in the temptations of Jesus. Luke 4:5–7 reveals a portion of this encounter. "So he took Him up and showed Him all the kingdoms of the world in a moment of time. The Devil said to Him, 'I will give You their splendor and all this authority, because it has been given to me, and I can give it to anyone I want. If You, then, will worship me, all will be Yours.'" Of course, Jesus did not succumb to that temptation. But I am intrigued by the fact that He never contradicted the right of Satan to make that claim. "All the kingdoms of the world belong to me." Where Christ is not known—where He is not acknowledged as Lord—the cultures and nations and peoples of the world are the kingdoms of Satan, under dominion to the powers of darkness.

He is opposed to the kingdoms of the world becoming the kingdom of our Lord.

When we arrived in Indonesia to begin our church planting ministry, we were committed to our call and believed in the power of the gospel to draw people to Christ. I envisioned arriving on the shores of Indonesia and the pages of Acts unfolding once again with multitudes being saved every day. They were just waiting for us to get there with the good news of the gospel. Well, obviously, it didn't happen that way. We had amazing opportunities to witness and to preach openly in this Muslim country, and yet the people were largely indifferent and even antagonistic to our message. I know my language skills were not exceptional, but the people would just look at me with blank stares on their face as if what I was saying did not relate to them. I wanted to shake them and say, "Don't you realize what I'm saying?" But I came to understand that to expect a Muslim in Indonesia to respond to the gospel was not unlike asking a blind man to read a newspaper. For the Scripture says the god of this world has blinded their eyes lest they should see and hear and understand and turn again and be saved. Second Corinthians 4:4 speaks of the gospels being veiled to those who are perishing, "Regarding them: the god of this age has blinded the minds of the unbelievers so they cannot see the light of the gospel of the glory of Christ, who is the image of God."

One doesn't have to go overseas to encounter those who are blinded to the gospel and whose hearts are hardened by Satan. When I was a youth minister in Fort Worth while in seminary, a student named Steve lived down the street from the church. Everybody knew him. He was a good friend to many of the church kids, but Steve and his family didn't come to church; he was unsaved and at the top of our prospect list. Almost on a weekly basis someone would call on Steve during visitation. As youth minister I tried to cultivate a friendship and often witnessed to him without success. He never came to church or showed any interest in becoming a Christian although I explained the gospel every way I could in appealing to him. He was finally persuaded to attend one of our youth retreats and made a profession of faith when a friend who played on the baseball team with him led him to the Lord. Of course we were all thrilled that Steve had finally been saved. At the conclusion of the retreat, various teenagers were giving their testimonies, including Steve, who shared about trusting the Lord. In his testimony he mentioned that he had never heard the gospel until his friend witnessed to him! I thought, *How could he say that considering how many times I, and many others, had shared the plan of salvation with him?*

Those who are lost are blind. They cannot see and understand the truth of the gospel in spite of frequent and clear communication. That doesn't just happen. Satan, the god of this world, is blinding their understanding. We have an adversary that is opposed to people giving their hearts and lives to Jesus Christ; he hardens their hearts and keeps them in bondage to sin and darkness. Paul said in Acts 26:18 what is really the essence of evangelism and missions. He said God had called him "to open their eyes that they may turn from darkness to light and from the power of Satan to God." The task of witnessing to the lost is a matter of opening eyes that are blind and to turn them from the darkness of sin to the light of the Savior, from the power of Satan to God. This is because one who is lost is in Satan's power.

In the parable of the sower in Luke 8, Jesus tells about the seed of the gospel that falls on the hardened, beaten-down pathway where it does not take root. Many missionaries are going to resistant cultures that do not readily receive the gospel. Those places are like that hardened soil, but many in our own community and neighborhood have hearts that are hardened and unreceptive. Jesus says that the birds come and take away the seed, even as it is sown, and then explains in verse 12 that the birds are the devil. Even when people are faithful to witness and share their faith with the lost, an adversary is actively taking away the truth of the gospel from their hearts and understanding, lest they should understand and repent. Satan would not want us to recognize his role in those who reject the gospel, but we must not discount his involvement among those who resist a Christian witness.

Attempting to share the gospel in most Muslim countries is difficult; the seed of the gospel falls on hard soil and does not readily take root. Even though the gospel may be clearly proclaimed, Satan is taking away the truth of the gospel by his deception and lies. He tells them that Christians believe in three gods which is blasphemous to their way of thinking or that an imposter, not Christ, died on the cross. They are fatalistic and do not believe they are responsible for their sin. They are convinced Christianity is a foreign religion that is characterized by the immorality seen in Western movies and American lifestyles. Satan sees to it that they are deluded in their perception and understanding. He influences them through their cultural worldview and traditional religion to believe his lies, taking away the seeds of the gospel from their understanding even when the message is communicated to them.

Such deception is especially prominent in Hindu and Buddhist cultures. I once witnessed to a student in India who was more receptive and enthusiastic upon hearing the gospel for the first time than anyone else I had ever encountered. He was thrilled to hear everything I told him about God's love and how Jesus had died for his sins. He affirmed every premise in my presentation and readily prayed to receive Christ. Then he said, "This is wonderful; now I've got a Savior among all my other gods." I thought, *Uh-oh, wait a minute. Let's back up; we missed something here.* Satan tells them in their pluralistic society that all religions are the same, and one can follow any or all of them. There is nothing unique or exclusive about Jesus, and once again the birds take away the truth of the gospel through Satan's deception and lies.

For years missionaries in Thailand and other Buddhist countries have felt that they are on the verge of a breakthrough, an evangelistic harvest, because the people seem so interested and receptive. But few step across the line and embrace faith in Jesus Christ. It is not so much a religious barrier but a cultural barrier that Satan uses. He uses his lies and persuasion to tell them that to become a Christian means to cease to be a Thai. Turning to Christ is to reject one's family, culture, and ethnic identity.

Certainly the gospel is the power of God to draw all people to Jesus Christ. We make a mistake in thinking that it is just a matter of gaining access, building relationships, and communicating the gospel. We must realize we have an adversary that is actively taking away the truth we are sharing and distorting the thinking and understanding of those to whom we witness. We have an enemy who is opposed to the gospel and the extension of God's kingdom. Satan easily uses pagan worldviews and concepts to filter and distort the truth of the gospel.

One of my colleagues in Bangkok had been cultivating a witness with a businessman for several years; he finally came to the point of a decision to accept Christ as his Savior. The first question he asked was, "What do I do with all this karma I have accumulated?" Satan had twisted his thinking to see good works as the factor determining one's eternal destiny. It is easy for the god of this world to distort the understanding, even of those who desperately want to believe the truth, in order to keep them out of God's kingdom.

Among many cultural Catholics throughout the world, Satan takes away the seed of the gospel by convincing them they are already Christians in spite of the fact that they have never been born again through a personal experience of trusting Jesus. He will allow them to concede that they must believe on Jesus but deceives them into believing that the sacraments of the church are also necessary. They accept the lie of a salvation of works and merit because it is cleverly disguised as the gospel, successfully enabling the adversary to keep them from a personal relationship with God.

The perverted and false concepts of other religious traditions are not the only tools Satan uses to keep people from coming to Christ. He also uses social barriers to stop people from entering the kingdom of God. Even in our own American culture, we should readily recognize where excuses come from when people say, "I don't need God," or they are unresponsive to a Christian witness "because there are hypocrites in the church," or give an endless number of other reasons for rejecting Christ.

I found a man in the city where we lived in Indonesia who was receptive to the gospel, and I sensed he was coming to the point of receiving Christ. But just before I pressed him for a decision, he asked, "If I do this and become a Christian, who will my daughter marry?" I had never considered that might be a problem. But in most cultures people will go into debt and commit a lifetime of earnings in order to marry their daughter well. This is essential for respect and social status. It's the ultimate shame if you're not able to find a good husband for your daughter. But if you become a Christian, a minority, an outcast, that destroys any hope of social status and community respect. And no one would want to marry his daughter.

Another question I often encountered by those considering becoming a Christian was, "Where will I be buried?" Obviously not in the community cemetery. That would be an apostasy to the Muslims. It would desecrate their cemetery for a Christian to buried there. And that would create a real dilemma for his family. This concern was a barrier to taking that step of faith and being willing to identify with Christ. The little ways that Satan can take away the seed and hope of the gospel are endless even as the Spirit is working in one's heart.

The most prominent barrier I found in every culture was the question, if a person accepts that Jesus Christ is "the way, the truth, and the life" (John 14:6), what does that say about one's deceased ancestors—parents and grandparents? They did not know Jesus, nor did they have an opportunity to be saved, so it is paramount to confirmation that they were lost and are in hell. That is difficult to accept since by embracing the truth of the gospel one is forced to accept that reality concerning those who died without Christ. It's easier just to deny the gospel and not accept it than to acknowledge the lostness of loved ones and ancestors. I learned to answer this objection by saying, "Because the Bible is true, and Jesus is the only way to God. Your grandparents and ancestors unfortunately are lost, but they now know that Jesus is the way to God and salvation. Don't you think they love you enough that they would want you to accept it now that you have an opportunity to do so?"

Satan is deceptive; he lies and distorts the truth of the gospel. He speaks to people in their minds, using cultural and social barriers to keep people from coming to Christ because he is an adversary, opposed to their being saved and bringing glory to God. He keeps countries closed to a Christian witness. He keeps people groups hidden from our awareness. He is opposed to the kingdom of God being extended and God being exalted among the nations, just as he is opposed to individuals coming to faith in Jesus Christ. He does everything he can among those who confess Christ to keep us from witnessing to the lost and God being glorified in our lives. Jesus quoted from Isaiah to alert His disciples in John 12:40 regarding this adversary, "He has blinded their eyes and hardened their hearts, so that they would not see with their eyes or understand with their hearts, and be converted, and I would heal them."

Many missionaries go to places that for centuries have been locked into a godless, spiritual darkness due to their rejection of God's revelation and as a consequence of playing into Satan's hands and purposes for generations. Second Thessalonians 2:1–12 speaks of the coming of the Antichrist and explains it will be in accord with the activity of Satan. We need to be alert about how the Bible reveals the activity of Satan in the world; verse 3 says, "Don't let anyone deceive you." The Scripture proceeds in verses 9–12, "The coming of the lawless one is based on Satan's working, with all kinds of false miracles, signs, and wonders, and with every unrighteous deception among those who are perishing. They perish because they did not accept the love of the truth in order to be saved. For this reason God sends them a strong delusion so that they will believe what is false, so that all will be condemned—those who did not believe the truth but enjoyed unrighteousness."

At face value it sounds as if God were responsible for the deluding influence. But this is similar to the nation of Israel facing the consequences of sin. When they sinned, when they disobeyed God, when they worshipped Baal and pagan idols, that rejection brought consequences: punishment due to God's moral nature. People who follow a false way and are lost have bought into a deluding influence that God is not going to contradict in judgment. Those who do not know Christ will be judged because of their rejection of the truth and embracing that which has deluded generations. For hundreds of years people have become acculturated into darkness and perverted religious beliefs that keep them from knowing God. Because they do not know God and for generations have rejected Him, even in their ignorance and due to a legacy passed down by their ancestors, they are still in their sin and will ultimately be judged and punished. But the gospel of Christ has the power to break through that stronghold and the bondage that has held them for hundreds of years. The gospel is the power of God unto salvation, and it is His desire for all to come to know the truth. Otherwise, we would not be sending missionaries to these places.

On a trip to Central Asia, I was traveling with the regional leader, who had been one of the early pioneer missionaries to enter that region following the breakup of the former Soviet Union. He and his family had located in Uzbekistan in the city of Samarkand for language study. Hundreds of years ago this area was a part of the Mongol Empire that extended throughout China, Russia, and most of Southwest Asia. Timberlane, known as Timor the Great, the nephew of Kubla Khan, became emperor and was a wicked, despotic ruler. He was determined to rid the Mongol Empire of any vestige of Christianity. By the time of his reign, a significant Nestorian Christian sect had spread from Syria, and there is still evidence of its existence in China in ancient times. With cruelty and hatred he wiped out churches, massacred Christians, and by his death in 1405 had successfully eradicated Christianity from the Mongol Empire, leaving this region in spiritual darkness for centuries. Not only did this ancient pagan empire become fertile ground for the Muslim faith, but that legacy was also overlaid with a veneer of atheism from seventy years of domination by the Soviet Union. A Christian witness had been prohibited for almost six hundred years, and multitudes had perished without hope.

The tomb of Timor the Great is located in Samarkand. When this new missionary arrived in the early 1990s for language study, he walked up to the tomb of Timor the Great and said in a mocking lilt, "We're back!" And we are back, indeed, with the gospel being proclaimed and churches multiplying among the peoples of Central Asia. Satan may prevail for a time, but his adversarial strategies cannot stand when God, in His providence and power, determines the time has come for His kingdom to be established.

Satan Is a Deceiver and a Liar

The Scripture also defines Satan as a deceiver and a liar. He is clever and can convince us that wrong is right and right is wrong. The Bible describes him as being disguised as an angel or messenger of light. As such, he can deceive us into justifying sinful, carnal attitudes and actions, thinking they are acceptable behavior. He can influence us to criticize and attack others, to create dissension and conflict, under the guise of serving God. He delights in getting us busy doing good things that actually divert us from God's will. He can also cause us to waste hours and days in carnal entertainment and activity without a word of thankfulness and praise. He plants unclean thoughts in our minds and makes us believe they are of no consequence since we are under grace.

Second Corinthians 11:14–15 says, "And no wonder! For Satan himself is disguised as an angel of light. So it is no great thing if his servants also disguise themselves as servants of righteousness. Their destiny will be according to their works." We all know of Christian leaders and pastors who have fallen and been agents of deception, living a lie. While presuming to be servants of righteousness, they live a life of deceit, all the while leading others astray. It is amazing that men of God, people who preach the Word of God, could live an alternate lifestyle of sin, but that is the power of Satan's deception.

In one of the Screwtape letters, Wormwood is advised how to defeat the Christian to whom he was assigned. "Delude him into thinking that he still has personal rights and can claim ownership of time and possessions instead of having died to self and yielded them to God. Nothing works so easily as to find a period of time which he reasons to have at his own disposal and then taken away from him by an unexpected visitor. Make him think his time is his own and it has been stolen from him. Always encourage the sense of ownership as this readily creates resentment when it must be shared or given away or is lost. Create a tendency to use personal pronouns for what really belongs to God—my house, my car, my family, my time" (paraphrased).

We would not think of justifying a right to personal time and space as something that is vulnerable to Satan's deceit. After all, we have a right to a little peace and quiet. My time is my own. Somebody interrupts our plans or makes demands of us, and it creates resentment, causing us to miss an opportunity God may be seeking to bring into our lives. Missionaries are especially vulnerable as most cultures overseas do not value privacy; every house is open, including theirs! People feel free to come and go at any time and have expectations of communal fellowship, readily responding to the needs of others. But we like to have our schedule and determine hours we're going to be available, and then we selfishly guard what we consider our own time. The resentment can begin to well up in our hearts toward those we are supposed to love and serve because Satan deceives us to think we have personal rights and privileges. Somehow we disregard Jesus' call

> *Anything in our mind that is contrary to the truth of God's Word is a lie and comes from Satan's deceitful nature.*

to His disciples to forsake all and follow Him as if it doesn't apply to us!

Paul expresses concern for the believers in 2 Corinthians 11:3, "But I fear that, as the serpent deceived Eve by his cunning, your minds may be corrupted from the complete and pure devotion to Christ." But that is exactly what Satan does. He leads us astray from a pure and simple faith. Believing in Christ and following Him, accepting what He has given to us, is really complete for giving us victory and everything we need to be devoted to Christ and to glorify God. It is a matter of believing and accepting what His Word tells us.

Beth Moore describes this prominent dilemma in her book *When Godly People Do Ungodly Things*.[1] The point of this book is that we are easily seduced to do things that are self-serving and actually are hurtful to others. That doesn't come from God and walking with Him. Satan deceives us to think that we have rights, that we have a right to our opinions; he tells us to stand up for ourselves no matter who is hurt by our actions. He convinces us that walking in victory and living for Christ is difficult. It is all a part of his deception. We have been taught to believe that victory is elusive, that the Christian life is always a struggle. We are deceived into thinking that we have always got to keep working at it but can never fully conquer sin and carnal impulses as long as we are in this life. We fool ourselves into justifying sinful behavior as if God is not aware of what we do. In the time of Ezekiel, God revealed this kind of deception among the leaders of Israel. "Do you see what the elders of the house of Israel are doing in the darkness, each at the shrine of his idol? For they are saying: The Lord does not see us" (Ezek. 8:12). However, that is not what the Bible teaches; God does indeed see us, and not only our deeds and behavior but also our attitudes and motives. We have so easily succumbed to Satan's deceit and lies.

Second Corinthians 10:4–5 gives us a clue to avoid becoming victims of Satan's deception: "We demolish arguments and every high-minded thing that is raised up against the knowledge of God, taking every thought captive to the obedience of Christ." Satan is speaking to us in our minds. He is deceiving us, convincing us to believe his lies and embrace the values of the world instead of what God's Word tells us. What's the antidote? Bringing those thoughts in captivity to what Christ has told us, to what His Word says will bless us, empower us, and glorify Him. Failing to do so subjects us to Satan's deceit.

I have been somewhat intrigued over the years that the principle of biblical inerrancy has been controversial within the Southern Baptist Convention. Maybe I have been naive or raised differently from others, but all my life I have understood that the Bible is the divinely inspired Word of God. God is not limited and deficient in being able to give to us the Word as He wants us to have it. Not only did He inspire those who wrote the original manuscripts, but He is capable of preserving the message intended for all generations. I have never been able to understand how anyone would see an errant, flawed Bible as reliable. I have always believed that the authority and reliability of the Bible are based on the nature of the God who inspired it. Certainly there are things I can't explain and don't understand, but that's my problem. It's not a problem with God or His Word.

This is likely what Paul is referring to in 2 Corinthians 10. Where do these speculations and arguments that rationalize away the truth of God's Word come from? We often hear people say, "Yes, that is what the Bible says, but . . . ," and they proceed to contradict the truth and meaning of the Bible or its clear intended application. If Satan can deceive us to doubt what the Bible says, he has readily defeated us because we are left to our own devices and fallible understanding. That is why we are told to destroy speculations, any high-minded thoughts raised up against Christ and counter to the truth of what God says.

First Timothy 4:1 warns us that this would happen. "Now the Spirit explicitly says that in the latter times some will depart from the faith, paying attention to deceitful spirits and teachings of demons." Paul reiterates this theme in 2 Timothy 3:13, "Evil people and imposters will become worse, deceiving and being deceived." Titus was alerted to the fact that he, too, would encounter this devious tactic of the enemy. Titus 1:10 says, "For there are also many rebellious people, idle talkers and deceivers, especially those from Judaism." He was indicating some of the most deceptive influences would be those that were characterized by religious piety.

Do you see where speculation and Satan's deception lead us? If certain verses and passages are thought to be erroneous and not really an authentic part of the Bible, it erodes the authority and reliability of Scripture altogether. Satan must be delighted when we come to that position because we no longer have the authority of God's infallible truth on which to base our faith and guide our life. It is easy for him to deceive us to embrace beliefs and values contrary to what would glorify God.

Do you realize how often the Bible says, "Do not be deceived"? Ephesians 5:6 tells us, "Let no one deceive you with empty arguments, for because of these things God's wrath is coming on the disobedient." Galatians 6:7 is a similar admonition that man will receive whatever he sows lest God is mocked and we are deceived. James 1:16–17 tells us not to be deceived; bad things do not come from God but only that which is good. Why do you think these verses and others, such as 1 John 3:7 and 1 Corinthians 6:9, begin with the phrase, "Do not be deceived," or, "Let no one deceive you"? Could it be because we may be deceived and think of this particular issue differently than it really is? The Bible is warning us that we could be deceived. We have an enemy that delights in deceiving us and even distorting the meaning of God's Word, just as he did in the temptations of Jesus. This is an alert. Don't be deceived. Understand and believe what God's Word says because this is the way it is; this is truth, not what our rationalizing minds manipulated by Satan would tell us. But Satan so easily and effectively deceives us with speculations and distorts even the Word of God.

When I was getting into church planting and beginning to see some results in Indonesia during my first term, I encountered a dilemma that was somewhat exasperating. After leading a group to confess Christ, we would follow with baptism, and a church would be formed. Now here were people that I had been teaching the basic claims of Christ—the plan of salvation, their sinfulness and separation from God, their need to believe on Jesus, and what that implies. At that point I had taught little about the subsequent Christian life, discipleship and growth, and the nature of the church. As I anticipated returning following the initial baptism in a village, I thought, *What's the first thing I need to teach them?* I started outlining and listing what I considered to be the most important lessons. I needed to teach them how to pray, about eternal security, how the church is to function, their relationships with one another, and on and on. When I finished, I had about three years of weekly topics, all of which were priority, and I felt needed to be taught immediately. Not only was it impossible to give priority to every subject, but I also didn't want to create ongoing dependency on my leadership by being the one to teach them for such a long period of time.

I was conscientious that Jesus told us in the Great Commission the responsibility of "teaching them to observe everything I have commanded you" (Matt. 28:20). God used that dilemma to help me understand that fulfilling the Great Commission doesn't necessarily mean we're to go through the Scripture and take all the teachings of Jesus and be sure that we've covered the whole comprehensive spectrum of lessons about the church and the Christian life. What He is saying is that we are to make disciples by teaching them obedience. When you teach new believers to be obedient to the Word of God, that includes everything Jesus taught and expects. I certainly continued to instruct them as I had opportunity, but having given them Bibles, I would tell them, "Read it, believe it, and do what it says." And they accepted that because this was the Word of God.

God began to teach me through the simple faith of these new believers. They would have questions. As I began primarily to relate to the group by discipling and training the leaders in a way they could pass on to others, they would struggle with the application of problematic passages, but there was never any question but they were to be obedient to what it taught.

I was in a group that was preparing to have a baptism. One of the men who had attended the group faithfully and made a profession of faith, Pak Sjamsul, was absent; and we were told that he was sick. He was an elderly man, had a high fever, was in a coma, and probably was near death as there was no access to medical care. I suggested that we pray for him, but as we started to have prayer for Pak Sjamsul, one of the members in the group interrupted. He pointed out that in reading the Bible he noticed that whenever they prayed for someone who was sick they laid hands on them. I saw this as a teachable moment to help them understand you can pray anytime, anywhere. But I had convinced them to do what the Bible said, and they were already getting up, filing out the door to go to Pak Sjamsul's house to lay hands on him as they prayed. The house was just down the little alleyway from where we were meeting; Pak Sjamsul was unconscious and burning with fever. The group gathered around his bed, put their hands on him, and prayed for him. There was nothing dramatic or emotional, just matter-of-fact prayers asking God to heal him. And having prayed, they went back to our Bible study.

I was rather distracted and disturbed by the experience because there was no medical attention for this elderly man, and obviously he was going to die. When I came back the next week for the baptism, how was I going to explain to these people why Pak Sjamsul had died when they, in simple faith, had obeyed God's Word and prayed for him to be healed? However, when I came back the next week, there was Pak Sjamsul alive, healthy, and ready to be baptized. It would not be possible for me to teach every church, every leader all the details and lessons throughout the Bible. But I found if one is locked into obedience to God's Word, Satan cannot readily deceive and lead one astray.

John 8:44 says, "You are of your father the Devil, and you want to carry out your father's desires. He was a murderer from the beginning and has not stood in the truth, because there is no truth in him. When he tells a lie, he speaks from

his own nature, because he is a liar and the father of liars."
Whatever comes into our mind that is contrary to God's
truth and the promises of God's Word is coming from Satan.
Remember who is the liar—it is his nature—and who is telling the truth.

We are told the final outcome of the battle with the one
who deceives us and the whole world in Revelation. "Then
war broke out in heaven: Michael and his angels fought
against the dragon . . . and there was no place for them in
heaven any longer. So the great dragon was thrown out—the
ancient serpent, who is called the Devil and Satan, the one
who deceives the whole world" (Rev. 12:7–9). The victory
is assured for this passage goes on to say in verse 10, "The
salvation and the power and the kingdom of our God and
the authority of His Messiah have now come, because the
accuser of our brothers has been thrown out: the one who
accuses them before our God day and night." Revelation
13:14 tells us, "He deceives those who live on the earth."
But we are not to believe his lies. We should not allow him to
put us on a guilt trip accusing us of our failure and defeating
us in our Christian life when Christ has given us the victory.
The victory comes when we believe the truth of God's Word
and what He has told us.

Bobbye and I were going through a time of crisis in which
we were subjected to a lot of highly publicized criticism that
was quite painful. I remember getting a note from one of
our longtime prayer partners, a little handwritten note card
that said, "Keep the view from the throne. All that is swirl-
ing about you is not reality." All the criticism and problems
confronting us were real, but this was a reminder—what was
God's perspective? When you go through trials and troubles,
Satan wants to deceive you, cause you to get discouraged,

to feel defeated and forsaken; but that is not God's perspective. He wants to use difficult situations to draw us closer to Him. He allows painful experiences and even criticism and opposition to teach us something. He wants us to grow. He wants us to experience His grace. What is His view and purpose? "Keep the view from the throne." If we will look at life's experiences from God's perspective and what His Word says, then we will not be deceived by Satan who is seeking to defeat us by his lies, distorting reality from God's kingdom perspective. It's really not difficult to believe God. Don't be led astray from simple and complete devotion to Christ.

CHAPTER 3

THE NATURE OF OUR ENEMY, PART II

*Do not love the world or the things that belong to the world. If anyone loves the world, love for the Father is not **in** him. Because everything that belongs to the world—the lust of the flesh, the lust of the eyes, and the pride in one's lifestyle—is not from the Father, but is from the world. And the world with its lust is passing away, but the one who does God's will remains forever.*
—1 John 2:15–17, emphasis added

The International Mission Board is located on Monument Avenue in Richmond, Virginia. It is a historic boulevard with Civil War monuments on prominent intersections. Often when I drive down this street and see the impressive statues of Stonewall Jackson, Robert E. Lee, Jeb Stuart, and others on their horses, I think of the story I heard a long time ago. A famous sculptor was renown for sculpting horses in various action poses, appearing realistic with their sinews and flexing muscles. Someone asked him how he had developed such artistry and skill. He replied with a rather simplistic understatement: "I just get a big block of granite and chip off everything that doesn't look like a horse!" This is what God wants to do in our life. He is seeking to chip away anything in our life that doesn't look like Jesus. He is glorified when we come to faith in Jesus Christ and accept His grace and provision for salvation. But He jealously desires that our lives be totally committed to Him and that we allow Him to be glorified by our living in His power, demonstrating His love, walking in holiness and appropriating a Christlike life.

Satan is countering that by getting us to live for self, indulging in sin and carnal gratification, adopting the values and standards of the world rather than living a separated life of holiness. He is adamantly opposed to the gospel being proclaimed to the nations and is an adversary to God's kingdom being extended. He lies and deceives, causing us to rationalize and doubt the truth of God's Word. He creates conflict, dissension, and disunity in the body of Christ, and is behind anything that keeps God from being glorified. Not only is he an adversary and deceiver, but the Bible also reveals that he is the one who entices us to sin by tempting that old sinful nature of the flesh. If he can't defeat us, deceive us, or defile us, then he simply tries to hinder us from doing what God wants us to do and living as God desires us to live.

Satan works in darkness and anonymity. Bringing to light and exposing his nature and tactics render him ineffective. A big part of claiming the victory in spiritual warfare is to be aware of the battle and understand his subtle schemes and strategy. The Bible reveals a great deal about his nature and methods and charges us to be vigilant and alert, always on guard that we might resist by recognizing and repelling his attacks.

Satan Is the Tempter

The Bible tells us that Satan is the tempter. This is a role with which we are probably most familiar as we are aware of what it means to be tempted. Since Satan is revealed as the source of temptation, we would be more than happy to relinquish any responsibility for yielding to his enticement to sin claiming, "The devil made me do it." Although Satan is behind every temptation, blaming him does not absolve us of any responsibility for sin and doing that which is contrary to God's will. In Christ we have been given power over sin, and Satan cannot make us do anything we do not choose to do!

However, Satan does tempt us to sinful behavior, actions, words, and attitudes because, obviously, God is not glorified when we sin. Satan attracts us to things of the world and tempts us to embrace carnal values. He persuades us to focus on ourselves, what we want, and our needs with a sense of entitlement that leads us to indulge selfish gratifications. First Thessalonians 3:5 says, "I also sent to find out about your faith, fearing that the tempter had tempted you and that our labor might be for nothing." As we will see later, Satan's first step is to undercut our faith, for only then can we justify doing things contrary to God's Word and what faith, or believing God, would lead us to do. Paul's labor and witness in bringing the believers in Thessalonica to salvation would have been in vain were they to yield to Satan's temptation and deny their faith.

James 1:13–15 says, "No one undergoing a trial should say, 'I am being tempted by God.' For God is not tempted by evil, and He himself doesn't tempt anyone. But each person is tempted when he is drawn away and enticed by his own evil desires. Then after desire has conceived, it gives birth to sin." Sin appeals to that old nature, providing gratification and satisfaction in something that is desirable but does not honor God. Satan, who is familiar with that old sin nature, entices us. He is the tempter. He begins just as he did with Eve, tantalizing her with, "Did God really say . . . ?" Yes, God really did say she was not to eat the forbidden fruit, but like Eve we begin to doubt what God said or that He really meant that to apply to our particular situation or desire. We begin to rationalize and justify what we do, never realizing that our enemy was behind those lustful thoughts, unrighteous desires, and self-serving motives.

The Bible reveals three basic categories of temptation. First John 2:15–17 tells us this: "Do not love the world or the things that belong to the world. If anyone loves the world, love for the Father is not in him. Because everything that belongs to the world—the lust of the flesh, the lust of the eyes, and the pride in one's lifestyle—is not from the Father, but is from the world. And the world with its lust is passing away, but the one who does God's will remains forever."

The lust of the flesh is that which is appealing to the gratification of our old sinful nature. It leads to adultery and unfaithfulness to one's spouse, physical indulgence that results in pregnancy out of wedlock, and a general hedonistic attitude that if something feels good, it's all right.

The lust of the eyes is the appeal to our aesthetic nature and leads to covetousness. Television ads are designed to stimulate this desire for something we do not have. The materialism that surrounds us at shopping malls creates the desire for things. Credit card appeals from financial institutions seek to convince us we can have it now and pay later, appealing to our lust for more and more possessions, comforts, and pleasures.

Then there is the pride of life, appealing to our innate desire not only to be liked but to be the center of attention. We compromise convictions and hurt others in order to get ahead, succeed in whatever we do for the sake of recognition and reputation. There is nothing wrong with leadership, recognition, and success if we give God credit for getting us where we are, remain faithful in living for Him, and humbly allow Him to receive the glory for our accomplishment.

Notice how this parallels the temptation of Eve in Genesis 3:6, "Then the woman saw that the tree was good for food"—the lust of the flesh, something her body needed and wanted—"and delightful to look at." It was attractive, appealing and desirable. "It was desirable for obtaining wisdom," the pride of life. To get her to doubt God, he proceeded to malign God's motives; in verse 5, "God knows that when you eat it your eyes will be opened and you will be like God, knowing good and evil." He made Eve believe that God was trying to deprive her of something. It is not Satan's nature to reveal the whole truth. Eve would know the difference between good and evil only when she sinned and succumbed to Satan's evil temptation to disobey God.

This also parallels the temptations of Jesus. When He was tempted to turn the stones into bread, it was the lust of the flesh and a desire to indulge in a physical need. He was hungry, He was human, His body needed something to eat, and it was a natural desire of the flesh. When Satan showed Him the kingdoms of the world, it appealed to the lust of the eyes—seeing that which He desired and wanted, the kingdoms of the world that He had come to claim for the kingdom of God. The sensationalism and pride of casting Himself off the pinnacle of the temple would have given Him instant acclaim and acceptance; there would be no need to go to the cross. So what's wrong with indulging these temptations? All of them seemed to be consistent with His purpose, His basic human nature and needs and what He wanted to accomplish. The problem was they were not of the Father; they were not His way and did not bring glory to Him. Later we will focus on the tension between the flesh and the Spirit which is the battleground for temptation. We will see how easy it is for Satan to use the flesh, our old sinful nature and selfish desires, to tempt us to do what is contrary to God's will and keep Him from being glorified in our lives.

In the Lord's Prayer, we are familiar with the supplication, "Do not bring us into temptation, but deliver us from the evil one" (Matt. 6:13). That gives us the perception that God is the one who is constantly tempting us and trying us. But the reality is that He is the only one that can keep us from being led into temptation and deliver us from evil, for He is the one who is more powerful and has overcome Satan. We have a confusing situation in Luke 22:31–32 when Jesus tells Peter, "Simon, Simon, look out! Satan has asked to sift you like wheat. But I have prayed for you that your faith may not fail. And you, when you have turned back, strengthen your brothers." Peter was about to be tempted, and his fallibility would be revealed in his denial of Jesus. But note that Jesus had to give Satan permission to try his faith and commitment. Why would Jesus do that? As He did, Jesus Himself was interceding for Peter that his faith would not fail, and Jesus also knew he would be stronger and be able to strengthen the brethren because of his own experience of weakness and failure. In Jesus Christ we have been given victory over temptation. When He allows us to be tempted, it is for our own growth in faith and equipping. Temptation reminds us of our own weakness and need to trust in God.

Later in that same chapter Jesus tells His disciples in the garden of Gethsemane, "Pray that you may not enter into temptation" (Luke 22:40). The Gospel of Mark defines the situation more explicitly, "Stay awake [alert] and pray so that you won't enter into temptation. The spirit is willing, but the flesh is weak" (Mark 14:38). Resisting temptation is not a passive exercise; we must be on the alert to recognize Satan's temptations, praying for God's intervention and strength, for only in His grace and power do we avoid indulging in that which is evil and contrary to God's will. We will see later how Satan uses our self-centered fleshly nature to entice us because that is where we are weak.

Second Peter 2:9–10 gives us assurance that "the Lord knows how to rescue the godly from trials and to keep the unrighteous under punishment until the day of judgment, especially those who follow the polluting desires of the flesh and despise authority." If we were on our own, we would not be able even to recognize the subtle temptations that appeal to our natural desires and instincts, but the Lord is the one who delivers us and rescues us from Satan's devious appeals. If we ever take pride in our own ability to withstand temptation, we have become vulnerable to certain failure, just as Peter was. Temptation should instinctively drive us to God to draw upon His grace and help. First Corinthians 10:12–13 gives us this beautiful promise and assurance: "Therefore, whoever thinks he stands must be careful not to fall! No temptation has overtaken you except what is common to humanity. God is faithful and He will not allow you to be tempted beyond what you are able, but with the temptation He will also provide a way of escape, so that you are able to bear it."

Satan Is a Hinderer

Satan is constantly deceiving us. He opposes anything in our lives that would glorify God and serve His kingdom. If he cannot get us to sin and yield to temptation, to indulge our carnal nature and live according to the flesh, he simply seeks to influence us in ways that hinder us from carrying out God's will or doing what God wants us to do. We may not indulge in an immoral lifestyle, and we may resist selfish gratifications that are contrary to the holy life to which Christ calls us. But a lot of things divert us, distract us, and keep us from doing what God would have us to do. There are sins we commit, but there are also sins of omission or failure to do what God would have us do. Often the things that hinder us seem to be circumstances that are natural, human obstacles. But remember, Satan is god of this world.

Many faithful church members know that God once called them to the ministry, but they were unwilling to abandon a successful career or allowed an unsupportive spouse to keep them from doing what God called them to do. I have met many who acknowledged that at some point in their life God had called them to missions, but they failed to be obedient to God's leading. They have been faithfully serving God in their church, honoring Him in their vocation; but they have allowed Satan to hinder them from what

anything to happen that God cannot use to fulfill His ultimate purpose of being glorified in your life and in the world.
We cannot always know, and we don't necessarily need to
know as long as we remain committed to being obedient
and walking by faith. The danger comes when the door is
closed because of our own disobedience or reluctance to do
God's will. But if we are fully committed and following by
faith to the place to which we discern He is leading, the end
result will be used of God for His purpose. We need to be
reminded that God is sovereign; nothing takes Him by surprise. He has the capacity to use closed doors to accomplish
His plan, just as He used Satan's schemes to crucify Christ
to provide redemption for a lost world. God is in charge, and
He can use Satan's efforts to hinder His will to carry out His
ultimate purpose.

Consider the case of a couple who felt led to serve in a
restricted country in Central Asia. They had prayed, stud-
ied the region, consulted friends and colleagues, discerned
their gifts relative to personnel needs, and were absolutely
convinced they were to go to Turkmenistan. They even stud-
ied the Turkmen language before they left. The government
assured them that they would be approved for a medical
ministry there. They were to enter the country on a tourist
visa and convert it to extended residency once their work
permit had been arranged. But the visa was never granted,
and after six weeks of bureaucratic hassle, they had to leave.
Eventually the whole team was deported, churches were
destroyed, and pastors arrested and tortured. Suddenly this
couple was in a dilemma. They had been in the appointment process for several years absolutely convinced where
God wanted them to serve. They were temporarily relocated
and spent the next six months in three countries. Eventually

they settled in a fourth country where their medical platform was well accepted—a place where God was beginning to work in significant ways. How does one know which one is the place of God's will? How do you make those decisions when you don't know if God is leading you contrary to your understanding of His will, or Satan is seeking to divert you from God's will and place of service?

When the International Mission Board began to use creative strategies to move some people into restricted countries, a new missionary family felt a strong call to a people group in a closed country. They thought everything had been arranged to begin their designated assignment when their visa was denied. We arranged for them to fill an interim assignment in Southeast Asia, and they were able to go in and out of their target country on a tourist visa for a month at a time, making contacts and trying to acquire a work permit. They took other interim assignments in the region, and finally after a year and a half their visa was granted. They just persevered, confident that was where God wanted them, even when we had tried to influence them otherwise. During that year and a half, they had lived in fifteen different places in five different countries. That's not a convenient lifestyle for a family with three small children. When we gathered to pray for them and see them off at the airport with that visa in hand, I remember him saying, "We never knew where we would be from one month to the next this last year and a half, but one thing God has taught us is that He calls us not so much to a place as to Himself!"

We need to take note of that attitude because places, situations, locations, and job assignments are not always going to work out the way we think they should and according to our understanding of God's will. Our plans are likely to be disrupted. We may be hindered from doing what we would choose to do. But if we have answered a call to the lordship of Christ, God's will cannot be thwarted. He will always use our location and our circumstances to fulfill His will and be glorified. It doesn't really matter where we are. He is going to see that we are in a place where He can use us as we follow Him. When Plan A doesn't materialize and we have to opt for Plan B, God has a way of making our Plan B His Plan A!

As a college student I had the opportunity to serve as a summer missionary in the Philippines. Because of my interest in missions, I arranged my overseas travel as an opportunity to visit several mission fields, hoping to discern where God might eventually be calling me to serve. Of all the places I visited, my heart was touched by India. The spiritual darkness was overwhelming, yet there seemed to be an amazing response to the gospel. Also Southern Baptists had just initiated work in the country, and such a pioneer assignment was appealing. As I prayed about my field of future missionary service, the conviction grew that India was the place. Our presence there was primarily limited to medical work, but coincidentally my future wife, Bobbye, was planning to go into medical technology, which would obviously be an open door for us to be attached to that ministry. This conviction and sense of God's leadership continued to be

> "We never knew where we would be . . . but one thing God has taught us is that He calls us not so much to a place as to Himself!"

strengthened throughout college and seminary studies and through pastoral experience in preparation for missionary appointment. However, as we moved toward appointment, it became evident that we would not be able to get a visa to serve in India.

This was extremely disappointing because we were so convinced this was God's will and where He was leading us to serve. We wondered why He had closed the door, or if this was Satan's way of prohibiting our witness in that country so desperately in need of the gospel. We assumed we had just made a mistake in interpreting God's will and now needed to discern where He wanted us to serve. The timing of our appointment occurred soon after an abortive communist coup in Indonesia, and missionaries there were reporting an unprecedented response to the gospel. We felt led to join the harvest there and fill one of the many urgent personnel requests for church planters. God richly blessed our ministry as we grew personally as well as in our understanding of effective strategies and church-planting methodology.

Toward the end of our second term, our mission board made some adjustments in its field organization, shifting work in India and South Asia from being under the administrative area for Northern Africa and the Middle East to Southeast Asia. Our area director had surveyed the area and realized India was experiencing an evangelistic harvest but was seeing little church growth. In each of the annual meetings of missionaries throughout Southeast Asia, he appealed for an experienced church planter to go to India and spend several months assessing the situation and training our medical missionaries and national evangelists to develop and carry out an effective church growth strategy. That was an open invitation in all the countries of Southeast Asia, but no one was interested in leaving his own assignment to spend several months in India. However, our hearts were stirred by such an opportunity; after all, this is where we had felt called to serve many years before.

We responded and found that all we had learned in almost ten years of church planting in Indonesia was relevant to the needs in India. We found a wonderful response to our training. In fact, we were asked to return two or three times a year to serve as consultants to the work, even while continuing our assignment in Indonesia. In the first ten years of Southern Baptist work in India, twenty-one churches had been started, all dependent on mission subsidy to build church buildings and pay pastoral support. As we were able to guide them in a more biblical approach of indigenous church planting, the number of churches multiplied to more than four hundred over the next ten years. We began to expand the training among Baptist partners in other places around India, and I eventually became associate to the area director, administering all our work in India and South Asia. What we thought was a closed door, a mistaken interpretation of God's will, or Satan hindering what we thought God wanted us to do, was really just God's plan, in His providence and timing.

Like our fellow missionaries, we would never have responded to the opportunity to go to India to provide training had God not planted that call in our hearts many years before. He knew what needed to happen in my own life before I was equipped to fulfill His call to India. In His sovereignty, He also knew the appropriate timing and circumstances for His will to be carried out in our going to India. A closed door is not necessarily a victory for Satan. If one is obedient to follow wherever God leads and trust Him, then Satan cannot hinder and divert God's will from being fulfilled in His way and His timing.

God is in control, and we are to be fully committed to Him and to follow His leading by faith. And even if Satan closes a door, God is able to use that. Satan is not going to get the victory. Paul wanted to go to Thessalonica, and even though Satan that hindered him from going, God used him where he was. The result wasn't any different from when the Holy Spirit hindered him from sharing the gospel in the province of Asia and Bithynia. Paul found himself in Troas wondering why in the world he ended up there when that was not his plan and intention. But he was obedient to the Macedonian vision, the gospel was spread into Europe, and in retrospect we can see God's purpose in that. More important than getting locked into a conviction about where we should be or what we should be doing is to be truly committed by faith to following the leadership of His Spirit, whatever God chooses to do in our life.

Satan does a lot of things to hinder us from doing what God wants us to do. He is the god of this world, the prince of the power of the air. Sometimes it's just circumstances, but he delights in taking normal events and using them to hinder God from being glorified through our obedience to His will. Some time ago I found an old newsletter from our first term of service in Indonesia. I had written about the way missionaries spend their time lest anyone think we were spending all our time witnessing, planting churches, discipling believers, and confronting a lost world with the claims of Christ. I was expressing my disillusionment that so many things infringed on my time and hindered me from doing the thing I had gone there to do.

The Nature of Our Enemy, Part II

It was time to pay the annual automobile taxes
and renew registration, so I set aside Tuesday
morning to drive to Bondowoso, about thirty miles
north of Jember where we lived, where this was
handled for a four-county area. The road was being
widened and under construction, which meant
several detours over muddy trails and long waits
for one-way traffic in many sections. Nevertheless,
I arrived after a couple of hours to be told that the
procedure had been changed and the registration
must be processed in Jember where we lived.
I returned home in time for lunch, and Wednesday
went to the tax office to receive all the necessary
instructions. I must have the original and two
photocopies—Indonesians love abbreviations for
official papers—of my STNK, my PBKB, my BBN,
my SKUM, and my residence card. The rest of
the day was spent gathering these documents and
having them photocopied. Thursday morning
I returned to the office where one clerk had the
job of processing the papers. Dozens of people
were crowded around his window while other
clerks were sitting around chatting with each other
or reading the newspaper. After an hour
I had edged my way through the mob to the front
of the line and handed over my folder of papers.
The clerk sifted through them, noting that I did
not have the original SKUM. When I replied I had
not found it with all my other documents, but I did
have photocopies, he explained, "Oh, the original is
on file in Bondowoso. You must get it from there."

I quickly left on another round-trip to
Bondowoso, which consumed the rest of the day.
Friday I returned to the tax office and miraculously
had the papers processed and taxes paid within a
couple of hours. I then hurried to the police station
to complete the registration renewal. Confused by
several windows all crowded with people,
I approached the information desk and was told to
go first to a certain window to buy the forms that
needed to be filled out. Finding the window,
I was told by the officer in charge, "I'm sorry, we've
just run out of forms. But come back tomorrow;
perhaps we'll have more then."

Saturday I returned to the police station early,
bought the forms, filled them out, and with my
other papers went to the next window. The officer
looked at what I handed him and said, "We can't
accept this. You have two vehicles to register. See
that sign? Papers for your Jeep must be in a green
folder and papers for your motor scooter must be in
a gray folder." I hurried to the office supply store to
buy the two proper-colored folders and rushed home
again. When Bobbye saw me crawling out from
under the car and turning the motor scooter over,
she asked what in the world I was doing. I explained
I had to rub over the motor and chassis number with
a pencil and thin piece of paper to prove I, indeed,
was in possession of these vehicles. Having done
this and placed everything in the proper colored
folders, I returned to the police station about
12:10 p.m. to be told, "I'm sorry, we close at noon on
Saturday. You'll have to come back on Monday."

The Nature of Our Enemy, Part II

Early Monday morning I got in line at the
proper window. After a while my turn came and
I was asked first for my owner's book, which had
to be stamped, signed, and recorded. I handed
it to the officer and noticed it was added to the
bottom of a stack about ten inches high. I leaned
against the wall and passed the next hour chatting
impatiently with the people. When I noticed in the
window that the stack of registration booklets had
not diminished, I calmly asked if they would be
finished today. The clerk replied, "Oh, the head of
the division who must sign them is out of the office
this morning, but they should be finished this
afternoon." That afternoon I returned skeptically,
but was delighted to find this preliminary step
was finished. However, the registration could
not be completed until I had the official receipt
from the tax office, which would not be ready
until Wednesday. As I returned home, not just a
little frustrated, I thought, *Well at least I have a
full day to do a little mission work and remobilize
my patience.* But then I remembered the monthly
financial report had been due last week, so the
bookkeeping for our mission station had to be
done. Bobbye reminded me that in all my running
around I had forgotten to buy rice, which we had
to get in one hundred kilogram sacks, and we
needed to exchange the butane gas bottles that I'd
also neglected to do. That wiped out Tuesday, but
Wednesday I was back at the police station with
high hopes for completing the registration and
getting on with more important priorities.

After negotiating my way through the mob of
people at the window, I was told that I would also
need photocopies of my letter of having registered
with the police since I was a foreigner. Getting this
taken care of took half the morning, but when
I returned, everything now seemed to be in order.
The Jeep being finished, I got in line for motor
scooters, and within another hour it too was
registered. Now it would take two days to process
the papers, so I must return on Friday to pay the
final fees. Friday, after much more waiting, I was
handed the final registration certificate, and that
two-week ordeal was over.

Now with that taken care of, this was the month
our visa must be renewed for another year. I'll
need to get twelve forms from the immigration
office, three for each member of the family, get
our passports, residence permit, immigration
certificate, and alien registration booklet and make
photocopies. I've already written our business
office and Baptist foundation for official letters
requesting our extension but haven't received
them. So I have to call the Jakarta office to get the
needed sponsorship letters in order to go to the
local Department of Religion and get a letter of
approval and file everything with the Department
of Immigration. And on and on it went!

Was Satan responsible for all of that? That may be debat-
able, but I certainly thought so in the midst of all that time-
consuming, bureaucratic red tape. Whether or not Satan was
responsible, he was absolutely elated. Anything that can

keep us from doing God's work, witnessing to others, and fulfilling His will fits his schemes against the kingdom of God. Satan is clever and subtle. We never think of the busyness of daily demands as spiritual warfare, but anything that hinders us and diverts us from God's will and what we should be doing for His glory is an aspect of the battle. Whether it is dealing with time-consuming bureaucracies on the mission field, or just the demands of taking care of our family and working to fulfill the aspirations of an American lifestyle, little time is left for serving God and sharing Christ with a lost world. Does Satan not have something to do with it? Someone has said, "B-U-S-Y means 'being under Satan's yoke!'" James 4:17 says, "So, for the person who knows to do good and doesn't do it, it is a sin."

How do we deal with these kinds of hindrances? Scripture gives us a couple of clues. We're going to discuss the steps to victory in spiritual warfare later, but let's consider a couple of ways of dealing with Satan's proclivity to hinder us from doing what God would have us do because this may be an area where we are most vulnerable. After all, we are not doing anything immoral or sinful. But if we have any conscientiousness about spiritual disciplines and our walk with the Lord, it will be recognized that Satan is actively opposing our witness, diverting our time and causing us to rationalize and justify not doing what we know we should be doing. We may not succumb to his deceit and lies in contradiction

> *To him who knows the right thing to do and does not do it, to him it is sin.*

to the Word of God. We may have gained a victory in resisting temptation. But Satan subtly distracts us and diverts us from doing what we should. If we recognized it was Satan, we would readily repel his efforts, so he allows us to see it as just the normal, demanding circumstances of life.

Discipline in Time Management

One of the keys to avoid being hindered by Satan is disciplined time management. That comes easier and more natural for some than others. A lot of people are rather laid back and spontaneous, which means they just flow with the circumstances and do whatever the impulse of the moment compels them to do. On the other hand, there are those, like me, who are compulsive calendar keepers and list makers. We have such a need to plan our time and control our schedule that we are not sensitive to God's Spirit seeking to lead us or flexible enough to respond to opportunities He may put in our path.

When we have no discipline in planning and managing our time, it is easy for Satan to divert us and hinder us from doing what we should. We never get around to fulfilling our tasks and responsibilities. Many Christians have had plans for serving the Lord, being a more conscientious witness, even going to the mission field, but they never get around to it. Paul said in 1 Corinthians 9:26–27, "Therefore I do not run like one who runs aimlessly, or box like one who beats the air. Instead, I discipline my body and bring it under strict control, so that after preaching to others, I myself will not be disqualified." I have always been intrigued that Paul, of all people, could be concerned about being disqualified and no longer useful to God—he who had planted churches and been used so effectively in evangelism. But this should be a helpful clue to us. Paul realized that he must stay focused on God's calling and purpose. That focused commitment is much more than time management, but he understood that unless he disciplined his body, even he could be distracted by secondary and trivial things and no longer useful to God.

So the discipline to stay focused on what God has called us to do is important. It must be the commitment and passion of our life, so that every day we are conscious of God's presence leading us and seeking to use us as we walk in obedience. We must not allow secondary and trivial things to divert us and a lack of discipline to allow Satan to hinder us from doing what God would have us to do. And for those control freaks, like me, who order every detail of their day, we need to realize we can be so locked into our own plans that we are insensitive to God's leadership. We often overlook spontaneous opportunities for witness and ministry because we are so focused on what we have determined to do.

One of my life verses has always been Proverbs 3:5–6, "Trust in the LORD with all your heart, and do not rely on your own understanding; think about Him in all your ways, and He will guide you on the right paths." That passage has always been an exhortation to trust in the Lord completely, confident He will guide my life in every way. However, I have discovered the most difficult aspect of this instruction is "do not rely on your own understanding." It is so easy to be diverted by our own plans, and, when we rely on our own understanding, it is easy for Satan to use our predetermined agenda to hinder us from what God would have us to do.

One's Mind Set on God

Satan also hinders us from doing God's will by getting us to focus on ourselves—our needs, our comforts, and our plans—rather than on God. In Matthew 16 Jesus was attempting to prepare His disciples for His crucifixion, but Peter could not accept it and objected. In verse 23 Jesus addressed Peter and said, "Get behind Me, Satan! You are an offense to Me because you're not thinking about God's concerns, but man's." That may appear to be a rather harsh reaction as Peter meant well. But we need to recognize who seeks to hinder God's will being done. How does the enemy keep God from being glorified through our obedience to what He wants us to do? Satan causes our minds to focus on our own interests, our needs, our comforts, and our safety; and we can get totally consumed in living for that instead of what God has called us to do. Jesus called Peter, "Satan," because He had the spiritual perception to recognize who was influencing him. Peter had good intentions and meant well, just as we often do, but his values were based on what seemed best from man's perspective; his proposal was contrary to what God desired to do. Peter was used by Satan as a stumbling block because his mind wasn't focused on God's interest but man's.

There is a prominent myth that the center of God's will is the safest place to be, but it's not necessarily safe to focus our life on God's purpose and glory. Just as being in the center of God's will led Jesus to the cross, obedience to God provides no guarantee of safety from a human perspective. In recent years eight of our missionaries have been martyred in their place of service, four of them in Iraq. Were they out of God's will because they were killed? Does God separate us like the tares and wheat, putting a hedge of protection around those in the center of His will and leaving the rest vulnerable to an evil and fallen world? I don't think so. God is not primarily concerned about our physical safety and security; His primary purpose is to be glorified in our lives and among the nations. Sometimes the only path to His being glorified is through suffering and even death. Our witness may be more effective when people see the reality of our faith in times of suffering and as we experience illness and trials. We are going to talk about adversity that is common to life as one of Satan's favorite fiery darts that He uses to defeat us. But don't be deceived by Satan and, like Peter, think we are entitled to comfort and safety. Don't let him hinder God from being glorified in your life by seeking to avoid the inconvenience and sacrifices involved in fulfilling His will. Focusing our mind, our concerns and affections on our needs and interests instead of God's is to forfeit doing what will glorify Him.

> *God is not primarily concerned with our safety and security but to be glorified in our life.*

Many of our missionaries have parents and family who have been opposed to their going overseas. They make them feel guilty for abandoning them as if having children and grandchildren nearby were more important than obedience to God's call. From their perspective their needs and what they want is more important than a lost world knowing Jesus. Sometimes those closest to us are the ones Satan uses to hinder us from doing God's will. Several years ago one of our families in orientation was served with a court injunction, filed by their parents, to keep them from going overseas. Satan will go to any extent to keep us from fulfilling and carrying out God's will and doing what will glorify Him. Satan uses circumstances, busyness, other people— even those who love us and mean well—to hinder God's purpose in our lives. But more often than not it is primarily that our minds and hearts set on our own interests, desires, and plans that keep us from being totally submissive to God and His purpose.

We have looked at just four characteristics of our enemy as revealed in Scripture. He is our adversary, opposed to God and His kingdom. He is a deceiver and liar seeking to create doubts, erode our faith, and keep us from believing God's Word and promises. He is the tempter who takes those old self-centered inclinations of our fleshly nature to entice us to sin. And he is the one that simply hinders us from doing what God would have us do that would glorify Him. There are other identities—thief, ruler of the world, god of this world, beast, prince of the power of the air, spirit of disobedience, evil one. And each description has implications regarding his nature that should alert us to his strategies and how he works.

The Son of God appeared for this purpose, that He might destroy the works of the devil. To yield and succumb to Satan's tactics is to believe his lies and deceit, contrary to what Christ has told us, because he has been defeated. Being aware of the battle and understanding the nature of the enemy is a major part of claiming the victory. The fact and assurance of victory, however, implies there is a battle, and a battle means there is an enemy, an adversary.

CHAPTER 4

THE STRUGGLE WITH THE WORLD

Such wisdom does not come down from above, but is earthly, sensual, demonic. For where envy and selfish ambition exist, there is disorder and every kind of evil. But the wisdom from above is first pure, then peace-loving, gentle, compliant, full of mercy and good fruits, without favoritism and hypocrisy.
—James 3:15–17

The second aspect of our tripartite enemy in spiritual warfare is the world because this is the domain in which we live and in which Satan works. Satan is against us, but he also uses the realm of this world as a context and powerful influence to distract us from living by the godly, Christlike principles and values that glorify God. Several years ago when I was coordinating our mission work in India, I clipped an interesting article from a New Delhi newspaper.

Every day thousands of Hindus flock to the shores of the great Ganges River where they drink and bathe in the holy waters as partially cremated corpses float past them, and nearby drains spew millions of gallons of raw sewage into the river. While the faithful seem unfazed, the Indian government is concerned that religious rituals and social customs have helped turn Indian's most sacred river into a fifteen-hundred-mile health hazard. They have designed the largest environmental project in Indian history—cleaning up the Ganges from its glacial source in the Himalayas to the mouth at the Bay of Bengal. The biggest challenge, according to environmentalists, comes not from the rapid urbanization along the river shores, but from the firm belief among many Indians that the Ganges is so spiritually pure it cannot be polluted regardless of how much garbage is dumped into it. . . . With sewage and half-cremated corpses being thrown into the river, people urinating, taking baths, washing their clothes and bathing their animals, they're beginning to realize that it's dirty. But the purity and sacredness of the river can never be destroyed or even diminished. Even a breeze from the Ganges is enough to wash sins away.

Our reaction may be to think how foolish and irrational such thinking is. "All the garbage and sewage going into the river cannot pollute it because it is holy." A lot of Christians rationalize a less than holy lifestyle the same way. We watch movies and entertainment that portray sinful and ungodly behavior and carnal attitudes. We feed on a television diet of murder, crime, and mayhem and rationalize, "It doesn't affect me. I'm a Christian; I've been born again and sanctified by the blood of Jesus. It's not real; it's just entertainment." To think that we can feed our minds and expose ourselves to all of the garbage and filth of the world and believe it doesn't affect us, our attitudes, and our thinking is as foolish as the Hindu pilgrims who think the Ganges River cannot be polluted. It demonstrates the effectiveness of Satan's deception.

Look again at the temptation experience of Jesus in Luke 4:5–7, "So he took Him up and showed Him all the kingdoms of the world in a moment of time. The Devil said to Him, 'I will give You their splendor and all this authority, because it has been given over to me, and I can give it to anyone I want. If You, then, will worship me, all will be Yours.'" Jesus didn't contradict Satan's claim that all the kingdoms of the world belonged to him. When did Satan gain that dominion, that authority, over all the earth? First John 5:19 says, "We know that we are of God, and the whole world is under the sway of the evil one." While the nations and peoples of the world who do not know Jesus Christ and have not come to a faith relationship with God are, indeed, under the power and deception of Satan, so are massive segments of our own society.

First John 5:18 tells us, "We know that everyone who has been born of God does not sin, but the One who is born of God [Jesus] keeps him, and the evil one does not touch him." Because we are born of God, we have assurance of victory; the evil one, although he has dominion in the world, cannot touch us because we are kept secure by the sinless Son of God who died for us, conquered Satan on the cross, and protects us from the allure of worldly values. However, Satan subtly and deceptively propagates his lies so that we readily compromise our values and become splotched by the sinfulness of the world rather than claiming the victory we have been given in Christ.

Jude warns us in verses 18–19, "'In the end time there will be scoffers walking according to their own ungodly desires.' These people create divisions and are merely natural, not having the Spirit." Timothy also alerts us to the extent of worldliness that will be apparent in the last days. "But know this: difficult times will come in the last days. For people will be lovers of self, lovers of money, boastful, proud, blasphemers, disobedient to parents, ungrateful, unholy, unloving, irreconcilable, slanderers, without self-control, brutal, without love for what is good, traitors, reckless, conceited, lovers of pleasure rather than lovers of God, holding to the form of religion but denying its power" (2 Tim. 3:1–5). That's a pretty extensive description of worldliness!

When did Satan gain dominion in the world? Obviously it was in the garden of Eden. It was God's intention that man have dominion over the earth. He created man for this purpose. "Then God said, 'Let Us make man in Our image, according to Our likeness. They will rule the fish of the sea, the birds of the sky, the animals, all the earth'" (Gen. 1:26). Man was intended to have dominion over all the earth, but in disobedience and listening to Satan's lies and influence, he relinquished that dominion to Satan. However, we can't just blame Adam and Eve because we are still doing it. The problem is that we are continually being enticed to choose to live for the false riches and godless principles of this world. We rationalize the clear instructions and admonitions of God's Word in how we are to live to eat of the forbidden fruit and indulge our carnal appetites. Satan continues to appeal effectively to the lust of the flesh, the lust of eyes, and pride of life.

James 1:27 tells us, "Pure and undefiled religion before our God and Father is this: to look after orphans and widows in their distress and to keep oneself unstained by the world." It is good to be reminded that religious piety, which is pleasing to God, is not accomplished just in our worship and faithful attendance at church but is expressed through ministry to those in need. But we are also to keep ourselves unstained by the world. Purity is a challenge when we are immersed each day in a world where sex is glorified and sensual gratification in entertainment is flaunted with little restraint. Corporate scandals reflect that business and economic leaders have no moral compass beyond self-aggrandizement and the accumulation of personal wealth. Politicians and government officials seem to have no hesitancy in mishandling the truth if it promotes personal advancement. The media put their spin on information to propagate postmodernism and a relativism in which there are no absolute moral standards. The result is religious expression being declared illegal in the public marketplace and sanctity of human life set aside in justification of abortion rights. Immoral relationships and aberrant homosexual lifestyles have become acceptable, and even Christians choose to reject the authority of God's Word in believing and following whatever is convenient.

Advertisements and credit card promotions persuade us to succumb to consumer indulgences. "Buy now, pay later" appeals entice us to increase indebtedness in our quest to accumulate more and more things. It is not to meet valid needs but to indulge the enticement of materialistic comforts, to enjoy the latest gadgets and attain status in the eyes of friends and neighbors. Families are being destroyed by indebtedness because they believed the lies of financial institutions and used credit to acquire all the desires of the "good life" now. Lives are being wrecked by the deceitful collaboration of the government with the gambling industry, which entices people, usually the poor, to take risks under the illusion of instant wealth.

We readily recognize the more obvious areas of sin such as pornography, lying, adultery, immorality, and such things. We may not be enticed to indulge in such sinful behavior; in fact, Satan knows these things do not appeal to us, at least they should not entice a child of God. But he is subtle, enticing us to embrace and justify worldly values that may not seem so obviously to contradict God's way and holiness, yet the end is just the same—spiritual defeat. Colossians 2:8 exhorts us to avoid becoming captivated by the deceptive values of the world. "Be careful that no one takes you captive through philosophy and empty deceit based on human tradition, based on the elemental forces of the world, and not based on Christ."

A worldly approach to money and financial management rather than practicing biblical stewardship is one of Satan's most prominent and successful strategies in this regard. Like you I receive daily "opportunities" for acquiring additional credit cards as well as appeals from financial institutions telling me how I can quickly become wealthy. This deluge of mail appeals to our fleshly desires for success, comfort, luxury, and status in society. Responding to these offers of "easy credit" puts many into bondage to indebtedness. Believing the lie, "You can have it all now," leads to stress, anxiety, broken marriages, and debilitating financial burdens. When we live beyond our means, we reveal that our priorities and values are not biblical but worldly and materialistic. We severely limit our options and inhibit our ability to serve God and to glorify Him as good stewards of all He has given us. Many missionary candidates who feel called of God cannot pursue that call because they have accumulated such a large indebtedness from maxing out their credit cards and living beyond their means.

Jesus told a parable in Luke 12:16–21 about the danger of being entrapped by the covetous desire for wealth and the material things of this world. The rich man accumulated more and more wealth but was condemned as a fool and lost his soul because he lived only for the things of this world rather than for God. Not only does one quickly begin to feel a sense of entitlement to more and more riches and luxury goods; there is a tendency to think that we have gained success and earned the right to such indulgences because of our own efforts and ability rather than God's blessings. It is difficult to keep material prosperity in the proper perspective of glorifying God as it usually feeds our selfish nature. Jesus said in Luke 12:15, "Watch out and be on guard against all greed because one's life is not in the abundance of his possessions."

Wealth and money are not evil in themselves. In fact, many notable philanthropists and dedicated Christian stewards recognize their success enables them to serve God and help others. But that is unusual because of the deceptive nature of wealth. All too often it lures us into the sticky web of worldly values. First Timothy 6:10 is an oft-quoted passage alerting us to this danger. "For the love of money is a root of all kinds of evil, and by craving it, some have wandered away from the faith and pierced themselves with many pains." We don't have to have a lot of money for it to lead us away from faith in Jesus Christ rather than using what we have to glorify God in obedience to His will. Few Christians continue to practice even the minimum giving of a tithe to God because they are so consumed in financial obligations in conformity to worldly materialism.

We can readily identify with the dilemma of the psalmist who said in Psalm 73:2–3, "But as for me, my feet almost slipped; my steps nearly went astray. For I envied the arrogant; I saw the prosperity of the wicked." One of the most prevalent tendencies that should alert us to being diverted from pure and holy devotion to God is our envy of those in the world who seem to have it so good in spite of the fact that God has no place in their life. We find ourselves wishing we were free to indulge in hedonistic pleasures that others seem to enjoy. We see promiscuous lifestyles portrayed on television; movie stars and prominent sports figures seem to flaunt their disregard of the basic spiritual values of holiness and godliness without retribution. A growing number of people never go to church and have no evidence of spiritual piety, yet they seem to prosper with beautiful houses, expensive cars and boats, vacations to exotic places and increasing wealth.

Someone has said the problem with things is just that; they are things. And that's what the world uses to appeal to us. We become possessed by possessions. Envy begins to distort our perspective even in childhood and in the early years of school when we want to be a part of the popular crowd, those who always wear the latest fashions and have the neatest toys. Students who are a part of elite cliques and indulge in drinking and partying without any apparent parental restraint are envied as the "in crowd" and those always having fun. We are losing the younger generation in our churches to the world as they view religion as legalistic standards and expectations of self-denial that only deprive them of what others are free to enjoy.

The pressures to conform to the world are powerful. They begin early when a child who chooses not to participate in some mischievous activity conspired by his playmates is taunted and ridiculed. A young person who values purity and seeks to honor God does not fit in with the crowd. And though the repercussions may not be physical, the ostracism and condescension will be felt just as severely. Too many Christians seek to straddle the fence and find some middle ground of compromise in order to be accepted by friends and colleagues at work. No one wants to appear pious and judgmental, and the pressure to fit in as one of the "good ole guys" is not always so subtle. To resist temptation in order to be true to the Lord is to be subjected to ridicule and disdain by others. Even the media is becoming more and more blatant in its scathing verbal persecution of people of faith.

What's the appeal here? It is the deception that you can have whatever you desire and are, in fact, entitled to it. Never mind that you are a Christian and should be guided by other values. The world convinces you that you can have whatever you want and believe to be essential for your happiness and comfort. And we never recognize that Satan is leading us astray through the lust of the flesh, the lust of the eyes, and the pride of life. How effectively he uses the materialistic and self-centered values of the world to create a sense of entitlement. "You deserve it. Everyone else is doing it." We fail to realize God is robbed of His glory because we give glory to things, the created instead of the Creator.

I would never tolerate pornography coming into my home. If it ever got into my mail, it would go straight into the trash. But society is becoming saturated with the attractions of sexual indulgence. Even many Christians are entrapped in a vicious whirlpool of sexual fantasies and lustful thoughts, being fed by readily accessible Internet sites. Perhaps it was a lot easier to maintain purity in our lifestyle when one had to search out places of carnal entertainment and intentionally drive to the more seedy areas of town to patronize adult-only bookstores or places of prostitution. The devious nature of our enemy has been successful in enticing many to participate in the same kind of gratification through forms that are not so open and blatant. It it hard to find movies and television programs without explicit sexual content. The entertainment world has gradually pulled us in to the point that we feed our minds with these reflections of worldly values and convince ourselves that it has no affect on us; it is just relaxation and entertainment. Not only the sexual content and innuendoes are enjoyable to many today, much of the programming is focused on murder and violence. What does that reflect about God's values and the sanctity of life?

In my travels and frequent speaking on weekends, I sometimes tune in to ESPN Sports Center to get an overview of the day's games. I've discovered that you can't surf the television channels on Saturday night, or any other time, without catching graphically sexual images. It's uncanny how Satan continues to plant those images in your mind. They are there and continue to surface in your memory for days. Satan has access to our minds and uses the things of the world—the lust of the flesh and lust of the eyes, the attractions that appeal to selfish gratification that are always around us—to deprive God of His holiness in our lives. In this way Satan constantly pressures us to conform to the world and its perverse standards.

One reason we are so vulnerable is because we readily expose ourselves to the things of the world and, in fact, enjoy doing so. We may invoke our freedom in Christ and the fact that we are under grace, not the legalism that would prohibit enjoyment of secular things. But Paul reminds us by his testimony in 1 Corinthians 6:12, "'Everything is permissible for me,' but not everything is helpful. 'Everything is permissible for me,' but I will not be brought under the control of anything." We are warned against having a casual attitude toward the sinful things of the world by the example of the Israelites who were destroyed in the wilderness. In 1 Corinthians 10 we are told that they indulged in eating, drinking, playing, and craved evil things, acting immorally. They were destroyed, and verse 11 says, "Now these things happened to them as examples, and they were written as a warning to us, on whom the ends of the ages have come."

Too many Christians succumb to moral failure, putting aside their marriage covenant to indulge in an adulterous affair or simply adopting the sensuality and sexual mores of the world. Our self-centered fleshly nature gives us a sense of entitlement, convincing us we deserve whatever gives us pleasure and enjoyment. Someone close to me went through a divorce recently, after many years of marriage. I was not just disappointed; I was devastated. I could not believe it was happening. I took the initiative to talk with my friend and try to understand what was going on. In an effort to justify the divorce, he said in the course of our conversation, "She was no longer meeting my needs." I replied, not without a tinge of indignation, "What does that have to do with it?" I felt we were close enough in our relationship to confront him rather harshly and went on, "When you were married, you made a covenant with your wife and with the Lord to give yourself to her. Your one concern and focus of your life was to be her welfare, her happiness, her joy. It had nothing to do with you and your needs."

Divorce is rampant, even among Christians. Many have embraced the worldly concept that marriage is a fifty-fifty type commitment of each spouse giving equally to the other in a beautiful reciprocal relationship. But I discovered the ratio of commitment is not even ninety-ten. I have no intention of going into all the details of how I discovered this reality, but I can remember the adjustments and struggle of suddenly having another person to share my life. I realized my obligation to love my wife and care for her and wanted to do that with all my heart. But I had some needs as well—expectations of affection, respect, and consideration. I was so in love, I think I was truly willing to give 90 percent to the relationship—my life, my time, and everything she needed—but I expected a little in return. It wasn't unrealistic to expect 10 percent of the relationship to be given to meeting my needs. But even that didn't work. It doesn't work because if giving of myself as a 90-percent part of the relationship is contingent on what I get, it is still about me. The only thing that will work in a marriage relationship is 100-percent devotion and commitment to one's spouse. That's what love is, giving of oneself whether you get anything out of it or not. And love is of God. We are capable of loving and giving ourselves to another, or to a lost world, only as we follow Him and are empowered by the Holy Spirit. Love doesn't allow any self-centeredness that leads to dissension, conflict, and sinful indulgences of the flesh.

The world convinces us that our needs should be met, that we have rights and it is all about us.

I can't think of anything that grieves me more than to hear that a missionary, pastor, or someone in Christian ministry has failed morally. I think, *How could this happen?* Not only do they forfeit their ministry and calling, and often destroy their marriage and family, but their behavior is destructive to a kingdom witness among the lost. On the mission field it contradicts the Christian witness that has been proclaimed, disillusions new believers being discipled, and often deters the impact on society of an infant church that is being planted. Can you imagine how elated Satan is to bring down a missionary or an influential pastor? All Christians are vulnerable, but those who dare to stand up against the powers of darkness and infringe on Satan's territory become prime targets. We alert our missionaries that they are venturing into Satan's territory; he doesn't want to relinquish his kingdoms of darkness, and those who presume to represent the kingdom of God will come under attack. Satan could do little to destroy one's witness and ministry as effectively as feeding the lusts of the flesh and leading a person to yield to a selfish act of physical gratification. Many respond with remorse and repentance, but the witness has been compromised, and Satan has won the victory.

Many attribute that seed of worldly lust to being planted by Internet pornography. It is something in which one can indulge privately without anyone else knowing. It leads to an addiction that poisons the mind, and too often leads to sinful behavior. Often a man and woman will be mutually attracted and find pleasure in just being in the company of someone other than their spouse. It moves beyond being together in groups to creating opportunities to be together, often in conscious denial that it was intentional. Enjoyable socializing, presumed to be innocent and without any intention of reaching the point of adultery, invariably leads to crossing the line, because one's heart and affections have been opened to Satan using a powerful aspect of our human nature inappropriately and contrary to the honorable and holy way God intended.

Decisions should be made ahead of time regarding activities, entertainment, and relationships, avoiding anything that is inappropriate. A guide for me is never to watch anything on television that I would not be comfortable with my mother, my wife, or my pastor watching with me. Other principles include never reading anything that I would be embarrassed to read to my children. I try not ever to be in a situation alone with someone of the opposite sex other than my wife. Get an Internet filter. Faithfully adhering to such commitments keeps Satan from having an opportunity to expose us to anything that would appeal to our basic nature. James 4:4 confronts us with a timely reminder: "Do you not know that friendship with the world is hostility toward God?"

Jesus told His disciples they would be hated by the world because they were not of the world. They did not live like others in the world, and their holiness was a reflection on the shameful behavior and values of those in the world. In the prayer of Jesus in John 17:15, He made an interesting appeal to the Father: "I am not praying that You take them out of the world but that You protect them from the evil one." As long as we are in this world we will encounter the appeal of the world that Satan uses to entice us to affections and desires that are not of God. Jesus is praying for us as He did for His disciples, and God is the one who protects us from the evil one.

One of the most effective deterrents to worldly indulgence is an accountability relationship. That's one of the reasons God has made us members of a body of believers. But such a fellowship is meaningless if we are not willing to be open, honest, and transparent. Every husband and wife should have a relationship of accountability with each other in which nothing is hidden. God has provided strength in numbers. It is hard to stand alone in our struggle against all the unwholesome influences and potential temptations to which we are exposed every day simply because we live in a sinful and fallen world. We need one another—a mission team, a church staff, Christian coworkers, our family, or a group of friends that will stand together, determine to live for the Lord, and hold one another accountable.

At the International Mission Board we do everything possible to assure that our missionaries will never yield to temptation and step across the line into moral failure that would ruin their ministry, potentially destroy their marriage, and erode a Christian witness on the mission field. We are thorough in our screening process, and I don't think we could be any more detailed and intimate in our questioning. We have explored whether there is more we could do in orientation, but we already discuss the issues pretty candidly. I've come to the conclusion that there is only one solution that guarantees success in maintaining a holy lifestyle that brings glory to God. It is to have such a desperation and heart for God that we can never take that first step in allowing our minds to nurture a temptation or a lustful thought that would divert us from the holiness and purity to which God calls us.

Andy Dietz, who is on the staff of a church in the panhandle of Texas, has been coordinating mission trips overseas for many years. On one particular trip with his young people, the project had been finished, and the kids had left for home, but Andy stayed over to visit with missionary friends in the area. He was coming back through a European city on his way home. Having an overnight transit, he went downtown for dinner, found himself in the wrong part of town, and was mugged and kidnapped. After taking all his money, and all he could get from the ATM machine, his captors had him wire his family to ask for $5,000 to secure his release. His family notified us, and we activated a prayer network and contacted our personnel in the city who were not even aware he was there. They notified the police, but before anything could be done, Andy was able to elude his captors and get away while they were eating and drinking.

I called him after he got home to talk through the experience and seek to minister to him. I asked him, after such a traumatic experience, if he thought he would go on any more mission trips. He said, "Oh yes. It's the most gratifying thing I do to take these kids overseas." He continued, "I was negligent and learned that I have got to be more vigilant about where I go." He described what it was like to be beaten, tied up, put in the trunk of a car, and his life threatened. He said, "They didn't know me. Nobody knew where I was. I meant nothing to them. My life was worthless. I realized they wouldn't think twice about getting rid of me, and no one would know." He continued, "You can imagine how desperate I was to get away. And all I could think of was God saying, 'Andy, this is how desperate you should be to know Me.'"

I held the phone in disbelief. I can only imagine the extent of desperation to escape a situation where your life is threatened. Can you imagine being so desperate to know

God in all of His fullness, to have a heart that is so passionate for Him and His holiness? I think that's the only thing that will be a fail-safe deterrent to immoral behavior. We are always vulnerable; Satan will see to that, but in Christ we have been given the capacity to walk in holiness and victory.

Satan knows that many of us would never be enticed by immoral behavior and carnal gratifications, but he is devious and clever and uses the humanistic and materialistic values of the world to entice us to live for ourselves and for

> *The most effective deterrent to the allure of the world is to have a heart that is desperate for God!*

what we can gain for our own comfort and benefit. Living in the world causes us easily to succumb to a sense of entitlement. We see others enjoying the comforts and pleasures of a worldly lifestyle and rationalize nothing is innately wrong with that. In fact, Satan will convince us we deserve it.

When the IMB was riding a wave of record missionary appointments and growth, it began to put a strain on our budget. I received an occasional letter from missionaries who would say, "If the number of missionaries being appointed would be restricted instead of sending so many, it would be possible to increase our support and better provide for the needs of those on the field." I was heartbroken that anyone would succumb to such an attitude. "It would be preferable to provide me a higher salary and more comfortable lifestyle, rather than sending more missionaries to reach a lost world; my needs are more important than sending more missionaries to reach more people groups and save them from hell!" Many never consider even going to the mission field because of an unwillingness to sacrifice the comforts and security in America that we have become convinced we deserve. As our financial crisis deepened and we had to restrict the number of new personnel being sent to the field, other missionaries wrote to say, "Why couldn't each missionary unit return part of his or her salary so the board would have funds to send more new personnel?"

New missionaries usually go out with great devotion to God's call. With a willingness to sacrifice and do whatever it takes to reach a lost world, they seldom even express interest in their salary and benefits. But after they have been on the field awhile and experience the reality of what sacrifice entails, their attitude sometimes begins to change. Making ends meet is hard. The dollar is weak, and inflation is high. They see others with more affluence shopping in the international markets, buying imported goods. One can quickly forget that Jesus calls us to a sacrificial lifestyle and to turn our backs on the things of the world. For a sense of entitlement to emerge is not unusual.

A missionary, serving in a high-cost economy, resigned, explaining he could not possibly live on the support being provided by the International Mission Board. As an illustration of how they could not make it on their missionary salary, he pointed out that it cost his family $57 to eat out at McDonald's each week. Where do we get into that mindset that we're entitled to what the rest of the world enjoys, and we have to have it to serve the Lord? Satan is able to seduce us into adopting the values of the world, in thinking we are entitled to a comfortable lifestyle and salary that enable us to own and enjoy the luxuries and amenities of others.

Jesus modeled the life of sacrifice we are to follow. Possessions and the material things of life are not sinful in themselves; God provides for our needs—houses, beds, kitchen appliances. But if we remember that they should be used for God's glory, it would probably deter us from excesses that the world propagates upon us. Above all, as we deal with the temptation to acquire more and more, even to the point of abusing credit and putting ourselves in a bondage to indebtedness, we should remember that Jesus calls us to sacrifice and self-denial, as expressed in this poem.

The Crown and the Cross

They borrowed the bed to lay His head when Christ the Lord came down;
They borrowed the ass in the mountain pass for Him to ride to town.
But the crown that He wore and the cross that He bore were His own,
The cross was His own.

They borrowed the boat for Him to sit when He taught the multitude;
They borrowed the nest for Him to rest, He had never a home so rude.
But the crown that He wore and the cross that He bore were His own,
The cross was His own.

They borrowed the bread with which He fed the crowd on the mountainside;
They borrowed the dish of broken fish with which He satisfied.
But the crown that He wore and the cross that He bore were His own,
The cross was His own.

They borrowed the room on the way to the tomb, the Passover lamb to eat;
They borrowed the cave, for Him a grave; they borrowed the winding sheet.
But the crown that He wore and the cross that He bore were His own,
The cross was His own.

The crown on His head was worn in my stead; for me the Savior died;
For the guilt of my sin, the nails drove in, when Him they crucified.
And though the crown that He wore, and the cross that He bore were His own,
They were rightly mine instead.

(Author Unknown)

Our mission organization was going through a church-growth-strategy study my first term in Indonesia, realizing we needed to make adjustments in our church-planting methodology. It was after the aborted communist coup, and churches were growing rapidly. However, we were not seeing significant growth in our own work and needed to get our strategy aligned with what God was doing. Yet, once we got into our study, God led us to look at other issues such as relationships, lifestyles, and organizational structure—things that were inhibiting our effectiveness. The Lord began to work in our hearts, especially regarding the matter of lifestyle. Some were resistant, but conviction spread and infected the whole group. It resulted in a resolve to move out of the big, pretentious houses in areas where foreign diplomats and businessmen lived. We realized we needed to adopt a lifestyle more compatible with our national pastors and the common people with whom we were ministering. Many made a commitment to move to the villages where there wasn't the convenience of electricity and indoor plumbing. As the momentum grew, it was obvious the Lord was at work.

A lady stood up in our meeting and spoke with emotion. With tears she said, "We've got to do this. We've got to move to the villages and *kampungs* (neighborhood ghettos) if we're going to be used of God. We can't isolate ourselves and continue the way we've been living." Then she blurted out between her sobs, "But I can't give up my refrigerator!" She had begun to realize the practical implications of such a commitment. The thought occurred to me that God knows what we need to serve effectively where He calls us. He is concerned about the health and the care of our family. He probably doesn't want us to give up refrigerators, but we had better be willing to give them up!

Anytime we say there is something we are not willing to give up, we draw a bottom line of commitment beyond which we are unwilling to go. The lordship of Christ demands full and complete surrender and relinquishment of all rights, but the world convinces us that we are entitled to what others have and that compromise is acceptable. I have seen families of six live in seven-hundred-square-foot apartments in places like Russia and Hong Kong, yet others will say I can't live in a house less than two thousand square feet. Some missionaries live in spacious houses in the capital city with lots of amenities. Those called to live among remote, isolated people groups can begin to feel deprived and resent the disparity and the sacrifice they have to make.

Where does the concept of equality and entitlement come from? Not from God; it comes from the world. Jesus calls us to eschew comfort and to die to self; His call to discipleship has always been a call to sacrifice. If everybody lived in the capital city and the more comfortable locations, there would be a lot of people who would never hear the gospel in the frontier areas of countries around the world. Satan is the source of jealousy, envy, and lust for what the world offers, even among missionaries, in ways that defeat us and deprive God of being glorified through our sacrifice and obedience.

One of our missionaries had gone to an unreached people group and had to commute a great distance to access the area where his assigned people lived. After a couple of years he was finally able to get a plot of land to build a house. Because it was an isolated area, a ministry center was needed in the house, as well as a school room and adequate space for all the children. He proceeded to design and build a house, about three thousand square feet, which by American standards isn't all that large, but well beyond the policy limits of sixteen hundred square feet the mission board feels is adequate in Third-World countries. The main problem was putting what would appear to be a mansion in the midst of people with nothing but mud huts and straw roofs for miles around. Mission leadership tried to persuade him to see that this was not only a violation of policy but an inappropriate lifestyle in the midst of his target people. His reaction was severe, expressing anger that the IMB didn't support his ministry and appreciate what he was trying to do. Administration didn't care about his family and their needs. He accused leadership of being legalistic and unspiritual. The impasse deteriorated until finally he came home intending to resign.

I happened to be with him at a mission conference, and he saw this as an opportunity to ventilate. He was really unloading about how unfair everybody was, how legalistic our policy was, and how we didn't care about his family, didn't support his ministry, and so forth. He went on to express his intentions to resign. When he finally paused, I addressed him by name and asked, "Do you believe God called you to that people group?" He responded, "Yes, that's why we were there." I asked, "Is anyone going to take your place?" He said, "No, I'm not aware of anyone else that is available to pick up the work." I continued, "Now let me get this straight. You are willing to be disobedient to what you have affirmed is God's call, and you are willing for these people to be deprived of hearing the gospel and go to hell because you can't have a big, comfortable house. Is that what you're saying?" He just stared at me, speechless, and later decided to go back to the field.

Our thinking can get so twisted and distorted, but it is really not surprising. Satan uses the values of the world to create wants and desires and to influence us to adopt the materialistic standards of the world, justifying it with a sense of entitlement.

While still in a leadership role overseas, I was conducting a pre-stateside interview with a missionary couple finishing their first term of service. After language study they had moved to a difficult assignment in a Muslim country and had essentially not had any success. They had not seen any results, and it had been a difficult term. The children had been sick, the community hadn't received them, they had been harassed by gangs of kids throwing gravel on their tin roof all night and that sort of thing. With a sense of dejection that they had nothing to show for their whole term of work, they said, "We've been thinking that maybe there is some place we could be used more effectively next term."

I responded with support for the possibility of a move. They were dedicated and gifted, and I could think of several places in that country and in neighboring countries where they could be used. As I began to discuss some optional assignments they might consider, they interrupted me and said, "Jerry, we want you to understand, we're willing to come back here next term." I had jumped to the conclusion that they weren't willing to come back to their present assignment. With disbelief I exclaimed, "In spite of what you have encountered and the difficulty your family would face with no assurance of results, you'd be willing to face another four years in this situation?" They said, "Yes. When we got here after language study and realized what we were up against, we had to reconcile ourselves to the fact that God had not called us to success or personal fulfillment but to obedience. And if this is where God wants us, we don't want to consider anywhere else."

That's not the kind of attitude that comes from the world. The world would say to plan your life and assert yourself to get what you want. You deserve success and fulfillment. If you don't find it, move to another location, take another job; don't let anyone deprive you of what you want. A willingness to sacrifice the comforts and conveniences others enjoy doesn't fit worldly values. But Jesus calls us to obedience, an obedience to follow wherever He leads. It may entail sacrifice and suffering, which is a contradiction of what the world desires. We will be constantly confronted with the allure of the world's values to the point of believing it is something we deserve. And it's all a part of spiritual warfare as Satan uses the world around us to divert us from God's will and a lifestyle that glorifies Him.

> "God has not called us to success or personal fulfillment but to obedience!"

First John 2:15 tells us, "Do not love the world or the things that belong to the world. If anyone loves the world, love for the Father is not in him." Only the heart that loves God and is desperate to know Him in all of His fullness will allow us to resist the appeal and attractions of the lust of the flesh, the lust of the eyes, and the pride of life. But we are not left to our own feeble efforts to overcome the attractions of the world. God has provided us the victory if we will believe and follow Him. First John 5:4 says, "Whatever has been born of God conquers the world. This is the victory that has conquered the world: our faith." We have that victory because of the One who is in us; He is greater than all the allure and enticement of those who are in the world that Satan would use to defile and defeat us. First John 4:4 says, "You are from God, little children, and you have conquered them, because the One who is in you is greater than the one who is in the world." We who are saved should heed the admonition of Titus 2:11–12, "For the grace of God has appeared, with salvation for all people, instructing us to deny godlessness and worldly lusts."

We have been born again and should have no excuse for being deluded by the attractions of the world. First Corinthians 2:12 says, "Now we have not received the spirit of the world, but the Spirit who is from God, in order to know what has been freely given to us by God." Revelation 11:15 reminds us that one day "the kingdom of the world [will] become the kingdom of our Lord and of His Messiah." That is what God is in the process of doing that He might receive all glory and honor and power. It is beginning in us, His people. We are to reflect the kingdom of God and His reign in our life, unspotted by the world.

We are encouraged in 2 Timothy 2:15 to "be diligent to present yourself approved to God, a worker who doesn't need to be ashamed, correctly teaching the word of truth." We do this by also heeding verse 16 that says, "But avoid irreverent, empty speech, for this will produce an even greater measure of godlessness." We work in the marketplace to support our families and to provide for our physical and material needs in this world. But we must remember that we live to serve God and bring glory to Him, even in the secular workplace. We are to be diligent in living in a way that is approved by God, avoiding even empty worldly conversation that contributes to ungodly attitudes and behavior and robs God of His glory.

CHAPTER 5

THE BATTLE BETWEEN THE FLESH AND THE SPIRIT

I say then, walk by the Spirit and you will not carry
out the desire of the flesh. For the flesh desires what is
against the Spirit, and the Spirit desires what is against
the flesh; these are opposed to each other, so that you
don't do what you want. But if you are led by the Spirit,
you are not under the law.
—Galatians 5:16–18

The third part of our tripartite enemy is the flesh. It is probably what immediately comes to mind when we think of spiritual warfare—that tension between the flesh and the Spirit. This is primarily where the personal battle is engaged. Satan is opposed to us and anything that would glorify God in our lives. The world is around us seeking to entice us to embrace its materialistic and self-serving values. But Satan's most subtle and effective strategy is to convince us that we are still in bondage to our old, unregenerate nature. When we believe this lie, we have already lost the battle.

In a few places in the New Testament, the word *sarx,* translated "flesh," actually refers to literal muscle and bodily tissue. But most of the time, it has reference to that old nature of the unregenerate man, the indwelling dynamic of sin that responds to the external environment of the world. The flesh is self-serving and is susceptible to Satan's temptation because it's totally self-centered. Any attitude that causes us to think that life is about me, my rights, my entitlement, my comforts, and standing up for self is the nature of the flesh. We all experience the tension between the Christ life, which is led by the Holy Spirit, and the self-life, which is controlled by the flesh.

Many Christians are disillusioned about their ability to live a God-glorifying Christian life upon receiving Jesus Christ as Savior because they fail to understand that as soon as they are born of the Spirit a battle begins. An enemy is seeking to deprive them and rob them of what they have been given in Jesus Christ. We need to understand that Satan is against us, the world is around us, and the flesh is within us—all collaborating together, conspiring to rob us of what God has already procured for us in Christ. Satan cannot off-set what God has provided and deprive us of the empower-ment Christ has given us over sin, except as he convinces us to believe his lies and forfeit the faith to believe what God has told us to the contrary. Satan influences us to inter-pret truth and reality by our feelings and experience rather than believing what God has told us about our life in Christ. The Bible has a lot to say about the battle between the flesh and the Spirit. Every reference affirms the victory we have already been given, but Satan distorts our understanding of God's Word, causing us to see the struggle as futile and to embrace defeat.

Galatians 5:17 says, "For the flesh desires what is against the Spirit, and the Spirit desires what is against the flesh; these are opposed to each other, so that you don't do what you want." What we're dealing with is clearly a battle between two natures—the spirit and the flesh. We have been born of the Spirit. He is within us—that is, the person of Jesus Christ, God Himself. The flesh is that old, unregenerate nature that wants to serve self and to sin. This verse is typically interpreted to say, "I know what I want to do. I want to live for Christ and live a holy life without sin, but because of the flesh, that sinful old nature within me opposing what I want, I can't do it." We are going to see that this is exactly opposite of what is being said, but first, consider a parallel passage in the seventh chapter of Romans.

Paul's testimony actually begins with verse 14, but the core of what he is saying is found in Romans 7:18–20, "For I know that nothing good lives in me, that is, in my flesh. For the desire to do what is good is with me, but there is no ability to do it. For I do not do the good that I want to do, but I practice the evil that I do not want to do. Now if I do what I do not want, I am no longer the one doing it, but it is the sin that lives in me."

All of us can identify with that. We know what God expects of us. We know what a holy life is supposed to be. We know what the law says and how we should live. We know what is right and wrong. We don't want to sin but constantly find ourselves failing, doing the very things we know are sinful and displeasing to God. If this was Paul's dilemma, who are we to think that it can be any different with us? That has been ingrained in my understanding most of my life; I have even preached on it from this perspective. It's always a struggle. The victory is elusive. Just keep fighting the battle because there will always be this dilemma due to our dual nature and the sinful nature of the flesh that is still attached to our born-again bodies.

We see these two passages as confirming the fact that the flesh is always going to win and deprive us of living the way we should and want to live. The existence of the fleshly nature assures we will continue in sin, and any hope of attaining a significant degree of holiness in this life is an illusion. But that is exactly opposite of what the Scripture is saying. In order to correctly understand what Paul is saying about the battle between the flesh and the Spirit, we must go back to the beginning of Romans 6. His testimony must be understood in the context of the unified message of Romans 6, 7, and 8.

Romans 6–8

Romans 6:1–3 says, "What should we say then? Should we continue in sin in order that grace may multiply? Absolutely not! How can we who died to sin still live in it? Or are you unaware that all of us who were baptized into Christ Jesus were baptized into His death." Now he's not talking about water baptism here. Water baptism symbolizes this, but he's talking about our experience of being in Christ; we are actually immersed in, participate in, His death on the cross. The Scriptures talk about "putting on the Lord Jesus Christ." We are in Him, and the best concept to describe that is being baptized or immersed in Christ. And this is true—we identify with His death because His death is actually our death to sin once we receive Jesus as Savior and have been born again.

Continuing in verse 4, "Therefore we were buried with Him by baptism into death, in order that, just as Christ was raised from the dead by the glory of the Father, so we too may walk in a new way of life. For if we have been joined with Him in the likeness of His death, we will certainly also be in the likeness of His resurrection." This is not a reference to our future resurrection to glory in heaven. Paul is talking about our life here and now. We have been resurrected to a new life that we have in Christ. If we died with Him, then we are also raised with Him. We are participants in His resurrection to a new life, just as we participated in His death. This is what Paul expresses in Galatians 2:19–20, "I have been crucified with Christ; and I no longer live, but Christ lives in me." We, like Paul, are still walking, moving, breathing, yet, as he said, "It is no longer me, but Christ who lives in me." This is no longer my life. We are immersed in the life of Jesus Christ and are one with Him.

We normally have no problem accepting the substitutionary death of Christ as our death, understanding that it was our sin for which He died on the cross. That is a basic, foundational belief of every child, man, or woman who makes a profession of faith in Jesus Christ. Why, then, is it so difficult to accept the substitutionary life of Christ, who was resurrected and has given us newness of life?

This is what is being affirmed in the verses that follow. Romans 6:6 says, "For we know [this is the truth, what we should know] that our old self [the flesh] was crucified with Him." Crucifixion is a death; it's an execution. Our flesh, not our bodily muscle tissue but that old sin nature, has been crucified. Notice how this continues to be reinforced. Continuing in verse 6, "In order that sin's dominion over the body may be abolished." So what happened to it? The power of sin over our life has been abolished. The passage goes on to say, "So that we may no longer be enslaved to sin." Then verse 7 explains, "Since a person who has died is freed from sin's claims." It is important that we understand what God's Word tells us about the flesh, that old sin nature—it has been crucified, it has been abolished, we have been freed from it, and we are no longer in bondage and enslaved to it. This is the reality of our being in Christ as a born-again believer!

> *God's Word tells us we have been set free from our old sin nature; it has been crucified, abolished, and we are no longer in bondage to it.*

Is this how you view that old sin nature? Is this how you understand it? Probably not. So Paul says in verse 11, "So, you too consider your-selves dead to sin, but alive to God in Christ Jesus." Some versions say "reckon" your-selves to be dead to sin but alive to God in Christ Jesus. Accountants or those in business management know that to reckon, or reconcile, the account means to bring the accounts into balance. Paul is saying that this is a true picture of how it is. You may not feel that the flesh is dead; it may not seem evident as you deal with temptation and ungodly thoughts that obviously come from that old fleshly nature of sin, but the Bible is saying, "Consider the flesh as being dead—think of it in this way—because that's the way it is!" Reconcile your perception of the flesh with the truth of what God has said about it.

How do you do that? How do you consider something? It's how you choose to think of it. Later we will see the role of our minds in the matter of faith and what we choose to believe, as well as how our minds are the target of Satan's lies and deception. And one of his primary approaches is to distort the truth of God's Word. God tells you one thing, and Satan tells you another, so which are you going to choose to believe? It is in your mind that the choice is made, based on the validity of your perceptions. We will follow up on this concept in discussing the victory we have been given over the flesh and how we are often admonished to renew our minds because that is a key element of claiming the victory.

Continuing this sequence in Romans 6:12, Paul says, "Therefore do not let sin reign in your mortal body, so that you obey its desires." We can begin to understand how we are to appropriate the victory consistently and walk in it. We have been told the reality of our experience in Christ and what He has done with regard to that old sin nature. We have to do two things to appropriate this and make it a practical reality. This is our part of claiming the victory. First, we have to accept it and think of it as God has told us it is. This is why faith is the victory, believing God and what He has said. Then we are told, "Don't let sin reign in your mortal flesh." The Bible doesn't tell us to do something that we're not capable of doing. You've been set free from it, so if you think of it that way, then you don't have any excuse for giving sin a place in your mortal body, that is, in the physical life you now live. Once again this truth is reinforced in verse 14, "For sin will not rule over you, because you are not under law but under grace."

We are going to observe this analogy to law and grace several times. The fact that Christ is within us and His Spirit has displaced and put away sin is an act of grace; it is not something we've accomplished by our effort to avoid sinning and obeying the law. It's the work of His Spirit. It's by grace. Under the law you have to do it yourself by the power of the flesh. Under the law, if you want to be righteous, live a holy life and not sin, then you have to try to do it by obeying the law through your own efforts. This is especially important to understand when we get back to Paul's dilemma in chapter 7.

Now look at Romans 6:16–18. "Do you not know that if you offer yourselves to someone as obedient slaves, you are slaves of that one you obey—either of sin leading to death or of obedience leading to righteousness? But thank God that, although you used to be slaves of sin, you obeyed from the heart that pattern of teaching you were entrusted to, and having been liberated from sin, you became enslaved to righteousness." This analogy, using the concept of slavery, calls on us to recognize and obey the one who is our master.

It may help to illustrate this by a time line. There was a point in which you were born physically as a living person and there's a point when you are going to die. That's the flesh, this body, this container we live in while in the world.

Born   **Die**

But there is also a point when you were born of the Spirit, and you were born again. At that point you received a new spiritual nature that is eternal and endless. We really can't do justice with the analogy of these lines, as the new spiritual nature should be a big heavy line, and the flesh would be a thin, little thread in comparison. Remember the relative nature of Satan as a fallen angel, a created being, compared with the Almighty God of the universe dwelling within us! The application of that is the relative nature of the flesh and the Spirit within us.

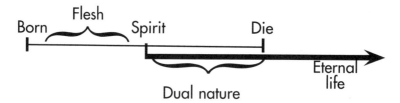

The Spirit dominates. It is the presence of God within us. He is all-powerful and has conquered sin, including our own sin nature. He has cleansed us; sin has been done away with. But between the two points of our being born of the Spirit and physical death, there is a dual nature because the Spirit resides in our mortal body. This bodily existence in the world is manifested with certain needs and desires. When our body is thirsty, it wants to be satisfied with a drink of water. When our body is cold, we want to put a sweater on to comfort and care for the needs of the body. But the flesh, or our human nature, manifests other needs as well. It wants us to guard our self-esteem. It desires recognition and praise. It wants us to be self-serving and stand up for its rights and provide gratification for its desires. While these may be natural inclinations, they do not necessarily glorify God. He has given us His Spirit and intends for us to bring all of life under the control of His Spirit so that everything we do will glorify Him. Paul said in 1 Corinthians 10:31, "Therefore, whether you eat or drink, or whatever you do, do everything for God's glory." All of those appetites of the flesh that are natural to our physical existence are to be brought into bondage to God's Spirit. We respond to them in a way that will honor and glorify Him. That would not allow for expressing one's sexual drive outside of marriage. It would not justify gluttony and debauchery in responding to one's need for food and drink. And this is where the conflict comes. The battle rages between the old, self-serving fleshly nature and the new power and control that has come into our life.

We must not miss the implication of the analogy of slavery. One cannot serve two masters. We are the slave of either one or the other. There was a time when we were in bondage to the flesh. There was no alternative because that was our nature; we had not yet come to faith in Jesus Christ and received the Spirit into our life. We served self and lived for self; sin reigned and had total dominion over us. But once we were born of the Spirit, we became enslaved and obedient, by choice, to the Spirit to live for Jesus Christ as slaves of righteousness. We are going to see how the continuing spiritual warfare is a matter of Satan manipulating our thoughts, tempting us to adopt perceptions that are contrary to the truth of what God has told us. He persuades us to believe what is false, to choose the self-serving things of the flesh. He convinces us that this is our nature, and we really can't help it when in reality that is a blatant lie!

The true relationship between our two natures is expressed once again in Romans 6:22, "But now, since you have been liberated from sin and become enslaved to God, you have your fruit, which results in sanctification—and the end is eternal life!" The only way one can be obedient and enslaved to God is by giving up one's enslavement and bondage to sin, and that is what we did when we came to faith in Jesus Christ. The benefit or result of doing so is sanctification or the holiness of life that glorifies God.

It is only because we are enslaved to God, controlled by His Spirit that we have the bonus of eternal life.

In chapter 7 the same truth is illustrated, but instead of the analogy of slavery, Paul uses the analogy of marriage. A woman is not free to marry another husband until the first husband has died. This lines up with the relationship of law and grace, the flesh and the Spirit. The only way we can be obedient to the Spirit—joined with the Spirit as in marriage—is having died to a marriage with the flesh. Though the Spirit indwells our mortal body, the Spirit cannot coexist in an equal relationship with the old nature of sin. But we have already been told that the flesh, or sin, has been crucified and is dead; that death is a necessary precondition, enabling us to be now united in "marriage" with the Spirit.

The point of rebirth or change from slavery to one master to the other, or from marriage to flesh to being married to the Spirit, is expressed in Romans 6:22 and then again in Romans 7:6. "But now we have been released from the law, since we have died to what held us, so that we may serve in the new way of the Spirit and not in the old letter of the law." Don't miss the point of this reference to the law. He is saying that we are released from having to keep the law, striving by our own futile efforts to live a holy and righteous life. There is now a higher power within us (by grace) that has given us victory over the old nature and enables us to fulfill the expectations of the law and walk in newness of life.

Note the following verse, Romans 7:7, as this is an important point of transition for understanding the rest of the chapter. "What should we say then? Is the law sin? Absolutely not! On the contrary, I would not have known sin if it were not for the law."

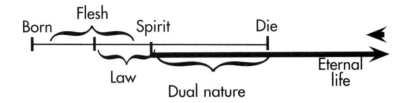

When on our time line did Paul become acquainted with the law and therefore became conscious of his sinful nature? It was prior to being saved and being born of the Spirit. After talking about the transition of being released from the law and being born of the Spirit in verse 6, he goes back to reflect on the role of the law. Once he had come to an understanding of the law and his accountability to live righteously according to the law, he tried to do so. At that point he knew what sin was and wanted to avoid committing sin, but there was no power within him—that is, in his flesh—that enabled him to do it. He wanted to do good, and even though he now understood the difference between right and wrong, he was still in bondage to the old nature of the flesh and was not able to do the good that he desired. In fact, he continually did evil and that which he did not want to do.

Beginning in Romans 7:7, he goes back to the point at which he became aware of the law, what was expected to fulfill righteousness and how God wanted him to live. What, then, was the value of the law? It made him aware that he was a sinner and that he was in bondage to sin. How does this line up with what he had already said about sin and the law in chapter 6 where he said he was freed from sin? He was no longer obligated and enslaved to sin; it no longer had control over him. But now, beginning in Romans 7:7, he is obviously still in bondage to sin. He had not yet been born again but had only come to an understanding of the law and expectations of God for righteousness.

In Romans 7:11 he observes, "For sin, seizing an opportunity through the commandment, deceived me, and through it killed me." Thinking he could obey the law and attain the righteousness of God, the law and his failure to keep it actually confirmed he was under condemnation. James 2:10 says, "For whoever keeps the entire law, yet fails in one point, is guilty of breaking it all." So the rest of Romans 7 is not talking about the conflict between the flesh and the Spirit. It is talking about the dilemma of one who has come to an awareness of the law, understands right and wrong and what sin is, but is striving to overcome sin in his own power and ability. That will always be futile as, in our own strength, the sin nature will prevail.

Romans 7:14 says, "For we know that the law is spiritual." There is nothing wrong with the law; it just doesn't provide the power in itself to enable compliance. "But I am made out of flesh, sold into sin's power." It is evident in verses 14–23 that Paul had not been born again because he is describing what it was like when he was still under the law and dependent on his own efforts to obey the law and try to overcome sin. There was no other alternative except to sin: "For I know that nothing good lives in me" (v. 18). There was no good within him or any power to do good because that comes only from the Spirit by grace. He was still in bondage to the flesh.

Being in this dilemma, with which we all can identify, of knowing the law and wanting to obey it but unable to do so, he comes to a dramatic and emotional climax in Romans 7:24: "What a wretched man I am! Who will rescue me from this body of death?" And what's the answer? "I thank God through Jesus Christ" (v. 25). All that Paul is talking about, in this discouraging testimony in Romans 7, is leading to this point, "I couldn't do it because I'm in the flesh, but praise God, Jesus Christ did when I was born of the Spirit. He did what I couldn't do."

It is disturbing that we allow Satan to distort our understanding of a passage of Scripture like Paul's testimony in chapter 7, causing us to accept defeat and see the Christian life as a continuous struggle rather than as a victory over sin that has already been won by Christ. We need to pause and examine the cleverness and the devious methods of Satan that he uses to defeat us and rob God of His glory in our lives. He even twists our understanding of Scripture to cause us to justify indulging in sin and carnal living, convincing us that is our nature and there is nothing we can do about it. When Satan tempted Jesus, he used Scripture, but he distorted its meaning and intent. He does the same thing to us, telling us that we can't really live in victory, that we are still in bondage to the sin nature and that even the Holy Spirit within us is not powerful enough to give us grace to overcome it.

In some versions of the Bible, editors have inserted a subhead before Romans 7:14, "The Conflict of Two Natures." That would lead us to believe that the dilemma Paul describes in the following verses is about the conflict between the flesh and the Spirit rather than the struggle under the law to live a righteous life through our own efforts. While there are scholars who make a strong case for this interpretation, it seems in conflict with the context of the expanded passage and would cause us to accept our battle against the flesh as a futile struggle rather than affirming our victory in Christ.

However, God wants us to see and understand in the Scripture that we've been given the victory in Christ. Romans 8 describes explicitly the contrast between the flesh and the Spirit. It begins in Romans 8:1: "Therefore, no condemnation now exists for those in Christ Jesus." As Christians we are in Christ Jesus. We have been immersed in Christ. We have accepted His death, have been crucified with Him, and have arisen with Him to a new way of life! Now what about expressions of that old sin nature? We are told there is no condemnation in Christ Jesus.

Many believers continue to struggle with the guilt of sin and their mistakes from the past, perhaps in rebellious student days or in a lifestyle prior to becoming a Christian. There may be experiences and things you have done in the past that continue to plague you with guilt. Where does that condemnation and burden of guilt come from? Who is it that keeps beating us up and making us feel unholy and unworthy? It is not God; it is Satan who accuses us and condemns us—trying to defeat us and keep us from accepting the grace and cleansing we have in Christ. God doesn't put us on a guilt trip. He says, "There is no condemnation if you are in Christ Jesus."

That doesn't mean we're not going to sin. And when we do, God's Spirit convicts us of sin. Satan is the accuser and wants us to live with a guilt complex because that denies the forgiveness and cleansing God has provided.

> *God does not put us on a guilt trip; there is no condemnation in Christ Jesus.*

But when the Holy Spirit, who is within us, convicts us of sin, what happens? He doesn't say, "I'm going to forgive you, but I'm not going to release you from the burden of what you have done; I'm going to let you stew in your guilt a little while and feel miserable." No, that is not how God responds to our sin.

When God convicts us of sin, our response is to confess readily, to acknowledge our sin. It doesn't even have to be a sinful or disobedient act. If something enters the mind in the way of temptation or a lustful thought, the Spirit alerts us, and awareness and conviction lead to confession. That leads to God's counter response of forgiveness, and it is not just forgiveness for what we may have done but complete cleansing. First John 1:9 says, "If we confess our sins, He is faithful and righteous to forgive us our sins and to cleanse us from all unrighteousness." Being forgiven results in restoration; we are restored to fellowship with God. The result of being restored to fellowship with God is joy. The Scripture tells us that godly repentance is a joyous experience. "For godly grief produces a repentance not to be regretted and leading to salvation, but worldly grief produces death" (2 Cor. 7:10).

As long as we're in this world and having to deal with the influence of the world around us, Satan will use the flesh to entice us to sin. He knows our weaknesses, where we are vulnerable, and how to get to us. But the Spirit of God is within us and alerts us to Satan's temptation and lies. We can't plead ignorance if we are in Christ. We know when a thought, an attitude, or an action is contrary to God's holiness and the nature of Christ; and the Spirit leads us to react with confession and repentance. And that's joyous because God gets to manifest His grace and forgiveness, and we are restored to fellowship with Him. So if you're living with guilt and condemnation, recognize that is one of Satan's fiery darts that just found its way into your heart and life. You have succumbed to one of his lies because there is no condemnation to those who are in Christ Jesus.

Romans 8:2–4 goes on to explain, "Because the Spirit's law of life in Christ Jesus has set you free from the law of sin and of death. What the law could not do since it was limited by the flesh, God did. He condemned sin in the flesh by sending His own Son in flesh like ours under sin's domain, and as an offering, in order that the law's requirement would be accomplished in us who do not walk according to the flesh but according to the Spirit." Doesn't this take care of Paul's dilemma in chapter 7? "What I could not do in the flesh, God did! What the law could not give me in terms of empowerment to live righteously, God did!" He did it in sending Jesus Christ to die and overcome that old sin nature for all who belong to Him. Paul had every basis for taking pride in the flesh and assuming he could do it himself. In Philippians 3:3 he alludes to his religious heritage, his genealogy, and his theological training but concluded, "The ones who serve by the Spirit of God boast in Christ Jesus and do not put confidence in the flesh." We are not in bondage to the flesh but have been given victory over sin.

Notice this victory is for those who do not walk in the flesh, that is, do not choose to go on living according to that old nature. It is for those who walk in the Spirit, accepting God's grace. We can understand how this happens by insight into the practical application that follows. In Romans 8:5–7, notice the frequent reference to the mind and how we choose to think. "For those whose lives are according to the flesh *think* about the things of the flesh, but those whose lives are according to the Spirit, [*think* is implied] about the things of the Spirit. For the *mind-set* of the flesh is death, but the *mind-set* of the Spirit is life and peace. For the *mind-set* of the flesh is hostile toward God because it does not submit itself to God's law, for it is unable to do so."

Four times in this passage—a fifth time implied—the Scripture refers to the mind and its function. What do our minds do? They are a physiological part of our anatomy, the bodily organ that processes information, perceives, thinks, reasons, and makes decisions. Our attitudes and actions are controlled by the volitional choices we make in our mind. The victory doesn't come automatically just because we are in Christ. The battle is in our minds and in our hearts. We are vulnerable because Satan speaks to our minds. He shapes our thoughts and perceptions, enticing us to be self-serving, to gratify carnal desires and embrace the values and things of the world. This was the way we lived by default before knowing Jesus Christ and being born of the Spirit. Ephesians 2:3 describes how our mind held us in bondage to the flesh: "We too all previously lived among them in our fleshly desires, carrying out the inclinations of our flesh and *thoughts*, and by nature we were children under wrath, as the others were also."

Through lies and deception Satan seeks to distort God's Word and erode our faith, distorting God's truth. As we pointed out in chapter 2, those who are blind to the truth and do not accept it have closed minds that are hardened to God's Word. Second Corinthians 3:14 refers to those today who are like the rebellious Israelites. "But their minds were closed. For to this day, at the reading of the old covenant, the same veil remains; it is not lifted, because it is set aside only in Christ." Openness to the truth of God's Word that lifts the veil of understanding comes only in knowing Christ. Paul describes this bondage to the flesh of those without Christ because they choose to set their minds on earthly things. Philippians 3:19, "Their end is destruction; their god is their stomach; their glory is in their shame. They are focused on earthly things."

It may be an oversimplification to say you choose what you focus your thoughts on and what you think about. You choose what to believe. Are you going to choose to believe what you're confronted with in the world and what human wisdom will tell you or God's truth and what He says? The difference is what you set your mind on. Do you set your mind on spiritual truth and reality, conscious of Christ's presence? Do you think about the assurance of victory God has given you, rejoice in being led by the Spirit, and celebrate the power to resist temptation that has come by His grace? Or are you constantly thinking about the things of the flesh, things of the world, those titillating, gratifying fantasies and images you're constantly exposed to? The difference is a life of victory and peace or a life that is rebellious and hostile toward God.

When I was a boy, I heard a story that has been around for a long time. It is about a missionary who led to the Lord a man who had been somewhat of a reprobate. The man said to the missionary, "Ever since I gave my life to Christ, I feel like there are two dogs fighting within me. There is an evil dog that wants me to return to my old habits and a good dog that wants me to live right." The missionary asked, "Which one is winning?" The man paused for a moment and replied, "The one I feed." It's just that simple. It is not something beyond our control. It's something we can choose to do, either to walk in the Spirit or not. We choose to believe God or not, to feed our mind on His truth or what the world and our old nature would tell us.

A contingency is expressed in Romans 8:9: "You, however, are not in the flesh, but in the Spirit, since the Spirit of God lives in you. But if anyone does not have the Spirit of Christ, he does not belong to Him." This conditional proposition is critical. If you have received Jesus as Savior, then He has come to dwell in you. If the Holy Spirit does not dwell in you, then you do not yet belong to God, and there is no way you can set your mind on things of the Spirit, for you are still in bondage to sin. As believers we ought to understand that Christ does, indeed, dwell within us. We no longer live in the power of the flesh but in the Spirit.

I have known many adults and young people in the church who come under the conviction that they have never been born again. It is so easy to go through all of the motions, the typical pattern of growing up in church— walking the aisle as a child, being baptized, joining the church, going along with all the programs and expectations, and presuming one has had a conversion experience.

The basic pivotal question is whether or not we have been born again and the Spirit of God is in us. This verse goes on to say, "But if anyone does not have the Spirit of Christ, he does not belong to Him." If you do belong to Christ, then the Spirit of God dwells within you, and the flesh has no power and control (except as you believe Satan's deceit to the contrary). So with that assumption Romans 8:10–11 says, "Now if Christ is in you, the body is dead because of sin, but the Spirit is life because of righteousness. And if the Spirit of Him who raised Jesus from the dead lives in you, then He who raised Christ from the dead will also bring your mortal bodies to life through His Spirit who lives in you." In other words, we have a new spiritual life in this mortal container of flesh that is our body. And because the Spirit of God is in us, verse 12 affirms, "So then, brothers, we are not obligated to the flesh to live according to the flesh." This is the simple, matter-of-fact conclusion: you have no obligation to the flesh. It has no power over you.

Who has been telling you otherwise? Who has been lying and convincing you that your old sin nature still has mastery over you—your thoughts, your attitudes, and your behavior? Instead of believing what God has said, has someone been telling you to turn all this around and interpret it by what you experience? Have you been deceived in believing as long as you are in this life there will always be a struggle with your sin nature because you are under bondage to sin? We need to realize the power of faith. When we truly believe something, it's amazing how it becomes a reality. Doubt is one of Satan's favorite fiery darts. He erodes our faith through constant failure so that we become skeptical about what God has said because that's not the pattern of our experience. The battle between the flesh and the Spirit begins by Satan's blinding us to the awareness of what we have in Christ and creating skepticism regarding what God has told us concerning the victory over the flesh. Just remember who is lying and who is telling the truth. God's Word is true, not what Satan has influenced you to think in your mind.

First John 5:4 says, "This is the victory that has conquered the world: our faith." Faith is believing what God says, even when all evidence is to the contrary. Romans 8:12 clearly says we are under no obligation to the flesh. We don't have to sin. We don't have to yield to Satan's temptations and to the allure of the world. It has no power over us except as we choose to allow it to have sway in our lives.

Satan wants us to think it's out of our control. But we've been given the victory in Christ and can choose to be led by His Spirit.

Galatians 5:13–25

Let us return to the parallel passage in Galatians 5 to understand better the battle between the flesh and the Spirit. "I say then, walk by the Spirit and you will not carry out the desire of the flesh. For the flesh desires what is against the Spirit, and the Spirit desires what is against the flesh; these are opposed to each other, so that you don't do what you want. But if you are led by the Spirit, you are not under the law" (Gal. 5:16–18). This appears to be echoing Paul's testimony in the seventh chapter of Romans. We know what we ought to do. We want to be led of the Spirit, but because of our dual nature, that old sinful nature of the flesh will not let us live for the Lord as we desire to do. We accept defeat in our efforts, acknowledge the victory is elusive, and concede that the Christian life is a constant struggle. However, just as we noted regarding Paul's testimony in Romans 7, this passage is telling us the exact opposite, that we have been given victory over the flesh.

To understand the context of this passage, we must first look at verses 13 and 14. "For you are called to freedom, brothers; [The Spirit has set us free, no longer in bondage to the flesh.] only don't use this freedom as an opportunity for the flesh, but serve one another through love. For the entire law is fulfilled in one statement: Love your neighbor as yourself." The tendency to exploit God's grace and use the security of our salvation to indulge in sin is more prevalent than we would like to admit. We indulge a lustful thought or even give expression to what we know to be sin, confident of God's grace and forgiveness.

Paul dealt with this twice in Romans 6:1, "Should we continue in sin that grace may multiply?" The response in the next verse is, "Absolutely not! How can we who died to sin still live in it?" Then in Romans 6:15, after explaining we are no longer under the law but under grace, he asks, "What then? Should we sin because we are not under law but under grace?" Once again the response is, "Absolutely not!" Freedom in Christ is not freedom to indulge the flesh and do whatever we want; it is freedom from the power of the flesh and the old nature.

I recall seeing a film on the life of Martin Luther years ago; he had discovered the reality of justification by faith and living by grace that is ours when we come into a personal relationship with Jesus Christ. He once commented in a scene in his seminary classroom, "Once you are a Christian, you can do anything you please." The class was indignant and responded vociferously to this apparent endorsement of licentiousness and libertarianism. After quieting them down, Martin Luther corrected their assumption and said, "No, that's not it at all. Once you are in Christ, what is it that pleases you?" Obviously, the implication is that once we have been set free from the old inclination to sin and bondage to the flesh, the Holy Spirit dwells within us, and we want to do what pleases Christ and brings glory to God.

Why is Paul talking here about loving one another? He says, "The entire law is fulfilled in one statement: 'Love your neighbor as yourself.'" What is love? It is not focused on yourself and meeting your own needs; it is not about you; it is about the beloved. Love is giving yourself to others. Your affection, your concern, and your interests are on the needs and welfare of the one who is the object of your love. It is the antithesis of the flesh, which is totally self-centered. Not only that, but love is the nature of God and comes from Him. This is one of those practical alerts that show whether we are being led of the Spirit or are still in the flesh. In fact, the Bible describes the person who does not love as dwelling in darkness, which is the domain of Satan! "But the one who hates his brother is in the darkness, walks in the darkness, and doesn't know where he's going, because the darkness has blinded his eyes" (1 John 2:11).

Several practical keys help us gain the victory in spiritual warfare, and love is one of them. If you love your husband or your wife, your family, your neighbor, your friends, your colleagues, your team members, a lost world, what are you doing? Taking advantage of them? Abusing them? Exploiting them for your own needs, your own comforts? No, you are giving yourself to them. Focusing our life on others in love makes it difficult for Satan to appeal to our self-centered, fleshly nature.

Then we come to Galatians 5:16, "I say then, walk by the Spirit and you will not carry out the desire of the flesh." That is matter-of-fact. Will the Spirit allow you to sin? If you're walking in the Spirit, will He allow you to take advantage of someone or abuse someone for your own gain or pleasure? No, that's not the nature of the Spirit. He leads us to do in word, attitude, behavior, and relationships only what will glorify

> *Love is a key to walking in victory because it is the antithesis of the self-centered nature of the flesh.*

God and please Him. So here two practical keys are given to guide us to victory—love others and walk in the Spirit.

This verse and verse 18 provide the framework for correctly understanding the primary passage—verse 17. Verse 16 says, "Walk by the Spirit and you will not carry out the desire of the flesh." Then we read in verse 18, "But if you are led by the Spirit, you are not under the law." In other words, it's not a matter of striving to do what is right through your own efforts. A higher power enables you to fulfill the law, love others, and serve God without the guilt or constant failure. It is the power that comes in being led by the Holy Spirit.

Typically we have read verse 17 in isolation and concluded that we cannot live for God as we desire because of that old sinful nature of the flesh that is still within us, manifesting itself in opposition against the Spirit. "For the flesh desires what is against the Spirit, and the Spirit desires what is against the flesh; these are opposed to each other, so that you don't do what you want." Why would we interpret this verse to say something that is exactly opposite of the previous verse and the one that follows? Verses 16 and 18 tell us the Spirit will not allow us to fulfill the desires of the flesh and has set us free from bondage to the law. Then we flip-flop the meaning of verse 17 to conclude the flesh has the upper hand. We reason, "I want to walk in the Spirit. I want to live a holy life. I want to gain the victory in righteousness, but the flesh is in me; it is opposing the work of the Spirit so I can't do what I want to do." But that is opposite of what the Scripture is saying: you have a fleshly nature, but it cannot make you do what you want to do in gratifying your self-centered, carnal nature. Why? Because you've got the Spirit within you, set in opposition to the flesh, empowering and leading you.

Once again it is evident how we have commonly distorted Scripture to excuse failure and say exactly the opposite of what it means. Could Satan have anything to do with this through his access to our mind and his desire to defeat us in our Christian walk? God's Word is telling us that we have victory over the flesh in the Spirit of God. You cannot continue living in the flesh except as you deny, reject, ignore, and grieve the Holy Spirit within you. You cannot go on indulging sin if you are acknowledging His presence and allowing Him to lead you. Spiritual warfare is not just the temptations of Satan trying to get us to sin. His deception and lies lead us to accept defeat and believe that we don't have the power to walk in victory.

Just so we can know the difference, the verses that follow make a clear distinction between what is of the flesh and what is of the Spirit. "Now the works of the flesh are obvious" (v. 19). And they are. You don't have to be taught this. You know what is not of God. "Sexual immorality, moral impurity, promiscuity, idolatry, sorcery, hatreds, strife, jealousy, outbursts of anger, selfish ambitions, dissensions, factions, envy, drunkenness, carousing, and anything similar, about which I tell you in advance—as I told you before—that those who practice such things will not inherit the kingdom of God" (Gal. 5:19–21). What or who is behind all of these attitudes, feelings, and behavior, including enmity, strife, jealousy, anger, dissensions? Satan is. All of these characteristics and behaviors reflect the self-centered nature of the flesh, which seeks personal gratification and takes pleasure in the things of the world.

In contrast, what the Spirit produces in our lives is identified. "But the fruit of the Spirit is love, joy, peace, patience, kindness, goodness, faith, gentleness, self-control. Against such things there is no law" (Gal. 5:22–23). As I have read this last verse over the years, I have always thought that final expression was strange. Of course there is no law against love, joy, faith, and so forth. What does the Scripture imply? It means that nothing can keep the Holy Spirit from manifesting these characteristics in our life. That could not be said if we were trying to love and express kindness and goodness through our own efforts because the law stipulated that is what we are supposed to do. In fact, if it were just the legalism of the law, that in itself would guarantee that we would fail. They are produced by the Spirit, and nothing can stand against them and deter the Spirit from producing this fruit in our lives because they characterize His nature.

When you find yourself trying to relate to a difficult colleague who is critical, always berating you and putting you down, you can't just say, "I'm going to love that person." No, you can't do it. All you can do is walk in the Spirit and allow Jesus to express His love through you. If you have a problem with temper or anger, you don't just decide, "I'm not going to do that anymore, but I am going to be patient and kind." No, something in that old fleshly nature guarantees if you try to do it by your own effort, you will fail. A power is working against love and patience and gentleness if we are doing it because we are supposed to. But when it is produced by the Spirit, He overcomes our weakness and inability to focus on anything other than oneself. Love, joy, peace, patience, kindness, goodness, faithfulness, gentleness, self-control—this is what our life will look like when we are walking in the Spirit. We can't make excuses or plead ignorance. We know the difference—what is of Christ and what is of the flesh.

This is affirmed in 1 John 3:7–9, "Little children, let no one deceive you! The one who does what is right is righteous, just as He is righteous. The one who commits sin is of the Devil, for the Devil has sinned from the beginning. The Son of God was revealed for this purpose: to destroy the Devil's works. Everyone who has been born of God does not sin, because His seed remains in him; he is not able to sin, because he has been born of God." Jesus has appeared and on the cross overcame the work of the devil. We are born of God, and His nature has been planted within us. Because of that, one who is born of God cannot just go on living in sin and indulging in those things that are in conflict with the righteousness of the kingdom of God. We are righteous, not because of our ability to live perfect lives but because the Righteous One lives within us, guiding us and enabling us to live righteously. Where does sin come from, that is, anything that is not righteous? It is from the devil because that is his nature. Once again the opening part of this passage alerts us to the fact that it is easy to be deceived in this regard.

In conclusion of our focus on the passage in Galatians 5, note verses 24–25. "Now those who belong to Christ Jesus have crucified the flesh with its passions and desires. If we live by the Spirit, we must also follow the Spirit." Circle back to what Paul expressed in the sixth and eighth chapters of Romans. If we belong to Christ, this is what has happened to our old nature. It is crucified not just theoretically in Christ's dying for our sins, but we have put to death and abolished its passions and desires. They were nailed to the cross, so don't let Satan lie to you and convince you to resurrect them.

The younger generation hasn't had the blessing to know of Miss Bertha Smith. Miss Bertha was a missionary in China for many years. She was part of the Shantung revival and had an anointed ministry of challenging Southern Baptists and others to appropriate the Spirit-filled life. Following retirement, she established a retreat ministry based in Cowpens, South Carolina, and was a frequent speaker at evangelism conferences and spiritual life conferences.

When I was a student at Southwestern Seminary, she was often invited to come and speak to the students. However, none of the students wanted to host her or provide airport transportation. When you got around Miss Bertha, you felt like it was obvious that you had not done your daily Bible readings or something. She did not engage in normal protocol in her no-nonsense approach to spiritual matters. She likely would reply to your greeting with, "Young man, are your sins confessed up-to-date?" Or she might say, "Are you filled with the Holy Spirit?" It just didn't seem appropriate or adequate to say, "Well, I want to be," or, "I think so," or, "I'm trying to."

I don't remember the context of her message, but I'll never forget an illustration she used while speaking in one of my classes. She told about a pastor who had a discipleship group of men in his church, and one of them had died. As they gathered at the funeral home, the pastor noticed late in the evening that the family had left. Only the members of this close-knit discipleship group were there. Without a word of explanation, the pastor walked over to the casket and addressed the deceased: "John, you've been a part of this group and been a faithful member of the church. But we really know it was all a pretense, that you were a hypocrite and nothing but a gossiping, backstabbing reprobate." Then Miss Bertha stopped, turned to the class, and asked, "And what did John do?" Someone replied, "He didn't do anything." Miss Bertha responded, "Why?" Of course, the reply was because he was dead.

Then she continued with the story and related how, after a moment, the pastor walked back to the casket and addressed the deceased again. "Actually John, of all these men you were the most genuine and godly; you were the finest Christian I have ever known—a faithful witness, an ideal husband and father, and the most wonderful supporter a pastor could have." Miss Bertha stopped and said once again, "And what did John do? Did he get the big head and swell with pride?" No, he didn't react or respond because he was dead.

She was illustrating what Paul has said in Galatians 5:24. "Those who belong to Christ Jesus have crucified the flesh with its passions and desires." People may slander us, abuse us, hurt us, or take advantage of us. We don't react in self-defensiveness, lash back, create conflict, and cause dissension because we are dead; we have died to self. If God should choose to bless us with success and we get accolades and praise, it doesn't feed our pride and make us feel that we are something special. That is because we are dead, and that self-centered nature of the flesh has been crucified. It's not about us if we are led by the Spirit.

This is the testimony Paul expressed in Galatians 2:19–20, "I have been crucified with Christ; and I no longer live, but Christ lives in me. The life I now live in the flesh, I live by faith in the Son of God, who loved me and gave Himself for me." So the victory is actually simple as expressed in Galatians 5:25, "If we live by the Spirit, let us also follow the Spirit." The Holy Spirit is within us—that is a reality—so choose to appropriate by faith what we have been given and allow Him to lead us.

We need to be reminded once again of 2 Corinthians 11:3 in which Paul said, "But I fear that, as the serpent deceived Eve by his cunning, your minds may be corrupted from a complete and pure devotion to Christ." Satan tries to complicate the Christian life and make it appear to be something difficult and even impossible. He has an amazingly successful record of convincing us we are in bondage to the flesh— that old, sinful nature—and have to continue to struggle to overcome it in our own strength and willpower. But we are to deny self and accept the life that Jesus Christ has given us. It is a simple walk of faith, believing what He has done for us and accepting all that He has given us through the fact of the Holy Spirit living within us.

CHAPTER 6

DENYING THE FLESH ENTAILS SUFFERING

Therefore, since Christ suffered in the flesh, arm
yourselves also with the same resolve—because the
One who suffered in the flesh has finished with sin—
in order to live the remaining time in the flesh,
no longer for human desires, but for God's will.
—1 Peter 4:1–2

The Bible has given us several practical keys for claiming the victory of the flesh. These have already been provided for us in Christ. We are to set our minds on things of the Spirit rather than focusing on worldly, self-centered desires. We are to love, which keeps us giving ourselves outwardly to others rather than becoming vulnerable to the self-centered nature of the flesh. And we are to be led by the Holy Spirit within us through yielding to Him and following by faith. Scripture gives us one other little practical element of advice: "But put on the Lord Jesus Christ, and make no plans to satisfy the fleshly desires" (Rom. 13:14). We have put on the Lord Jesus by receiving Him into our life as Savior, but a part of being vigilant is not placing ourselves in situations where we would be tempted to indulge the flesh.

When I was growing up, I remember hearing a youth evangelist advise, "If you want to live a pure life for the Lord, stay away from drive-in movies." There aren't many drive-in movies these days, but we knew then what he was talking about. He was saying, "If you don't want your passions aroused in a way that would lead to hard-to-resist temptation, don't put yourself in a situation where that is likely to happen by parking with your date in a dark car at a drive-in or anywhere else." If you want to live a pure life, don't make provision for what would appeal to your carnal, sinful nature.

It comes down to the choices we make. If we desire to walk in the Spirit, then we have to choose to avoid situations that would cause the flesh to be tempted. Avoid being alone with someone of the opposite sex who is not your husband or your wife. Don't put yourself in a position where inappropriate emotional attachments would excite you or gratify you. Be discrete about watching television programs and movies that would stimulate lustful thoughts and actions. Internet pornography has become so prominent and destructive because a person can indulge in it in privacy without anyone knowing. Just don't go there! Don't pause and scan the covers of pornographic magazines on the newsstand. A familiar proverb says, "You cannot prevent birds from flying over your head, but you can prevent them from building a nest in your hair!" The Holy Spirit will readily alert us when the birds are flying over our head seeking to alight in our minds.

Too often, however, we are building the nest for them, inviting them to make themselves at home in our minds. But most of the time temptation comes in subtle, unexpected ways that are not readily recognized. If we make the decision beforehand that we are not going to put ourselves in a position that would expose us to temptation, we have made a big step toward walking in victory.

In emphasizing the victory of which we are assured, we must not diminish the reality of the warfare. There is an ongoing battle between the flesh and the Spirit. Satan is opposed to our doing anything that glorifies and exalts Christ. He uses that self-centered nature of the flesh within us and the carnal values of the world around us to defeat us and cause us to sin. Where we are most vulnerable is not in the temptation or allure of the world but in believing the lies and deception of Satan that convince us we cannot walk in victory. Some reject the truth of what God's Word is saying because it appears we are advocating living a perfect, holy life without sin, and we know that is impossible. Only Christ was capable of being sinless because He had the Spirit without measure.

When I was on the high school debate team, I learned there was a real advantage in taking the initiative in defining the argument. You could readily get the upper hand by defining the issue in a way that would put the other team on the defensive, forcing them to spend their time trying to counter your position rather than positively advocating their own. This is exactly what Satan does. He gets us to accept defeat by his accusations, "Well, you can't expect to live a perfect life, can you?" We have to answer, "No, of course not," and have immediately accepted defeat and justification for sin. But that is the wrong question.

The issue is not whether or not you can live a perfect life and never sin. The question is, Does Jesus live within you? Has He defeated the power of sin on the cross? Can you walk in the Spirit? The answer to all three is "yes!" Don't let Satan twist the truth by defining the issue with the wrong question.

Yes, we will sin. We will make mistakes. We will fall not only in things we do but in attitudes of jealousy, anger, or resentment. Ungodly attitudes may never be expressed beyond our heart, but due to our fleshly nature we may allow them to come into our mind and influence our life and attitudes in a way that is not Christlike and does not glorify God. But if we are led of the Spirit, we have instant awareness when something is not aligned with God's holiness. It's amazing. Before you can actually indulge and take that step of sin, the Holy Spirit lets you know it; one of His roles is to convict us of sin. We may try to rationalize and justify it. Though we know it is wrong, we may be presumptuous in assuming we can just confess it and be forgiven. But if we are led of the Spirit, He will guard us from allowing sinful attitudes and things of the flesh to come into our heart and become a part of our life. The Spirit will put a

> ### *Practical Keys to Victory over the Flesh*
>
> *1. Believe Christ has conquered sin for us.*
> *2. Set your mind on things of the Spirit.*
> *3. Counter self-centeredness with love.*
> *4. Be led by the Holy Spirit.*
> *5. Make no provision for the flesh.*

hedge around us, and we will find that anything contrary to the character of Jesus has no attraction to us. When Satan places something in our mind that should not be there, we may not naturally be able to resist, but the Spirit will alert us and enable us to resist because He is that greater power dwelling within us.

Claiming victory over the flesh has another side. It hurts to deny the flesh, the needs of our body. Sacrificing what would be comfortable and gratifying is painful. If you have had any experience with fasting, you know what this means. At least the first couple of days before your digestive system shuts down, you'll feel gnawing hunger pains. That is not comfortable because it hurts to deny the flesh the food it wants to satisfy the natural needs of the body. Fasting is a practical illustration of what it means to deny the flesh. But the flesh is not just our natural, physical body; it is also our ego, our self-centered nature. Selfish desires often cause us to hurt others. Standing up for ourselves, our opinion, our rights, what we want creates conflict and dissension with others. It is not natural to deny ourselves, to sacrifice what we feel is our right and entitlement. This is another way Satan undercuts us and robs us of the victory, for who wants to suffer? No one wants to be inconvenienced, to be taken advantage of, to deny himself pleasure and comfort. We want to stand up for our rights and defend ourselves when someone challenges us or offends us.

We concluded our study of the flesh and Spirit in Romans 8 with verse 12, which affirms we are under no obligation to the flesh. Romans 8:13 goes on to instruct us about how this becomes a practical reality. "For if you live according to the flesh, you are going to die. But if by the Spirit you put to death the deeds of the body, you will live."

At this point you may be wondering how a person walks in the Spirit. We know Jesus conquered sin on the cross, and the Holy Spirit lives within us, but how do we really let Him control and guide our life completely? We walk in the Spirit by constantly crucifying—putting to death—the desires, the gratification, the comforts of the self-centered life, and denying our own rights. And that hurts. It's not natural. Sacrifice is not what our human nature is inclined to do. So self-denial—putting to death the deeds, inclinations, desires of the flesh—entails suffering. The only way we can do this is in the power of the Spirit because we have a physical body of flesh and live in a fallen world. We cannot make a once-for-all decision to deny the flesh when we become a Christian. It is a constant process every day and throughout the day of choosing to deny the flesh. We do that by choosing to accept the leadership and power of God's Spirit as He leads us to think, speak, and act in ways that are not self-serving but glorifying to God.

Paul explains this clearly in 2 Corinthians 4:11, "For we who live are always given over to death because of Jesus, so that Jesus' life may also be revealed in our mortal flesh." The only way our lives will be a living testimony of Jesus Christ is if we constantly die to the personal, selfish gratifications we would naturally follow and choose to indulge in. As the preceding verses described, our physical bodies will be "pressured in every way" (v. 8). We will be "perplexed . . . persecuted . . . struck down" (v. 8–9). Is that not a picture of suffering? But in suffering and denying the flesh rather than following the comfortable, broad way of the world, we never reach the point of despair. We are not forsaken, and we are not destroyed because Jesus has given us the victory. However, we claim victory only by embracing the cost of self-denial. Verse 10 explains that we must "always carry the death of Jesus in our body, so that the life of Jesus may also be revealed in our body." That is the only way to be conformed to the image of Christ and to glorify God in the physical existence in the world. It demonstrates, as stated in verse 7, "that this extraordinary power may be from God and not from us."

Satan deceives us into thinking that we can have it both ways—that we can live for self and yield to worldly standards and still be faithful to God. If the Spirit is in control, He will always lead us to deny the base desires of the old nature. The Bible doesn't mince words when it describes this as literally putting to death the flesh. It describes this death as a crucifixion, a painful way to die. In this way the Scripture graphically portrays what must constantly happen to the fleshly nature when we are in Christ.

This is affirmed and explained further in Romans 8:16–17, "The Spirit Himself testifies together with our spirit that we are God's children, and if children, also heirs—heirs of God and coheirs with Christ—seeing that we suffer with Him so that we may also be glorified with Him." We believe in Jesus Christ; we are heirs of our eternal inheritance and know that our salvation is secure. We have trusted Him as Savior, but Satan wants to obscure the cost and implications of our salvation and life in Christ. We have the reality of all the blessings that accompany salvation in Christ, which we discussed in chapter 1, only if we suffer with Him. Jesus was sinless not just because He was the Son of God but because He was constantly denying the flesh. The victory is not in a theoretical identification with the cross and Christ's crucifixion but in a willingness to deny the old nature and desires of the flesh as He did.

Paul explained this truth in his letter to the Philippians, "For it has been given to you on Christ's behalf not only to believe in Him, but also to suffer for Him" (Phil. 1:29). We don't usually present that aspect of the Christian life in our appeal to someone to consider becoming a believer. Paul expressed the passion of his life and calling in chapter 3, verse 10: "My goal is to know Him and the power of His resurrection and the fellowship of His sufferings, being conformed to His death." We often feel that passion to know Christ in all of His fullness and to experience the power of the resurrected life but stop short of embracing His sufferings. But you can't have one without the other. We cannot know the fullness of the resurrected life of Christ without dying to self and crucifying the flesh as He did.

This is why Paul could say in Colossians 1:24, "Now I rejoice in my sufferings for you." His statement reminds us of the response of the apostles to persecution in the early chapters of Acts. They were beaten and ordered not to speak in the name of Jesus. Acts 5:41 says, "Then they went out from the presence of the Sanhedrin, rejoicing that they had been counted worthy to be dishonored on behalf of the name." Other translations say, "They rejoiced that they had been considered worthy to suffer shame for His name." Could it be that we are not worthy to suffer for Christ because we do not deprive ourselves of worldly pleasures in order to live an unpopular, holy, and separated life?

When temptation comes, it grows in intensity until a person yields. Jesus never yielded, though He was tempted in every way as we are. And indeed He experienced an intensity of temptation to gratify the flesh, to satisfy His needs and His comforts far beyond anything we encounter. But He denied them, and it entailed suffering in the flesh. He was hungry after forty days in the wilderness, but He did not yield to temptation to turn the stones into bread. He chose to suffer. We are called to suffer with Him because we are called to deny the flesh just as our Lord did. The writer of Hebrews speaks of Jesus' enduring the cross, despising the shame, for the joy that was set before Him. Then he chastises us, pointing out, "In struggling against sin, you have not yet resisted to the point of shedding your blood" (Heb. 12:4). No matter how painful self-denial may be in order to avoid sin; we don't even approach the extent to which our Savior suffered in resisting sin.

Back in Romans, Paul puts this suffering in perspective with a concluding observation, "For I consider that the sufferings of this present time are not worth comparing with the glory that is going to be revealed to us" (Rom. 8:18). Satan tries to distort our perspective. As we engage the battle, we must keep the reward in mind. We must remember that the gain and the glory we bring to God is worth the suffering, self-denial, and deprived lifestyle for the sake of the kingdom. We would do whatever it takes to be obedient and experience the power of God's Spirit. But Satan causes us to lose that perspective by persuading us to focus on the here and now and to indulge in what we want and what brings us pleasure. This may be why we're so weak and are so often defeated. This may be why we find the Christian life such a struggle. No one naturally wants to deny themselves and suffer when we readily have the option of satisfying our wants.

Believers in America may wonder, where is all that being hated and reviled and persecuted for righteousness sake that the Bible speaks of? To serve Christ and to walk in the Spirit will put us in conflict with the world's standards. Those who stand up for justice, speak against abortion, homosexual behavior, and a hedonistic lifestyle are not only not appreciated and respected; they are also criticized and reviled. Believers around the world are persecuted because they choose to follow Christ and do what He identifies as holy and right. It is becoming more common in our own country. It may not be physical persecution, but social ostracism and condescending comments will come if we are led of the Spirit to stand for convictions and values that honor God. The easy way is to compromise, fit in, and not take a stand, and Satan is delighted because he has fooled us into thinking we can follow Christ and live for Him without being inconvenienced or suffering ridicule.

In some religions ascetics intentionally abuse the body, thinking that it will bring merit and righteousness. That's not what we're talking about. Self-denial is not an end in itself. It is the natural outgrowth of walking in the Spirit and denying self in order for God to be glorified in our lives.

Some of our missionaries are deployed in places where they have to share a vehicle. A schedule is worked out determining who has the car on which days or at specific times. Such a situation is obviously subject to abuse. Is anyone ever going to infringe on someone else's time? Will someone have a need for the car when it's not their day and find others unsympathetic and unwilling to inconvenience themselves to allow another team member to use the vehicle to meet their needs? How do you feel when people take advantage of you, abuse you, or are insensitive to your needs? Do we reflect a servant heart, putting aside our own needs with a humble, Christlike spirit?

Many of our missionary personnel are deployed in assignments that are designed to serve others, such as bookkeepers, guesthouse managers, MK teachers, or volunteer coordinators. It is unfortunate that they do not get a lot of affirmation, appreciation, and praise. Colleagues often take them for granted. How does that make them feel when people treat them like servants? It reveals whether or not they truly have a servant heart and are willing to give of themselves in self-denial. It is the flesh that wants to get recognition and to be appreciated. It hurts to be taken advantage of. We do not want to deny ourselves; it is not natural to embrace the suffering and hurt that results. That self-centered nature of the flesh is powerful and wants to be recognized and served. That's why the victory calls for self-denial, walking in the Spirit and living for God's glory alone.

God is glorified and one is blessed when selfish gratification and comfort are denied.

First Peter 2:21 reveals something that everyone is looking for. At some time we all find ourselves asking, "What is my purpose in life? What has God called me to do?" But the answer is probably not what we would expect. This verse begins, "For you were called to this." I frequently ask our new missionaries, "For what purpose has Christ called you as a missionary?" That would be a relevant question for others as well—"For what purpose has Christ called you to Himself as a believer?" While a missionary might answer it is to proclaim the gospel, plant churches, or reach a lost world, seldom would any of us answer as Peter does, "For you were called to this, because Christ also suffered for you, leaving you an example, so that you should follow in His steps" (1 Pet. 2:21).

This concept was set up in the previous verse when Peter implies that there is no merit in enduring being beaten for sin or doing wrong, "But when you do good and suffer, if you endure, it brings favor with God" (1 Pet. 2:20). How do we bring glory to God? It is in bearing suffering for doing what is good and right.

Timothy is exhorted, "Share in suffering as a good soldier of Christ Jesus. To please the recruiter, no one serving as a soldier gets entangled in the concerns of everyday life" (2 Tim. 2:3–4). The only way to glorify God and to please Christ who saved us and recruited us into His kingdom is to avoid entanglement with things of the world, and that entails hardship and denial.

Christ has called us, not just missionaries but all believers, to follow His example of suffering. What is the Scripture referring to as the example of Christ in suffering? The cross was the ultimate expression of suffering, and we are called to take up our cross of self-denial, but none of us is likely to be literally nailed to a cross. We suffer in denying the flesh, in denying ourselves, and denying the things of the world.

Hebrews 5:7–9 paints a poignant picture of Jesus. He is identified as God's Son, the perfect high priest after the order of Melchizedek. Verse 9 says, "After He was perfected, He became the source of eternal salvation to all who obey Him." How did He become perfect and earn the right to die for the sins of the world, providing eternal salvation to all those who come to Him in faith? It is explained in verses 7 and 8: "During His earthly life, He offered prayers and appeals, with loud cries and tears, to the One who was able to save Him from death, and He was heard because of His reverence. Though a Son, He learned obedience through what He suffered." It wasn't easy. We must never think that because Jesus was the

Son of God He did not have to struggle and resist temptation in order to be obedient to the Father. Peter goes on to portray this example of Christ in 1 Peter 2:22–23: "He did not commit sin, and no deceit was found in His mouth; when reviled, He did not revile in return; when suffering, He did not threaten, but committed Himself to the One who judges justly."

That's not easy. People abuse us, slander us, malign and criticize us. How do we respond? Our tendency is to become defensive, standing up for ourselves and lashing back with a harsh and judgmental word or with quiet calculating sarcasm. That's the response of the flesh. That's the way of the world. Satan would like to use that fleshly nature to create conflict and dissension by telling us to stand up for our rights and our reputation. Instead, we are to trust ourselves to Christ. He is the judge. He is the one who vindicates. It hurts to suffer abuse, to be taken advantage of and maligned. Christ endured suffering His entire life and ministry, always resisting Satan and temptation, never indulging the flesh and therefore suffered the consequences of self-denial.

Chapter 4 picks up this same theme. "Therefore, since Christ suffered in the flesh, arm yourselves also with the same resolve" (1 Pet. 4:1). We are going to examine the spiritual armor later, but how do we arm ourselves in the warfare that is constantly raging against the flesh, enticing us to a self-centered life and actions? Obviously, by choosing to suffer instead. That's not natural. No one is inclined to suffer. We enjoy comfort. We like attention. We crave being served and having our needs met. However, a willingness to embrace and endure inconvenience and suffering in order to walk in the Spirit is the example that Christ set for us. It is the model He gave to us for walking in victory.

The Scripture goes on, "Because the One who suffered in the flesh has finished with sin—in order to live the remaining time in the flesh, no longer for human desires, but for God's will" (1 Pet. 4:1–2). This is a clear statement of the victory we have been given, but a contrast is stated in these two options. The will of God is for us to walk (live) in holiness; we cannot do that and live for our human desires, that is, the ways of the world. But we cannot choose the former without experiencing the suffering that comes with self-denial. The flesh wants to sin, to indulge in the selfish gratification of worldly pleasures. That's the easy way, the comfortable way, the common way, the natural way. To deny it is to give up that which is comfortable, convenient, and enjoyable; and that hurts.

"Dear friends, when the fiery ordeal arises among you to test you, don't be surprised by it, as if something unusual were happening to you. Instead, as you share the sufferings of the Messiah rejoice, so that you may also rejoice with great joy at the revelation of His glory" (1 Pet. 4:12–13). Don't be surprised when you suffer as if God has let you down. Suffering is the natural consequence of walking in the Spirit in this world. It is a given for us just as it was for Christ. This could be why we're so weak in the spiritual battle, always failing in our efforts to live holy lives, and defeated in our desire to walk in the Spirit. No one likes to suffer. We don't want to be inconvenienced. So we continue to indulge the self-centered nature of the flesh.

Paul observed in Romans 8:18 that our suffering in denying the flesh was not worthy to be compared to the glory that is to be revealed to us. We must not think of this as simply the heavenly glory of our eternal reward, but also as the present glory that is revealed when we walk in victory over the flesh day by day. Peter affirms this same truth following his basic statement regarding spiritual warfare in chapter 5: "Be sober! Be on the alert! Your adversary the Devil is prowling around like a roaring lion, looking for anyone he can devour" (1 Pet. 5:8).

Satan is not trying just to trip us up or get us to sin. We are to be serious and alert to the fact that he wants to take control. He wants dominion over the world. He wants our fleshly, self-serving nature to dominate our life. He is trying totally to consume our life, our attitudes, and our behavior so that nothing we do will bring glory to God. We are told to resist him. How? Firm in our faith—believing what God has said rather than what we feel or want. We are to resist the enticement to live by the values of the world, indulging and serving ourselves. We are to be firm and steadfast in believing what God says and not accepting anything contrary to His Word.

Now notice what follows. "Resist him, firm in the faith, knowing that the same sufferings are being experienced by your brothers in the world" (v. 9). Those who belong to Christ—who are living in the world—are suffering. It goes with the territory, with denying the flesh and walking with Christ. This should encourage us. We are not the only ones. God hasn't isolated us. He hasn't abandoned us. He is not seeking to punish us when we suffer. Although Satan is trying to defeat us, destroy our faith, get us to deny God and doubt His faithfulness when we suffer, we should be encouraged that this is common to the experience of believers, particularly those who are truly glorifying God by a Spirit-led life. God allows us to suffer to strengthen our faith; He is glorified when we choose to appropriate His grace in time of need rather than striving in our own strength.

He gives us the victory, not in lieu of suffering but in spite of suffering, and sometimes because of suffering!

"Consider it a great joy, my brothers, whenever you experience various trials, knowing that the testing of your faith produces endurance. But endurance must do its complete work, so that you may be mature and complete, lacking nothing" (James 1:2–4). The same theme is emphasized by Peter in his introduction because this is a basic principle of the Christian life. "Blessed be the God and Father of our Lord Jesus Christ. According to His great mercy, He has given us a new birth into a living hope through the resurrection of Jesus Christ from the dead, and into an inheritance that is imperishable, uncorrupted, and unfading, kept in heaven for you, who are being protected by God's power through faith for a salvation that is ready to be revealed in the last time" (1 Pet. 1:3–5). That is a wonderful assurance: our salvation is imperishable, protected by God. Even though our eternal inheritance is secure, notice how Peter goes on to describe what we have to go through in this life. "You rejoice in this, though now for a short time you have had to be distressed by various trials so that the genuineness of your faith—more valuable than gold, which perishes though refined by fire—may result in praise, glory, and honor at the revelation of Jesus Christ" (vv. 6–7). God is glorified when our faith is tested and proved genuine in the crucible of suffering.

I remember one of our mission leaders telling me about someone who was complaining. This family had moved to a new assignment in a remote location, without the conveniences others took for granted. They had no fellowship, social interaction, or support group. The electricity was off more than it was on, there was no running water, and privacy was practically nonexistent. It took a major effort just to survive. The couple was pouring out their complaints about their inconveniences and suffering when other missionary families got to enjoy nice, comfortable living conditions. This leader listened patiently and then quietly said, "You know, Jesus didn't like nails." That put their suffering in perspective. Jesus didn't like nails. He didn't enjoy being crucified. He didn't relish suffering. He would have preferred to avoid it, as was obvious in the garden of Gethsemane. He struggled with self-denial and suffering as we do, but Hebrews 12:2 tells us that He endured the cross for the joy that was set before Him—the joy of a redeemed world bringing glory to the Father. However difficult our life, we haven't suffered to the point of being crucified on the cross and shedding our blood, as He did.

Peter goes on to observe: "Now the God of all grace, who called you to His eternal glory in Christ Jesus, will personally restore, establish, strengthen, and support you after you have suffered a little" (1 Pet. 5:10). Realize that it is only temporary. After you have suffered a little while, God responds to your desire for Him—your desire to walk in the Spirit and glorify God in your life. He personally perfects you, confirms you, strengthens and establishes you. Why would we sacrifice that to avoid a little pain, indulge in a little pleasure, or avoid being inconvenienced? The Scripture says of Jesus' temptation experience in the wilderness, He suffered forty days and returned in the power of the Spirit.

Every believer should have an intense longing for the anointing and power of God in their life. I would hope that every missionary we send out goes with an overwhelming sense of inadequacy and spiritual mediocrity that makes them desperate for God's power in their life. If they don't when they leave home, when they arrive overseas and face the challenges of language study, a deprived lifestyle, and frustration in trying to communicate the gospel among people antagonistic to their Christian witness, they will inevitably acknowledge the need for the power of God's Spirit. But God cannot entrust His power to someone who doesn't want it enough to be willing to deny self and embrace suffering and sacrifice.

We have a choice to be made. The writer of Hebrews gives us the example of Moses, who chose suffering in order to identify with the suffering and reproach of his people and to receive the reward of obedience and glorifying God. "By faith Moses, when he had grown up, refused to be called the son of Pharaoh's daughter and chose to suffer with the people of God rather than to enjoy the short-lived pleasure of sin. For he considered reproach for the sake of the Messiah to be greater wealth than the treasures of Egypt, since his attention was on the reward" (Heb. 11:24–26).

Second Peter 1:3–4 provides us a summary of all we have been discussing. These verses clarify and affirm the victory that God has provided us in the matter of spiritual warfare. They can be outlined in five statements.

1. "For His divine power has given us everything required for life and godliness" (v. 3). God has already provided everything we need to live a holy and righteous life. He has not just assured us of eternal life but has given us everything we need to glorify Him here and now.

2. How is this granted to us? "Through the knowledge of Him who called us by His own glory and goodness" (v. 3), that is, by the experiential knowledge of knowing Christ and accepting Him by faith as our

Savior. Our life of victory is in Him, not through our own efforts. In Christ we have peace, joy, holiness, victory, power—everything we need for victory.

3. Therefore, "by these He has given us very great and precious promises" (v. 4). The Bible has revealed God's truth. All that we have is based on the promises of God; having come to know Christ, we have them and can claim them as a reality in our life in contrast to the lies and deception of Satan.

4. Why? "So that through them [these promises] you may share in the divine nature" (v. 4). We are immersed in Christ, baptized in Him; He dwells within us, and we walk (live) in the Spirit because that is what these promises of God's Word tells us about the relationship and victory we have through the experiential knowledge of Christ.

5. And the result of being partakers of Christ's divine nature is "escaping the corruption that is in the world because of evil desires" (v. 4). That is the victory in spiritual warfare. We are no longer dominated by the desires of the world; we can claim the victory over sin and no longer live under corrupting carnal influences and condemnation.

Fasting as an Example of Denying the Flesh

If you have had any experience with fasting, you understand how denying the flesh entails suffering, but encouragement and teaching regarding fasting have been neglected. While acknowledging the validity of fasting, we tend to relegate it to the category of an unnecessary, legalistic discipline. After all, we are under grace, and we don't have to earn merit and favor with God through such outdated practices. The Bible says a lot about fasting. In fact, even Jesus said, "When you fast," not "You should fast" or, "If you fast." Satan, our adversary, has likely had something to do with this de-emphasis, for he knows how effective fasting is for walking in the Spirit. That is because it is an intentional, deliberate decision to deny the flesh for a spiritual benefit. When you fast, you deny yourself food, something that is needed by your body. Why would someone do this? It is because of a greater desire for that which is spiritual.

I disagree with a lot that has been written on fasting because one doesn't fast to get something from God. God is sovereign. He does answer prayer, but we don't obligate Him to do anything because of what we do. He is going to do what He, in His providence, chooses to do. We don't fast in order to obligate God to meet a need. The only motivation for fasting is a desire for God, period! When your soul longs for God, to experience intimacy with Him, to be assured of His presence, and to be led by His Spirit, and you desire Him more than food and satisfying bodily comforts, that is fasting.

Maybe you are struggling with trials and unanswered prayer—a rebellious child, a sick mother, or an important decision. In the midst of that need, God's Spirit leads you to give yourself to prayer and fasting. It is likely God will answer your prayers but not because you have engaged in a legalistic discipline. When you have a heart for God that exceeds the desire for physical food and you allow hunger pains to be a trigger to focus on Him instead of the needs of the flesh, He honors your passion and desire for Him. And the amazing thing is that He does meet needs in our life as well.

We are familiar with the disciples' futile attempt to cast out the demon in a boy, recorded in Matthew's and Mark's Gospels. After the incident Jesus chided them, explaining, "However, this kind does not come out except by prayer and fasting" (Matt. 17:21). Although this verse is not included in some translations, we should not misunderstand the implications regarding the place of fasting. This is often interpreted as a legalistic application that if we pray and fast enough we can work miracles. I think what Jesus is teaching is simply that we should not expect God to empower our life and ministry if we don't have such a desire to know Him that we devote ourselves to prayer and even fasting, denying ourselves food because our passion for Him is greater.

I'm not sure when I began to give attention to fasting, but it was probably soon after our arrival on the mission field in Indonesia. We were alone and isolated from other missionaries. We were struggling, experiencing discouragement, doubt, and frustration. I found myself praying, "God, what am I doing here?" I remember one day coming into the house, falling on my face on the floor and saying, "Lord, I've been obedient to Your call. I've sacrificed to come to Indonesia and bring my family here, but You are just not keeping Your end of the bargain." I expected the least He could do was give a little fruit and response to our efforts. I was feeling a lot of needs, but the overriding impression was that I had lost touch with God. I longed for a vital relationship with Him and just wanted to restore a relationship of confidence and faith in Him, whether we saw results from our witness or not. God led us to begin fasting one day a week. It was just a simple matter of not eating that whole day and, instead of eating physical food, intentionally seeking spiritual food.

> *We fast not to obligate God to do something but because our hunger for Him exceeds our desire for food.*

On that day my somewhat defined devotional time became more open-ended since I didn't have to take time to eat three meals. It was amazing how the Scripture, just normal devotional reading, began to come alive. Fasting meant having time to meditate on His Word and sitting quietly to listen to the impressions God spoke into my mind instead of quickly running through my list of petitions and getting on with the day. Mealtime hunger was a trigger to focus on God rather than on what we were having for lunch or dinner. It was a cause-and-effect behavioral type thing. You have hunger pains—they are a reminder you are not eating in order to focus on God and seek Him. Fasting made such a difference that my wife and I began, periodically, once every two or three months, to have a three-day personal retreat of prayer and fasting. We would not necessarily go anywhere; often we would be at home engaged in our normal responsibilities, caring for the children and interacting with the neighbors. But we would block out other nonessential activities for an extended time of focusing on the Lord and spending time with Him. Fasting seemed to facilitate a sense of intimacy with God, not because we weren't eating but due to a heartfelt expression of wanting God more than food to satisfy our fleshly nature. The flesh, the body, needs food. But in the same way our spirit needs the sustenance of God's Spirit. Walking in the Spirit as the key to victory in spiritual warfare is a strange concept because we treat it as something that happens passively rather than something we choose to do.

I'm not legalistic about fasting. I drink juice in the morning and drink water constantly. Seldom have I been led to an extended fast; those occasions have been because of a strong sense of God's leadership, and rich blessings came out of the experience. When I realize I am operating primarily in the flesh, reacting to criticism in anger, and not reflecting a Christlikeness in my attitudes and relationships, I realize a need to get back in touch with God and allow Him to have control of my life. It's not a matter of engaging in a religious ritual but just deciding that I'm not going to eat. All of my priorities change, and invariably an awareness of God's presence emerges. Fasting is not a legalistic commitment; that's not what brings spiritual results but simply having a heart for God more than a desire for food. It is a matter of having a heartfelt desire for God and following Him in what He leads you to do.

A few years ago my son, who was overseas at the time, came to the States for a wedding in Oregon. He came to Richmond to visit with us and confer with our staff. He was to leave on the weekend prior to when I was to lead the sessions in our missionary training on spiritual warfare. I always fast during that week, not because I am unfamiliar with the material or in order to get God to do something extraordinary but because I dare not presume to deal with such a subject without being confident of my own walk with the Lord. As usual I had decided to start fasting on Saturday, so that the weekend would be focused on spiritual preparation for the week. As I was driving him to the airport, he asked if I would stop by Krispy Kreme as his wife had missed the doughnuts overseas and wanted him to bring some from Richmond on the plane. He got out of the car to buy a box of a dozen doughnuts, but when he came back, he had two boxes. He explained, "I asked for a dozen and paid for them, and they said, 'We have a two-for-one special. Here is your second dozen.'" He said, "I don't need to take two boxes back on the plane with me, so I'll just leave a dozen here with you." I hadn't eaten for eighteen hours, since supper the day before. After not having had breakfast or lunch, I was at the stage when the hunger pains were most intense. I dropped him off at the airport, and here was this box of steaming, aromatic Krispy Kreme doughnuts on the car seat. I ate half the box, rationalizing, "I can start fasting tomorrow." So much for discipline!

It is not the legalism of observing a fast but our commitment to deny the flesh and its physical needs because of a hunger for spiritual food that God honors. Fasting is such an obvious way of denying the flesh. It's a biblical way of expressing our heart for God. When I sense God leading me to fast, most commonly it is for three days. One day is often not significant and can be done rather perfunctorily, but three days is a real opportunity to refocus. Usually the last meal I eat is supper the day before fasting. By the next evening I have already been fasting twenty-four hours but have always felt that a day of fasting should be the whole day. I once got to the end of the third day of fasting; the experience had been a blessing, but nothing really special, so I decided to break my fast and eat supper with Bobbye that night; after all, I had already fasted for seventy-two hours. However, there was a catch in my spirit, and I felt God wanted me to honor my commitment to fast that entire day, so I decided against eating supper that night.

I normally get up at 4:30 each morning, but the next morning I awakened at 3:30, fully alert. My usual pattern is to go downstairs, put on the coffee, then kneel and spend some time just worshipping the Lord. Then with a cup of coffee, I read the Bible and move through my prayer list. But when I awakened that morning, I sensed God saying, "I'm waiting for you." When I knelt in prayer, I felt that I was putting my head in the Father's lap.

It was such a precious experience. I could have eaten the night before and that would have been all right with regard to having completed a God-led fast. But God seems to choose to reveal Himself in a way we desperately need when we demonstrate our desire for Him is greater than our desire for physical food, and we fast in obedience to His leading. When we are feeling that we are losing it, life is becoming unraveled—characterized by strained relationships, tensions, conflicts, filled with anxieties and frustrations—why don't we do the obvious and deny the flesh in order for God to reveal Himself to us? Do we ever come to the point when our desire for Him is greater than for the food that we eat? How many times do you find yourself wondering, "What's for lunch?" Or, "I wonder what we're going to have for dinner tonight." Is what you are going to eat, indulging the fleshly, physical appetites of more concern than fellowship with the Father and feeding on what He has to offer spiritually?

Fasting is just one obvious way of denying the flesh in response to our desire for God. We can deny the flesh and what we desire in our natural self-centered, carnal tendencies in many other ways. Fasting is an example of what it means to deny the flesh, and it helps us understand how suffering is a consequence of self-denial. It is an effective discipline to help us express our desire for God and, through self-denial, experience His power and the blessing of intimacy with Him. That is why I think perhaps Satan has something to do with the current, subtle de-emphasis on this biblical practice. We dismiss it as Old Testament legalism or pharisaical piety. We think that we can be passive with regard to indulging the flesh and still receive an outpouring of God's spiritual blessings. Fasting is a wonderful, practical way to demonstrate our longing and need for God through the denial and sacrifice of normal fleshly desires in our battle to claim the victory over the flesh.

CHAPTER 7

SATAN'S FAVORITE FIERY DARTS

In every situation take the shield of faith,
and with it you will be able to extinguish the
flaming arrows of the evil one.
—Ephesians 6:16

Satan is against us, seeking to defeat us; the flesh is within us, seeking to defile us; and the world is around us, seeking to distract us. They are all in collaboration, influencing us to choose selfish and carnal values and deprive God of His glory in our lives. To reinforce the nature of our enemy and understand his subtle and devious tactics, we need to examine what the Scripture tells us about some of his favorite schemes that are so effective. A lot can be said about how he works to deceive us, tempts us to sin, and influences us to justify living an unholy and self-centered life; but we especially need to heed what God tells us in His Word. The Bible alerts us to several ways the enemy often defeats us in our desire to live a victorious and obedient Christian life. We dare not ignore these warnings or neglect doing whatever it takes to repel these fiery darts of the enemy because they highlight areas in which we are obviously most vulnerable.

Second Corinthians 2:11 says, "So that we may not be taken advantage of by Satan; for we are not ignorant of his intentions." Satan had wreaked havoc in the church at Corinth. They were aware of Satan's schemes. They had experienced moral problems, dissension, carnality, pride, the perversion of gifts, and other problems. So they would be aware of his tactics and his schemes.

Unforgiveness

When Paul says, "So that we may not be taken advantage of by Satan," he obviously is referring to the previous verse. This concluding statement follows verse 10 which says, "Now to whom you forgive anything, I do too. For what I have forgiven, if I have forgiven anything, it is for you in the presence of Christ, so that we may not be taken advantage of by Satan." Unforgiveness is one of Satan's most effective schemes. When we fail to forgive, it gives Satan an advantage because we are holding on to our anger and hurt, and this is contrary to what our reaction should be. When we are unforgiving, our thoughts are on self: "I've been offended. I've been hurt. Someone has infringed on my rights." Our old fleshly nature, which is crucified with Christ, has rolled off the altar and come alive.

Satan has entrapped many believers into a constant state of defeat with its attendant loss of joy. We forfeit God's blessings and peace because of an unforgiving attitude toward someone in our past. Feelings of unforgiveness are often suppressed, causing us to presume we have gained the victory over them. But each time an abusive parent comes to mind or we think of a former business partner who betrayed us or a friend who took advantage of us, we know we have not gained the victory. Satan brings such past hurts to mind even after we think we have gotten over them and have moved on. He is the accuser who, at every opportunity, will stir up feelings of anger, hurt, and shame and then reproach us, making us feel guilty for our unresolved feelings. In contradiction to the clear testimony of God's Word, Satan whispers—maybe even shouts, "You are not really free!" The bitterness and resentment are easily rekindled when we are focused on ourselves.

Someone shared with me the tragic experience of having lost a child who was killed by a drunken driver. This mother said, "I went through the pretense of forgiving him, but I realized the bitterness still gnaws at my heart; the pain reminds me that I haven't forgiven, and that is inhibiting me from accepting God's healing."

Forgiving someone when we have been wronged or mistreated is unnatural according to the world's way and contrary to the natural inclination of our flesh. This is why Jesus had a lot to say about forgiveness. In the Lord's Prayer it is the only conditional clause. We can't expect God to forgive us if we don't forgive others. In Matthew 18 Jesus told the disciples that they were not just to forgive seven times, which would normally be considered complete, but seventy times seven. I don't think He meant we were to forgive up to 490 times but that we are to keep on forgiving, endlessly and indefinitely. Any time we stop forgiving, Satan gains a foothold and takes advantage of us. This is because when we stop forgiving we are once again focusing on self. Jesus follows this exhortation with the parable of the two servants. One servant was forgiven much and then refused to forgive his fellow servant a minor debt. Do you recall what Jesus called the unforgiving servant? In Matthew 18:32 He called him "wicked." Wickedness is of Satan. And all he did was to be unforgiving. He also threw the servant into prison. How many of us are locked into a prison of bitterness because of unforgiveness?

We can pretend to live a holy life and serve the Lord but never experience real joy and victory due to harboring an attitude of unforgiveness toward someone who has hurt us. The sad reality of this situation is that too often it is over an offense that is trivial or occurred in the distant past. We have probably learned to control the outward expression of our feelings and may not respond in anger when we are hurt, but our feelings continue to seethe within us. Others may not even be aware that they have offended us or notice that we give them the cold shoulder. But who is affected by unforgiveness? Not the person who has wronged us. I once read that unforgiveness is like drinking poison and waiting for the other person to die. We are the one affected. We may have every right to be mad, but we are the one who loses the blessing of an intimate relationship with the Lord. And that relationship is what, in jealousy, Satan is trying to destroy.

Why did Jesus pray on the cross, "Father, forgive them, for they do not know what they are doing" (Luke 23:34)? The religious leaders and Roman soldiers were not saved because Jesus forgave them as there was no evidence of their repentance or belief. So why did He say, "Forgive them"? Certainly it was an example for us. I think it was to guard His own heart. Even in winning the victory over sin and death on the cross, if He had failed to forgive, Satan would have had an element of victory in that experience—in a heart that was unforgiving. It is one of his favorite tools.

God's Word exhorts us, "And be kind and compassionate to one another, just as God also forgave you in Christ" (Eph. 4:32). We are also told, "Pursue peace with everyone, and holiness—without it no one will see the Lord. See to it that no one falls short of the grace of God and that no root of bitterness springs up, causing trouble and by it, defiling many" (Heb. 12:14–15).

Anger

Another one of those flaming missiles is found in Ephesians 4:26–27. Once again the Scripture explicitly identifies one of Satan's strategies. "Be angry and do not sin. Don't let the sun go down on your anger, and don't give the Devil an opportunity." Like unforgiveness, anger apparently is something that also moves us from walking in the Spirit to giving an opportunity for Satan to defeat us. We usually are not too concerned about this because the Scripture doesn't prohibit anger; in fact, it seems to acknowledge that we will be angry. We simply are admonished to process it and get over it by the end of the day.

We rationalize that anger is an involuntary reaction. I don't know of anyone who has said, "Here is the situation: I have been offended, so I think I'll be angry." That's not how it happens. When something ticks you off, you don't process it and come up with an angry reaction. Anger is an involuntary emotion; it is a psychological defense mechanism. You have been threatened; it may not be a physical danger, but your self-esteem has been challenged; your rights have been offended. Someone has been disrespect-ful, infringed on your space, or demeaned your idea. You respond with an emotion that is anger. We can easily justify it, and often we disregard it by claiming, "I'll get over it." But James 1:20 reminds us of the obvious, "For man's anger does not accomplish God's righteousness."

Let's consider how Satan uses anger to get an upper hand in our life and attitude. Anger always has an object. It's focused, not on something but usually on somebody. Hopefully you have never given expression to road rage when someone cuts you off in traffic, but how did you feel? I remember riding with one of our veteran missionaries soon after arriving in Indonesia. There was no such thing as orderliness in the midst of the traffic congestion there. This missionary beat on the side of his car and yelled, "Get out of the way. Don't you know we came to help you?" His actions certainly didn't reflect a servant heart of love and respect. What triggers rage? It is the need to assert yourself or defend your rights. It is the opposite of dying to self and is obviously not a reaction that is led by the Holy Spirit. Anytime we cease allowing the Spirit to lead, we are back into the selfish nature of the flesh.

The object of our anger is usually a person. Someone is at fault; someone is to blame. The verses that follow this passage in Ephesians say, "No rotten talk should come from your mouth, but only what is good for the building up of someone in need, in order to give grace to those who hear. And don't grieve God's Holy Spirit, who sealed you for the day of redemption. All bitterness, anger and wrath, insult and slander must be removed from you, along with all wickedness" (Eph. 4:29–31). Anger leads to a root of bitter-ness and a critical spirit. Outbursts of criticism, venomous put-downs, verbal abuse, and harsh, judgmental words do not glorify the Lord! That is why anger is one of Satan's favorite weapons. You are the instrument he is using, but God is being deprived of a patient, selfless spirit in you that would bring Him glory.

You don't have to lose your temper to express anger. Anger can be expressed with gentle condescending remarks, cutting sarcasm, or a judgmental attitude. Anger is about self and standing up for one's rights, consistent with the nature of the flesh. It's not serving and loving others, bearing wrong, and giving of oneself. I hope you have learned never to use the "why" question in your home or with colleagues. It is a subtle way of expressing anger. "Why did you leave that glass on the edge of the cabinet where it would fall and break?" "Why did you park the car where it would get dented?" How can anyone respond to a question like that? It puts people in a position of having to say, "Well, I'm stupid. I'm dumb. I was negligent." How can they defend themselves? You're expressing anger in a subtle way that puts down someone else. It is not edifying and usually precipitates dissension.

People who have a problem with anger are not just those with a short temper; they usually fly off the handle and then get over it. I've known and worked with a lot of such people, even among missionary colleagues. When they lose their temper, they usually realize it immediately, acknowledge it, and ask for forgiveness. That is a testimony of their walk with the Lord. A great many other people are seething with anger within, whether due to low self-esteem or a sense of rejection. Something within them is characterized by anger. This can be a much greater problem because it gives Satan a stronghold in their life.

The apostle Paul advised those in Corinth to "put up with it if someone enslaves you, if someone devours you, if someone captures you, if someone dominates you, or if someone hits you in the face" (2 Cor. 11:20). In 1 Corinthians 6:7, he challenges them with the rhetorical question, "Why not rather put up with injustice? Why not rather be cheated?" The implication is that it is better to suffer passively the consequences than to bring dishonor to Christ by reacting in anger and attacking someone in response and creating conflict.

When it comes to the matter of anger, we need to be careful about expressing what we justify as "righteous indignation." Yes, I get angry when I see the courts approving homosexual marriages. I get angry about abortion rights and other moral social issues. But we had best leave indignation up to the Lord. He said, "Vengeance belongs to Me, I will repay" (Heb. 10:30). That's not our task. He has not authorized us to express anger; we are to walk in holiness, selflessness, loving one another and led of the Spirit, the fruit of which is self-control.

Doubt

Another weapon, which may indeed be one of Satan's most effective, is doubt. If faith is the victory, then all Satan has to do is erode our faith. He seduced Eve in Genesis 3:1 by creating doubt regarding what God had said. "Did God really say, 'You can't eat from any tree in the garden'?" When Eve confirmed what God had said, Satan countered with a lie, contradicting God's truth, "'No! You will not die,' the serpent said to the woman" (Gen. 3:4). And he proceeded to malign God's motives in the next verse, "In fact, God knows that when you eat from it your eyes will be opened and you will be like God, knowing good and evil."

In the same way Satan is constantly leading us to question what God has said. He gets us to justify sinful living and attitudes by convincing us that we will not suffer consequences or God's judgment since we are His children and have been born again. We succumb to doubt when we indulge in speculations, seeking to rationalize the Scripture rather than accepting what God has said as truth. We are to bring every thought in obedience to Christ. God's Word says that we can have peace that supersedes understanding, that Jesus gives us an abiding peace; but Satan creates doubt and convinces us we cannot have peace in the situation we may be going through. We are told we have been given authority over all the power of the evil one, yet in disbelief we accept defeat in our Christian walk and never claim the victory.

In one of *The Screwtape Letters*, Wormwood is instructed: "Keep his mind off Jesus. It doesn't matter what he thinks about—even good things—just keep him from meditating on God's Word and promises. Keep him trying to produce feelings by his own actions. Get him to try to manufacture loving feelings instead of accepting Christ's love, trying to feel forgiven instead of simply accepting the Savior's promise. Create skepticism regarding prayer because what is prayed for doesn't always happen."[1]

Doubt is one of Satan's favorite weapons because it erodes the foundation of our victory. Believing God and trusting the truth of His Word as reality are the defensive weapons He has given us as a shield of protection to repel Satan's lies and deception. Our enemy is casting darts of doubt into our mind, constantly throughout every day. That's why we must abide in His Word and believe what God says, even when all evidence is to the contrary because faith is the victory.

Satan's attacks are deflected by a shield of faith. We are admonished, "Don't be led astray by various kinds of strange teachings" (Heb. 13:9). Anytime we stray from the Word of God and begin to embrace other teachings, Satan uses them to feed doubt and erode the foundation of our victory. Second Peter 3:17 expressed it well: "Be on your guard, so that you are not led away by the error of the immoral and fall from your own stability."

Pride

Another weapon of Satan, which no one should find as a surprise, is pride. We have referred to James 4:7 a number of times: "Therefore, submit to God. But resist the Devil, and he will flee from you." The previous verse says, "God resists the proud, but gives grace to the humble." Who are the humble? They are those who recognize their own inadequacy and unworthiness. They acknowledge a need beyond their own abilities. Humility is the characteristic that leads us to submit to the Lord and trust Him.

It's like Paul's thorn in the flesh. In 2 Corinthians 12 he tells us about an extraordinary spiritual experience in which he had an exalted vision of being lifted to the third heaven. Such an intimate experience with God could lead one to feel that he had arrived, been anointed with the Spirit, and was really something! That's dangerous. We are extremely vulnerable to pride when God chooses to manifest Himself in our life or ministry. God said, "Well Paul, I'm going to give you a thorn in the flesh that will keep you humble." So Paul prayed that God would deliver him from this affliction, and he really believed that God was all-powerful and able to take it away. But God replied, "No, there is something more important for you to learn. You must learn that My grace is sufficient. Only when you're aware of your weakness can the power of Christ be manifest in you."

Notice that Paul identified his thorn in the flesh as a messenger of Satan. "Therefore, so that I would not exalt myself, a thorn in the flesh was given to me, a messenger of Satan to torment me so I would not exalt myself" (2 Cor. 12:7). God did not impose suffering on Paul, but in His sovereignty He did allow the enemy to afflict him. God could have put a hedge of protection around Paul. He could have removed his thorn in the flesh, but Paul likely would have become more and more exalted and prideful. God had a greater purpose for him. He wanted Paul to experience the fullness of God's power and to find his strength in Jesus Christ Himself. The only way that would happen was to bring him to the end of himself and humble him to the point that he would recognize his own weakness and inadequacy. Adversity may be one of Satan's most commonly used tools to defeat us and discourage us. It is not a matter of whether or not we can escape adversity and live above hardship and trials but how we respond to it. If we humble ourselves, acknowledging our weakness and need, God gets the glory and is able to entrust His power to us in giving us the victory in such circumstances.

> *Pride assures we will be defeated because we try to win the battle in our own strength rather than the power of God.*

God will not share His glory with anyone. We dare not take credit for doing anything that comes only by God's blessings and favor. He alone is worthy of all glory and honor for every success and anything worthwhile in our lives. Pride may not necessarily be limited to someone who is arrogant or conceited; it is more typically an attitude of self-sufficiency. To presume that we can do anything in ourselves, especially in Christian ministry, is extremely dangerous. Satan will feed our success and gloat in the recognition and attention we get. It leads to a feeling of self-confidence. We begin to believe we are an outstanding leader or that because of our gifted preaching the church or ministry is growing. When we are not humbly submitting to God and relying on the Holy Spirit, pride will bring ultimate defeat.

This was a prevalent problem in the Old Testament. The attempt to build the tower of Babel in Genesis 11 was driven by pride to "make a name for ourselves" (Gen. 11:4). God dealt graciously with His people in the wilderness, as He explained to them, "In order to humble and test you . . . [Otherwise] you may say to yourself, 'My power and my ability have gained this wealth for me,' but remember that the LORD your God gives you the power to gain wealth" (Deut. 8:16–18). Pride was also the reason God instructed Gideon to diminish his troops. "The LORD said to Gideon, 'You have too many people for Me to hand the Midianites over to you, or else Israel might brag: "I did it myself"'" (Judg. 7:2). Pride led David to conduct a census of his people; the Scripture reveals who was behind those prideful acts and decisions in 1 Chronicles 21:1, "Satan stood up against Israel and incited David to count the people of Israel."

The prophets often confronted the pride of the people and especially of the leaders. They made it clear that it would bring God's judgment: "For a day belonging to the LORD of Hosts is coming against all that is proud and lofty, . . . it will be humbled" (Isa. 2:12). "Woe to those who are wise in their own opinion and clever in their own sight" (Isa. 5:21). God condemned the king of Assyria in Isaiah 10:12–13 saying, "'I will punish the king of Assyria for his arrogant acts and the proud look in his eyes.' For he said, 'I have done this by my own strength and wisdom.'"

In another one of *The Screwtape Letters*, Wormwood is advised to use pride to defeat the new Christian to whom he had been assigned. "Vanity and spiritual pride are one of our most useful tools. If you can't prevent spiritual growth, allow one to experience such depth he begins to feel he has arrived. Or allow him to be a part of such an enriching group of believers, they begin to look down on outsiders as those who have not arrived and are not as spiritual as they are."[2]

Pride has brought division and dissension into many churches. Such an attitude is not unusual, even among missionary colleagues. I get uneasy when one of our missionaries begins to experience spectacular success to the point they and their ministry are given publicity. They are in demand at mission conferences and other events when they come home. Pastors and churches flock to join them in the sweeping harvest and miraculous church growth that is occurring. But time after time I have seen these servants of God fall morally or succumb to pride to the point where relationships are strained, accountability diminished, and they become no longer useful to God.

Paul realized this danger: "Therefore I do not run like one who runs aimlessly, or box like one who beats the air. Instead, I discipline my body and bring it under strict control, so that after preaching to others, I myself will not be

disqualified" (1 Cor. 9:26–27). He had successfully evange-
lized the known civilized world, had preached the gospel
from Jerusalem to Illyricum, and planted churches throughout Asia and Europe. But Paul realized that pride could
cause him to be cast aside if he should ever cease humbling
himself in a disciplined life that was a contingency for God's
blessing and power.

We are so vulnerable to pride because, like unforgiveness and anger, it is aligned with the nature of our flesh,
that old nature that is centered on self. We should recognize the caution light is flashing when we are obsessed
with what people think of us, find ourselves living for the
approval of others and have a constant need for acclaim
and recognition. God gives us everything we need to live
life to its fullest; He blesses us with results and success,
but we dare not take credit or think that it is due to our
own ability. Whether we experience success or failure, both
should stimulate us to yield in humble submission to God
and His lordship.

The story of Ananias and Sapphira is a good example of
the danger of pride. They saw Barnabus getting accolades
and praise for selling land and giving it to the church. They
decided they would like to have that kind of recognition. So
they sold some property and pretended to give all of the proceeds to the church while actually withholding some of it
for themselves. In Acts 5:3 Peter said, "Why has Satan filled
your heart to lie to the Holy Spirit?" He is revealing where
self-deception and pride come from. Believing we're something we are not, pretending to sacrifice something when
we really aren't, assuming we are gifted and qualified for a
task and can do it ourselves—all of this comes from Satan.
He is the father of lies. There is no truth in him or in the

deceit he plants in our minds causing us to think we are anything apart from God.

The Bible doesn't indicate that Ananias and Sapphira outwardly lied. It was more an issue of self-deceit in pretending to be giving their all when they were not. But what about us? We may fool others—colleagues and fellow church members—pretending to be dedicated and serving for the sake of the Lord alone, when we relish the praise and recognition we get for our faithfulness and service. We alert missionary candidates to their vulnerability in this regard. People will put them on a pedestal, praise them for their dedication, be impressed by the sacrifice they are making to follow God and serve Him overseas on the mission field until they may really believe they are giving their all. When people talk about their devotion to the Lord and how they are sacrificing to leave behind a beautiful home, a successful business, and a comfortable lifestyle, they begin to think it is really true: they are wonderful and making a significant sacrifice. All the while in their hearts they know what they are holding onto; they know they really haven't gone all the way in sacrifice and devotion. "For if anyone considers himself to be something when he is nothing, he is deceiving himself" (Gal. 6:3).

God has not given the same discernment to spiritual leaders today that He gave to the apostles to reveal the insincerity, hypocrisy, and self-serving motives that are behind much of what we do for the Lord. This experience in Acts taught the church a lesson. The Scripture says, "Then great fear came on the whole church" (Acts 5:11). We ought to shudder in fear of taking credit for anything that belongs to God or any attitude of self-sufficiency that would deprive Him of the glory He desires in blessing our life and ministry.

However, a reverse side of pride is expressed in a kind of pseudo-humility. One can even take pride in humility. I recall hearing someone give a testimony and saying, "I'm just a zero with the rim knocked off!" He was seeking to acknowledge that he was nothing for the sake of Christ. But his testimony came across as one taking pride in expressing humility. I thought, *What an insult to God, who has made you, created you, gifted you, indwelt you, and empowered you by His Spirit.* I have seen Satan render more missionaries ineffective by low self-esteem than anything else. When we develop the idea that we don't have any abilities or talents and we can't be like others who are more gifted, Satan has claimed the victory, and God has been robbed of His glory in our lives. Being humble is not having low self-esteem. God has created each of us as someone of immeasurable worth to serve Him and live for His glory. We are to have a self-confidence that gives us boldness but only because our confidence is in God.

Satan's scheme is to get you to focus on yourself. It may be through pride in accomplishments and personal abilities or through feeling sorry for yourself because you are not like others and cannot do things they can do. But when we die to ourselves and live only for God's glory, Satan cannot tempt us with pride. God is able to entrust us with His power and use us effectively for His kingdom because He knows we will not claim the credit but will give all the glory to Him.

Unholy Living

We are expected to live holy and godly lives. Our position in Christ makes us holy, not based on our own efforts to become sanctified but because we have become the righteousness of Him. The Holy Spirit lives within us and empowers us for holy living that glorifies God. Holiness is separation from worldly lusts and a life of selfish gratification; therefore there is the expectation that our lives will reflect that holiness. First Peter 1:14–16 says, "As obedient children, do not be conformed to the desires of your former ignorance but as the One who called you is holy, you also are to be holy in all your conduct; for it is written, 'Be holy, because I am holy.'" God is holy and has come to live within us and, therefore, expects us to be holy in all our behavior. And why not, since He provides the means for us to do so through the Holy Spirit who guides and empowers us.

Paul expressed amazement at the sin he found in the lives of the Corinthian believers and said in 1 Corinthians 3:16–17, "Don't you know that you are God's sanctuary and that the Spirit of God lives in you? If anyone ruins God's sanctuary, God will ruin him; for God's sanctuary is holy, and that is what you are." It is unthinkable that we would allow our bodies to be used for sin since they are the holy abode of God's Spirit.

Being from the deep South, I remember a colloquialism that was commonly used when I was growing up. If someone did something that was foolish or kind of stupid, we would say, "Well that was 'ignernt.'" It was not ig-nor-ant, but "ignernt!" This is what Peter is saying. He is saying, brothers, it's just "ignernt" to go on indulging the flesh. Beforehand, when you were still in bondage to the flesh, you didn't have an option. You were living in ignorance of the Spirit's power and provision. You didn't know there was anything else. But now that you are children of God, don't conform to those lusts and desires of the flesh that were characteristic of your former life. We are to be holy because we have been called to be holy, and the Holy One dwells within us.

Peter expresses how special and precious we are to God. We are described in 1 Peter 2:5, "As living stones, [you] are being built into a spiritual house for a holy priesthood to offer spiritual sacrifices acceptable to God through Jesus Christ." In verse 9 we are identified as "a chosen race, a royal priesthood, a holy nation, a people for His possession," and it is for the purpose "that you may proclaim the praises of the One who called you out of darkness into His marvelous light" (1 Pet. 2:9). The next verse explains, "You were not a people, but now you are God's people; you had not received mercy, but now you have received mercy" (1 Pet. 2:10).

Here we are, the people of God, a special possession, indwelt by His Holy Spirit, a holy nation of people—God's own possession. Immediately the significance of who we are is expressed in an appeal: "Dear friends, I urge you as aliens and temporary residents to abstain from fleshly desires that war against you" (1 Pet. 2:11). There is a warfare against the people of God, one that is attacking our soul, the heart of our being. The allure of fleshly lusts is carried over from our former life apart from God before we became His people. We are to treat these lusts and desires as things that are alien to our nature as strangers because they no longer are a part of who we are. They have no place in our life. He is saying, "Don't even be associated with them."

In mentoring young Timothy, Paul warns him to recognize the danger of sensual desires and the tendency of many to live for worldly pleasures; he urges him, "Give the adversary no opportunity to accuse us. For some have already turned astray to follow Satan" (1 Tim. 5:14–15). The importance of being a holy people, separated from what is sinful and unclean is also stressed by Paul in 2 Corinthians 6:16–17: "For we are the sanctuary of the living God, as God said: I will dwell among them and walk among them, and I will be their God, and they will be My people. Therefore, come out from among them and be separate, says the Lord." Then he goes on to say, "Therefore dear friends, since we have such promises, we should wash ourselves clean from every impurity of the flesh and spirit, making our sanctification complete in the fear of God" (2 Cor. 7:1). When we realize that our physical body is the container in which God Himself dwells, it is unthinkable that we would allow ourselves to be enticed into sin. Out of the fear of God, we ought to be compelled to strive for holiness and avoid anything that would defile His temple.

> *Satan renders our witness to a lost world ineffective when we live unholy lives no different from the rest of the world.*

Indulging in fleshly lusts is not only inappropriate for a born-again Christian; it also grieves the Holy Spirit who jealously desires to control and empower our behavior. It also deprives God of being glorified in our life and renders ineffective our witness to a lost world. This may be the real reason Satan works so hard to keep us in bondage so that sin characterizes our attitude and actions. Holy living and behavior have tremendous implications for a Christian's witness in the world. "Conduct yourselves honorably among the Gentiles, so that in a case where they speak against you as those who do evil, they may, by observing your good works, glorify God in a day of visitation" (1 Pet. 2:12).

Holy living and good behavior are especially important for missionaries who live among peoples and nations that do not know Jesus and do not respect the Christian faith. But it is also important for Christians everywhere. "Gentiles" refer to the nations or the non-Jewish peoples of the world, those who do not know God. This is relevant to the fact that God's purpose and desire are to be exalted and glorified among all peoples. Satan's intent to deprive God of being glorified among the nations is successful when he can deprive God of being glorified in our lives by unholy living.

Many cultures and places, such as Muslim societies, consider Christians apostate, and they slander and speak evil of Christians. God, who wants to reveal Himself to all people, desires that they, too, will accept Him and glorify Him. That's why we send missionaries to these people and are confident that one day—the day of visitation—God will manifest His glory among them; Jesus Christ will be made known. Some commentaries interpret "the day of visitation" as the return of Christ and the manifestation of the new heavens and new earth. However, I think it's appropriate to interpret this as the day in which God reveals Himself and makes His presence and sovereignty known among that people group through the proclamation of the gospel.

What will allow those who blaspheme and slander Jesus Christ and the Christian faith to embrace the gospel and glorify God when He is revealed to them? It is the way we live, our behavior. This is why we send missionaries to plant their lives in an incarnational witness and live among them. There is no more effective witness than someone living out his faith in the midst of people who are lost. This is not to disparage the power and effectiveness of distributing Bibles and proclaiming the Word, or media broadcasts, or other methods of witness. But giving people an opportunity to see lived out before them the reality of a living Savior within us, and the difference He makes in our life is what gives credibility to the witness of our words. I think the reason Jesus told us to "go," is that a lost world, even to the ends of the earth, may not just hear the gospel but see the reality of it in lives that reflect the holiness of God.

Several years ago one of our personnel serving among a restricted Muslim people group in Northern Africa called to share that one of his workers had prayed to receive Christ. I responded with an expression of joy but then realized he was somewhat distraught. He replied, "You don't understand. He's the sixth local person who has made a decision to follow Christ; each of the others has been killed within a few months." He was struggling with the dilemma of how he could conscientiously lead someone to faith in Christ knowing it would result in his possible death. He went on to explain that the young man had come to him that morning and said, "I've been working with you for two years, and I've been watching your life and how you live. You are different from anyone else I have ever known in our society, even the religious leaders in our community. I have never known anyone with such integrity and genuine compassion and concern for others. I've come to realize in observing your life that it is because you're a follower of Jesus Christ." Then he went on to say, "I want to be like you; will you tell me how I can be a follower of Jesus?"

This took place in a country where it is illegal to share Christ with a Muslim and for a Muslim to become a believer; but confident the young man was sincere, the missionary shared with him the claims of Christ and the way of salvation. However, before he led him in a sinner's prayer to confess Jesus as Savior, he said, "You know, if you do this, you're likely to be killed." The young man replied, "I know, but there is no other way, and I must follow it."

How do Muslims, those who consider the gospel corrupt and who slander Christians as apostate and evil, come to that kind of conviction? Only by seeing in someone else the truth of the gospel lived out before their eyes, the holiness of God and the character of Jesus Christ in us that is the fruit of being led by the Spirit. On the other hand, what kind of witness do we have when we live like the rest of the world? When we are self-serving, embroiled in dissension and conflict, have condescending attitudes toward others, or experience a moral lapse in behavior, we give the "Gentiles" every reason to reject our witness. When the nations observe the moral decay in our nation as it is portrayed through movies and in the news media, that materialistic and promiscuous lifestyle becomes the witness of what Christianity is perceived to be. It is an insult to our Lord Jesus Christ and doesn't attract anyone to our faith.

The distinct witness of our holiness, as a contrast to the world, is what will turn the nations to God. "'The nations will know that I am Yahweh,'—the declaration of the Lord God—'when I demonstrate My holiness through you in their sight'" (Ezek. 36:23). How we live makes a difference in the world's knowing Jesus. Satan doesn't have to create religious opposition and government restrictions to inhibit the kingdom of God from being established among all peoples. If he can just get us to live like the world, indulge the flesh and treat sinful behavior as normative, he has deprived God of His glory and diminished the potential of others receiving the gospel. When will the nations know that He is Lord? Only when they see in us, Christians and a Christian nation,

His holiness—the difference that Christ makes. We need to claim the victory Paul expressed: "For our boast is this: the testimony of our conscience that we have conducted ourselves in the world, and especially toward you, with God-given sincerity and purity, not by fleshly wisdom but by God's grace" (2 Cor. 1:12).

One day we will be with Christ in heaven, delivered not only from the penalty of sin and power of sin but also from the presence of sin. "Dear friends, we are God's children now, and what we will be has not yet been revealed. We know that when He appears, we will be like Him, because we will see Him as He is" (1 John 3:2). John goes on to say in the next verse: "Everyone who has this hope in Him purifies himself just as He is pure." He explains that Christ appeared to take away sins, and in Him is no sin. It is inconsistent to look forward to our sinless glorification in heaven and be careless about living a holy life here. "The one who says he remains in Him should walk just as He walked" (1 John 2:6). And that is in holiness and purity of life.

Creating Dissension

The nature of the flesh contributes to conflict and dissension. If Satan can get us to manifest our self-centered nature by being defensive and insisting on our rights, it invariably results in disrespect and hurting others. The Bible is prolific in its admonition to love one another and give honor to others. Especially within the body of Christ, our fellowship is to be characterized by mutual submission and respect. First Peter 2:13–14 highlights a practical manifestation of spiritual warfare: "Submit to every human institution because of the Lord, whether to the Emperor as the supreme authority, or to governors as those sent out by him." This reflects a parallel admonition from Paul in Romans 13:1 and following: "Everyone must submit to the governing authorities, for there is no authority except from God, and those who exist are instituted by God. So then, the one who resists the authority is opposing God's command, and those who oppose it will bring judgment on themselves" (vv. 1–2).

One of our most serious challenges to victorious, Spirit-filled living may be the difficulty we find in being submissive to authority and to one another in the body of Christ. The Holy Spirit brings unity because wherever He is leading, He lifts up Jesus Christ and centers everything around bringing glory to Him and to the Father. Dissension, conflict, and disunity emerge out of self-serving attitudes of standing up for our own opinion, demanding our rights, seeking to dominate or control others and their actions.

As Christians we are quick to champion equality and equal standing in our church fellowship. But often we use the precious concept of the priesthood of the believer to justify our personal convictions and noncooperative attitudes. Each of us has free access to God without having to go through any other human agent or priestly mediator; being indwelt of the Holy Spirit, each believer is free to be guided in the interpretation of Scripture and to make decisions as we perceive God is leading us. That should not contradict or supersede the fact that the Holy Spirit leads us into unity. Divisiveness, factions, and conflict are not authored by God. They are created by a human nature that is driven by the inclinations of the flesh to view our own position as correct and to presume an exclusive claim to truth without respect for others. James 4:1 identifies the source of quarrels and conflicts as envy and "the cravings that are at war within you."

We need to be reminded that both Paul and Peter were speaking of being in submission to pagan, government authorities who were creating problems and even persecuting the early church. These rulers demanded allegiance and even worship of Caesar, and yet the church was instructed to be submissive, recognizing that civil authority existed because it was ordained of God for our welfare. God has also called and put in place those gifted to provide leadership as spiritual authority within the church. "Obey your leaders and submit to them, for they keep watch over your souls as those who will give an account, so they can do this with joy and not with grief, for that would be unprofitable for you" (Heb. 13:17). "Now we ask you, brothers, to give recognition to those who labor among you and lead you in the Lord and admonish you, and to esteem them very highly in love because of their work" (1 Thess. 5:12–13). Satan is having a heyday in destroying the witness of many congregations whose church members are following their fleshly instincts and attacking one another, especially those in leadership, instead of seeking Spirit-led conflict resolution.

Jesus had a lot to say about mutual submissiveness, calling us to bear persecution, insults, and evil, even when it is false and unjust. He instructed us to love our enemies and pray for them. In Romans 12 we are reminded not to think more highly of ourselves than we ought (v. 3); we are to bless those who persecute—and disagree—with us (v. 14). We are to identify with one another and rejoice with those who rejoice and weep with those who weep (v. 15); we are individually each responsible for being at peace with all men (v. 18), and we are not to be overcome with evil but to overcome evil with good (v. 21). In Philippians 4:2 Paul admonished two women in conflict, Euodia and Syntyche, to live in harmony. In chapter 2 he made it clear that unity and mutual submissiveness were basic to our corporate Christian faith. "If then there is any encouragement in Christ, if any consolation of love, if any fellowship with the Spirit, if any affection and mercy, fulfill my joy by thinking the same way, having the same love, sharing the same feelings, focusing on one goal. Do nothing out of rivalry or conceit, but in humility consider others as more important than yourselves" (Phil. 2:1–3).

Paul recognized the vulnerability of the church to dissension and warned the leaders at Ephesus: "I know that after my departure savage wolves will come in among you, not sparing the flock. And men from among yourselves will rise up with deviant doctrines to lure the disciples into following them. Therefore, be on the alert" (Acts 20:29–31). The antidote is described in the Scripture passages above and in Ephesians 5:21 that says, "Submitting to one another in the fear of Christ."

Why does Satan work so hard to create dissension? The picture of submissiveness and unity portrayed in these passages, and many others, glorifies God. This kind of relationship within the body enables God to work through us in the world. Not only is it an empowered synergy of witness; it is a testimony that glorifies Jesus because it is a blatant contrast with the ways of the world. The world says to stand up for yourself and your rights, defend yourself, don't let anyone take advantage of you. But God says, as expressed by Paul in 1 Corinthians 6:7, "Why not rather put up with injustice? Why not rather be cheated?" He said in the previous verse that it is already a defeat for you when you go to law against a brother. Why is this so difficult? Satan uses the values and pattern of the world around us to convince us the importance of our rights and that the cause for which we are fighting is more important than the testimony of unity that comes from mutual submission and respect. He uses the prideful nature of the flesh to cause us to hold on to our rights and our opinions, even attacking and maligning others who do not see things as we do. Yes, there will be conflict, even within the body of Christ and among believers, but God has given us biblical guidelines to resolve conflict, and the Holy Spirit will always lead that process in a way that will minimize hurt, respect diversity, and preserve unity if we approach disagreements in humility rather than pride.

If any organization is going to function effectively and efficiently, there has to be structure, and that means having people in places of leadership. It is not unscriptural for there to be a hierarchy of leadership responsibilities and accountability. It is reflected in the diversity of gifts that God gives to the body and His calling of leaders to various functions such as pastor, teacher, and evangelist. It goes all the way back to when God instructed Moses to put leaders and judges over groups of fifties and hundreds. However, the flesh makes it hard to be in subjection to leadership.

Especially in a large organization like the International Mission Board, with more than five thousand missionaries all over the world, there has to be structure, organization, accountability of leadership at various levels if we are to stay focused and fulfill our prescribed objectives. Someone once said we, like many churches and other organizations, had a biblical organization like that described in the book of Judges: "Everyone did whatever he wanted" (Judg. 17:6)!

It is amazing how many times we adopt that attitude to justify independent decisions and actions: "God has called me, and I'm accountable only to Him; no one can tell me what to do!" That is just not biblical. When God calls us to be part of the body of Christ, He calls us to mutual accountability within the body, the church. He calls us to be in submission to those He has ordained and called to provide leadership and spiritual direction.

When we reorganized our field structure into local people group teams, we found that assigning people to a team did not necessarily make them a team. Our goal was an effort to simplify and decentralize our organization so each component could be more focused and mutually accountable to one another rather than to a hierarchy of leadership. But reorganizing did not eliminate an independent spirit that continued to challenge teamwork and unity.

Why is it so hard to be submissive? In our relationships we tend to act out of the flesh and our self-centered nature rather than having the mind of Christ (as the Holy Spirit would lead us) "who . . . emptied Himself by assuming the form of a slave. . . . He humbled Himself" (Phil. 2:6–8). It is not only the far too prominent moral failures among Christians that bring shame to God and deprive Him of being glorified in our lives but simply the lack of Spirit-led submission to one another. Our independent, self-centered attitudes create dissension that paralyzes the work of God and makes us no different from the world.

In conclusion the Bible speaks of these effective tools of Satan as strongholds in our life that must be destroyed. I have been blessed in reading many psalms that assure us that God is powerful and gives us victory over the strongholds of the enemy. We normally think of strongholds in our life as those habits or addictions that control us. I have interests and passions in my life other than a unilateral focus on God. I am a passionate sports fan and stay connected with what's happening with my favorite teams. I have a passion for my grandchildren, a committed devotion to wife and family; the compulsion that drives my involvement in our mission task supersedes all other interests to the point of almost totally dominating my time, energy, and attention. However, I don't think any of those interests and commitments infringe on my commitment to the lordship of Christ and glorifying Him and, in fact, may be led by Him for the sake of blessing me with a wholesome and balanced life.

But there are things that get control of us, things that do not bless us or glorify God, things that are obviously of the enemy. Smoking, drinking, drugs, and overeating are destructive to our health and a body that is the temple of the Holy Spirit. Many in our society are addicted to sex, resulting in promiscuity or involvement in pornography. These weapons of Satan can be strongholds that have gained a power over us. Unforgiveness, anger, and pride are strongholds that need to be destroyed. Doubt and skepticism may be so strong that they have become strongholds fortifying our hearts from believing God and His Word. If anything has become an obsession in our life, which may not be evil in itself, such as acquiring wealth, moving up the corporate ladder of success, an infatuation with beauty and fashion, the enemy will use it to draw us away from God and get life out of balance. Psalm 101:3 says, "I will not set anything godless before my eyes. . . . It will not cling to me."

CHAPTER 8

ADVERSITY, SATAN'S MOST EFFECTIVE WEAPON

I have told you these things so that in Me you may have peace. You will have suffering in this world. Be courageous! I have conquered the world.
—John 16:33

We may recognize the villainous nature of unforgiveness, anger, and pride and be mature in our ability to recognize and resist these tendencies of our fleshly nature with the help of God's Holy Spirit. We would like to assume that we have grown in our faith and can believe and claim the Word of God as truth and reality in our lives, regardless of our feelings and experience so that doubt never erodes the foundation of our victory in Christ. We can readily understand how unholy living and dissension in the body of Christ are used by our enemy to erode our witness and the advance of God's kingdom. However, adversity can blindside the most dedicated Christian; create doubts concerning God's love, faithfulness, and power; and bring about reactions in attitudes and behavior that forfeit the victory by which God would be glorified. This is Satan's most prominent flaming missile because he doesn't have to do anything but distort our perception of circumstances that are common to life.

As stated earlier, it is contrary to God's moral nature to bring hurt, harm, and destruction upon us; neither has He empowered Satan to afflict our bodies physically apart from His sovereign control and permissive will. We bring the consequences of physical pain on ourselves by sinful choices and because we live in a fallen, imperfect world in which accidents, illnesses, tragedies, and natural disasters occur. When these happen, we can claim the promise of Romans 8:28 and believe that God works in all things for good to those who love Him and are called according to His purpose (which allows Him to be glorified). But if we fail to respond in faith, believe God's promises, and reflect our love for Him, even in difficult circumstances, Satan can use those same situations to destroy our faith, rob us of the victory, and bring discouragement and defeat. It is all contingent on our reaction to the negative experiences of life.

Satan delights in practicing his deception by speaking to our minds so that we indulge in a pity party, feeling abandoned by God and losing all hope. It is so easy for Satan to use adversity to defeat us because his deception leads us to believe we are entitled to health, comfort, and security. Because we belong to God and He is sovereign and all-powerful, we think He should put a hedge of protection around us so that we never have to suffer or go through trials and hardships. Satan keeps us from recognizing that God allows us to suffer because it is our greatest opportunity to grow in faith, experience the depth and sufficiency of His love and grace, and glorify Him by demonstrating the victory we have in Christ in spite of the most horrendous tragedy and loss.

We alert new missionaries to expect adversity because it is inherent in their role. We are simply disillusioned to think we are exempt because we belong to Christ. Jesus alerted His disciples to this in John 16:33. He said, "You will have suffering in this world." He said earlier, as He prepared to send them out to carry on His mission, that they would be hated and persecuted just as He was hated and persecuted because "a slave is not greater than his master" (John 15:20). So it is not a matter of being exempt and avoiding adversity. It is not a matter of walking in victory when we are blessed, prospering, and everything is going our way, while to experience tragedy and trials means being forsaken by God and defeated in our Christian life. That's what Satan wants us to believe. It is not whether or not we experience adversity but how we respond to it.

Tragedies seem to be a daily occurrence among our large missionary family. I write more than a dozen condolence letters every week to missionaries who have lost parents, siblings, and sometimes immediate family members. That's difficult for anyone, but when families are separated by great distances, the grief and pain of such a loss can be even more severe. Missionaries succumb to strange debilitating illnesses. While traveling in West Africa, I heard the missionaries discussing malaria everywhere we went. It wasn't a matter of whether or not they had contracted malaria, but their conversation was about the last time they had it and what they were doing to treat it. It went with the territory. When you arrive at a foreign destination, enthusiastic about sharing the gospel and giving yourself to be a fervent witness, it is hard to understand why you are constantly beset by sickness, harassment, a traffic accident, or legal problems.

When we moved to our assignment after language study in our first term of missionary service, enthusiastic and committed to our task, our family began getting staph infections. Boils would break out on our bodies and faces. I even got them on my eyelids. They would drain at night, giving me a grotesque appearance that frightened the children in the neighborhood. The doctors advised us to wash our sheets and clothes. Then they said, "You need to burn your sheets and clothes." Finally they decided the infection was in the water and had gotten into our blood stream. It was quite an irritation and inconvenience.

Missionary friends had come to celebrate with us our first Thanksgiving. We had just been seated for a late afternoon dinner with Russell, our son who was about two years old at the time, sitting between my wife and me. He had a little boil on his forehead, and Bobbye and I, sitting on each side of him, both happened to notice how it was protruding. We looked closely and noticed a red streak going down toward his eye. We were disturbed and, intuitively, perceived this was not good. So we called our mission hospital in Kediri and notified them we were coming. It was five hours away, so we jumped in the car and left immediately leaving our guests there at the table. When we got to the hospital, Russell's head had become swollen, and both eyes were swollen shut. The doctors began to pump him with antibiotics. They didn't tell us until a couple of days later, when he was all right, that if we had not come immediately, we could have lost him. That part of the face is called the death triangle; because there is no lymph system, the infection drains into the brain.

Coming close to losing our son was a disturbing experience. Since we were at the hospital and our annual physicals were overdue, we decided to have our physical examinations. We discovered that Bobbye needed emergency surgery. That delayed our going back home for a couple of weeks in order for her to recover fully. We finally got home the week before Christmas, and Bobbye and I both came down with dengue fever. Dengue is sometimes called breakbone fever or hemorrhagic fever because you feel like every bone is breaking, your head is about to explode, and sometimes blood oozes out of the pores. There is nothing you can do but just let it run its course, usually for ten days. That first Christmas in our assignment, Bobbye and I were miserable, wallowing in bed with a burning fever; fortunately we had household helpers caring for the children. The day after Christmas we got a phone call at our neighbor's house. It came to our neighbor's house because our phone didn't work. The local operator knew where we lived, so if we got a long-distance call, it was connected to our neighbor's house, and they would come over and get us. We decided it was easier for me to get dressed and take the call, which turned out to be from our mission administrator in Jakarta. He said, "The office received a call from Bobbye's family; her parents had been in an automobile accident. Her dad was killed, and her mother was in critical condition."

I came back to the house and cannot describe how devastated and forsaken we felt. Here we were, finally fulfilling our call to missions, ready to share the gospel with the people in our area of Indonesia. We had been obedient to God's will and, with a sense of sacrifice, had left our families and the comforts of America to serve Him. Now we were battling staph infections, had almost lost our son, had emergency surgery, suffered dengue fever at Christmastime, and now received word that one of our parents had been killed. Our administrator had called other missionaries and told us they were on their way to care for us. They got there that night, packed us up, and took us home with them to Surabaya to minister to us and care for us.

Bobbye didn't know if her mother would live, but she felt that she had to get home to see her. Arrangements were made for her to travel with a missionary colleague who was returning to the states. So while still recovering from surgery and the lingering effects of dengue fever, she and the children flew home. When she got to the hospital, her mother was unconscious, still in critical condition. Bobbye immediately knelt down by her bed to pray, intending to plead with God to heal her. But as she knelt there to pray, she was overwhelmed with a sense of peace and God's presence. She felt that she had no need to voice a prayer, as God's presence and grace were so real. Her mother survived and lived to see us at every stateside assignment, attended the college graduation, weddings, and missionary appointment of her grandchildren before she passed away at eighty-eight years of age.

These experiences are not something anyone would desire. We could not understand why God would allow them to happen to us when all we wanted to do was to serve Him and share the gospel in Indonesia. But as we have reflected on that time, we realized that through adversity we came to know the reality of God's presence and the sufficiency of His grace in a way that we would have never otherwise known. Was it worth it? No one would ask for suffering. We don't desire to go through times of adversity, but it is one of Satan's favorite fiery darts because that's what he can use to defeat us. It can readily destroy our faith and cause us to doubt God's love and faithfulness. It often brings bitterness to our heart. It can lead us to throw in the towel and walk away from serving God in obedience. But it can also deepen our faith and teach us to walk in the Spirit.

As I look back on these first-term experiences, our personal trials pale in comparison to the grief and disappointments we felt when new converts would turn their back on following Christ or newly planted churches dissolved in conflict and dissension. As Paul reflected in 2 Corinthians 11, he was subjected to imprisonment, stoning, being beaten, shipwreck, hunger, and hardships, but also the daily pressures of concern for the churches. All we wanted was to serve the Lord and to be used of Him. But it seemed we were constantly subjected to suffering, grief, and affliction.

Did God know this would be our course when we answered His call? These experiences did not take Him by surprise. He knew what we needed to survive for the long term. He knew what we needed to experience if we were going to lead and to minister and to encourage others in the future. He knew we needed to discover the depth of His love and that we needed a stronger faith to withstand what would become a continuing pattern of personal challenges. We had no clue as to what God had for us in the future, but He did. The Bible says plainly that walking with the Lord does not exempt us from suffering. In fact, it is assured. It is a lie of Satan that tells us, "If you live a holy life and are committed to obeying God's will, He should be expected to put a hedge of protection around you; He is obligated to prosper and bless you." The whole health, wealth, and prosperity doctrine is a distortion of God's Word. To the contrary, to walk with Christ is to suffer. Why? Because it necessitates denying the flesh, the comforts and conveniences that come from compromise and living for oneself. Suffering does not mean that God has forsaken us, that He is no longer in control, or that He doesn't love us. It's just that He has something better for us, and we can never learn that and acquire that deeper relationship with Him apart from suffering.

> *Adversity is Satan's favorite weapon because it is common to everyone and causes us to focus on ourselves and doubt God.*

This needs to be understood in the context of what we identified as God's purpose in the first chapter. God's desire for your life is to be glorified. Does He know how He can be most glorified in your life? Yes, and it's not by putting a hedge of protection around you so that you never have any challenges and struggles. God's desire is to be glorified and exalted among all peoples throughout the world. But His greatest glory doesn't come by missionaries living in nice Western-style houses, having the affluence to shop for whatever they need at the international market and, when trouble comes, using their American passport to retreat to the comfort and security of home. Focusing on our own comfort and welfare does not result in God being glorified among the nations. However, when people see us suffering and experiencing adversity, when they see us with a debilitating illness or reacting to the loss of a loved one, it is an opportunity for them to see the reality of our faith and the victory we have in Jesus Christ.

It is not a matter of whether or not we suffer but how we respond and react.

That's how He was glorified in Christ. *The Passion of the Christ* film focused on the agony, the brutality, and the suffering of Jesus. But only Christ realized it was all for God's glory. Through His obedience and suffering God was glorified by redemption being provided for a lost world. This is what Peter wants us to understand regarding our suffering and afflictions. "Dear friends, when the fiery ordeal arises among you to test you, don't be surprised by it, as if something unusual is happening to you" (1 Pet. 4:12). We should not presume God has abandoned us as He may be providing an opportunity for you to claim the victory, the reward of faithfulness and obedience.

Outside the cafeteria at our missionary training facility near Richmond, Virginia, is a display titled, "So Great a Cloud of Witnesses." It commemorates all those missionaries over the years who died in active service. Beside the display is a plaque in honor of Marianna Gilbert and Darla Lovell, two journeymen who were killed in a plane crash in China. All of us remember September 11, 2001 when terrorists hijacked commercial airliners and crashed them into the World Trade Center in New York and the Pentagon in Washington, D.C. That morning we were scheduled to have an administrative team meeting. We were gathering about 9:00 a.m. Someone came in and said, "Turn on the television monitor; something has happened in New York." We sat there through the morning, horrified, as we watched the events of that day unfold. But when we gathered that morning, we were already grieving because the night before we had been notified that Genessa Wells, a journeyman in the Middle East, had been killed in a bus crash just two weeks before her term was to be completed.

One of my heroes is Charles Beatty. Charles left his insurance business to go to Northern Africa as a witness to the Tunisian Arabs. Before he had completed his first term of service, he was diagnosed with cancer. He came home for treatment, later was told the cancer had gone into remission, but it shortly recurred with a vengeance. At age thirty-four he died, leaving his wife and four small children. About that time you may remember reading about Jim and Ronnie Bowers, missionaries serving in Peru with ABWE. The missionary plane they were in was mistaken for drug runners and was shot down; both Ronnie and her baby were killed. We have mourned the tragic death of Bill Hyde, a church planter who died in a terrorist bombing in the Philippines, the assassination of three of our dedicated hospital staff at the Jibla Baptist Hospital in Yemen in 2002, and a short time later four of our personnel who dared to go to Iraq to minister to the despair and hopelessness of the people there. Janet Shackles, a doctor from Alaska, arrived in West Africa to give badly needed reinforcement to our medical team at the Baptist Medical Center in Nalerigu, Ghana, but was killed in a traffic accident before she had been on the field a year.

In the last year reports came of two separate incidents in which a missionary was involved in a traffic accident, a pedestrian was killed, and they went to prison. In a lot of foreign countries, there is no appeal; it is not a matter of innocent until proven guilty. If there is a fatality, the driver of the vehicle goes to jail. In one of these, a missionary was in an African jail for ten days before his release could be arranged. These, and many others, could readily identify with the apostle Paul who envisioned going to Rome and preaching the gospel and then on to Spain but instead found himself in a prison in Caesarea. We all have visions and dreams of where we are going in life, expecting to enjoy health, prosperity, and success only to be blind-sided by tragedy and adversity. How do we deal with it? Do we use it for a victorious testimony that glorifies God, or do we turn our back on Him in bitterness and let Satan claim the victory?

Gary and Gloria Sloan, as new missionaries in Mexico, had been on the field about nine months when they were celebrating their daughter's birthday with a party at the beach. Their daughter, Carla, got caught in the undertow, and Gary went out to try to save her. Three student summer missionaries working with them also went to help. All five of them drowned. The next year there was a feature on Charles Beatty and Gary Sloan in *The Commission* magazine. When the doctor informed Charles that his cancer was terminal, he said that he wanted to run through the finish line. He returned to Tunisia and witnessed boldly to everyone he knew, knowing he had nothing to lose. In the magazine was a picture of Gary Sloan's body lying on the beach after it had been recovered. People had come out from the seaside villages in the neighborhood and were crowded around. There in the picture was Gloria witnessing to people. She was saying, "If this were you, where would you be? Let me tell you where my husband is now." Even at the moment of having lost her husband and daughter, she began to tell them about the glories of heaven and why he had assurance of being there. And after a period of time in the U.S., she returned to Mexico, more zealous than ever to carry out her missionary call.

How do you respond to the tragedies of life? When we lose a loved one, are diagnosed with an incurable disease, or experience misfortune, we are somehow able to dig down deep and access a reservoir of faith and the magnitude of God's grace. The intensity of the need seems to turn us to God as our only hope. But it is not necessarily the major catastrophes that defeat us. Rather the constant trials, disappointments, infirmities, and conflicts seem to defeat us. A husband and breadwinner loses his job. A fire or tornado destroys precious heirlooms and belongings. An accident leaves a child an invalid for life. A missionary is deported from his field of service, or his visa is denied. Drought destroys prospects for a harvest. Debts and poor financial management threaten foreclosure on one's home. A wayward child chooses an immoral lifestyle and abandons his faith upon reaching adulthood. A daughter finds she is pregnant out of wedlock. And the list goes on and on.

Being president of the International Mission Board gives me access to information regarding our missionaries and an awareness of many of the challenges they experience. I remember tracking the pilgrimage of a new first-term missionary family in West Africa. They had been assigned to Liberia, but during their first year on the field, tribal warfare broke out, and they had to evacuate. It was a perilous escape as they left behind all their belongings that were plundered and looted. They took an alternate assignment in Guinea across the border, but the war soon spread, and they had to evacuate from Guinea as well. So they went to yet another country for an interim assignment, and while they were there, a political coup overthrew the government, putting everything in disarray. The infrastructure deteriorated to the point that it was difficult to buy food and basic supplies. Finally, when that yearlong interim assignment was over, conditions had settled down in Liberia, and they were able to return to their original assignment. However, a short time later they had to evacuate again as the warfare escalated; it was close enough to their scheduled stateside assignment that they returned to the States. I met this missionary at a mission conference and commiserated with all that they had been through. He smiled and said, "Isn't it amazing what God allows you to experience so you can identify with the people to whom He calls you?" The peoples of West Africa were suffering. His attitude toward his own suffering and inconvenience was that it was just God's way of allowing him to identify with them and minister to them.

Note how Paul commended himself as a servant of God: "But in everything as God's ministers, we commend ourselves: by great endurance, by afflictions, by hardships, by pressures, by beatings, by imprisonments, by riots, by labors, by sleepless nights, by times of hunger" (2 Cor. 6:4–5). Why did these things commend him? Because he dealt with them in a way that would give, "no opportunity for stumbling to anyone, so that the ministry will not be blamed" (verse 3). He had stated the proper perspective toward adversity in 2 Corinthians 4:17–18, "For our momentary light affliction is producing for us an absolutely incomparable eternal weight of glory. So we do not focus on what is seen, but on what is unseen; for what is seen is temporary, but what is unseen is eternal." Satan wants us to see things only from the perspective of the suffering and inconvenience at the moment. The victory comes in keeping adversity in the context of God's eternal purpose and the glory that accrues through our faithfulness.

Our fleshly nature is so self-centered that we tend to focus on our comforts and conveniences and feel sorry for ourselves when our plans are disrupted, and we suffer the loss of material things. We fail to realize that God may have a higher purpose in allowing adversity to come into our lives. He sees the need for us to grow in faith and learn to trust Him rather than our life being focused on things and what we want. He wants us to be equipped to serve others and minister to those in need, but that is difficult if we have never experienced trials and needs ourselves. Satan takes the attitude of the world and deceives us into believing that we are entitled to comfort, safety, health, and prosperity. He would use our unexpected trials to make us doubt God and succumb to hopelessness rather than seeing them as an opportunity for greater spiritual victory and growth.

Paul also put the matter of affliction and suffering into the proper perspective of the comfort that God provides in 2 Corinthians 1:3–5. Obviously God could protect us from suffering, but in His providence He allows it for a greater purpose—that of being able to identify with the sufferings of Christ as well as being equipped to comfort and minister to others. His response to adversity was to praise and thank God, just as he demonstrated in response to his thorn in the flesh. "Blessed be the God and Father of our Lord Jesus Christ, the Father of mercies and the God of all comfort. He comforts us in all our affliction, so that we may be able to comfort those who are in any kind of affliction, through the comfort we ourselves receive from God. For as the sufferings of Christ overflow to us, so our comfort overflows through Christ." Just as God allowed Paul to be afflicted with a thorn in the flesh to keep him from becoming proud, He uses adversity to remind us of our inadequacy and the need to rely upon Him. Paul said, "However, we personally had a death sentence within ourselves so that we would not trust in ourselves, but in God who raises the dead" (2 Cor. 1:9).

Adversity is often manifested in disrupted plans. Paul experienced this in his desire to go to Rome and preach the gospel there and then on to Spain. "Whenever I travel to Spain . . . I do hope to see you" (Rom. 15:24). In verse 28 he repeated his confidence in those plans, "I will go by way of you to Spain." As far as we know, Paul never made it to Spain and later to Rome only as a prisoner. Instead, he found himself in a prison in Caesarea. Like Paul, many of us have had plans and visions of serving God or pursuing a course of life that never was fulfilled because of adversity and unexpected circumstances. Many new missionaries respond to God's call and with passion say, "I am going to China and join a church planting movement. I'm going to the Muslim world to teach English and devote my life to bringing people to faith in Jesus Christ. I'm going to join the growing harvest in Africa or Latin America. I'm going to engage an unreached people group and work to share the gospel with those who have never heard of Jesus." The reality is that some, with the deepest commitment, strongest vision, and most sincere intentions, like Paul, never make it.

A few years ago toward the end of orientation, a new missionary began to have severe headaches. An examination revealed a brain tumor, and his missionary career was aborted. Some, like those we mentioned above, arrive on the field but never finish their term. Others, confident of their calling to a specific country or people group, have their visa denied. When our plans, that we feel confident are God's will, go awry, we probably feel like Paul did in that dungeon in Caesarea. He probably went through times of doubt initially, wondering, "Where is God? Why did He allow this to happen?"

Fortunately few of us have to go through major catastrophes in our lives. Yes, the day will come when we will lose parents and other loved ones, sometimes unexpectedly. We likely will have to go through an illness, financial setback, or suffer the pain of an estranged relationship due to conflicts and misunderstanding. But as I mentioned before, the major tragedies don't defeat us; but the little trials and irritations every day upset us, rob us of joy, and cause us to succumb to un-Christlike behavior and attitudes. Satan delights in bringing criticism and conflict into our life, impeding our plans and aspirations, and other disappointments because we tend to take our mind off of Jesus, thinking only of ourselves. When we do that, it is easy for Satan to lead us to expressions of anger, to plant a seed of bitterness in our heart and harbor unforgiveness toward those we identify as being responsible. Satan is successful because we have turned our back on faith, rejecting God and His promise of help, strength, comfort, and victory.

Dr. Baker James Cauthen, former president of the Southern Baptist Foreign Mission Board, told us when we were appointed as missionaries, "It's not the elephants that will get you but the termites." He was speaking of the little irritations that are constant and common to life. They are always there, eating at us, robbing us of joy and peace, consuming our emotions in a defeatist attitude. We can usually deal with the elephants—those major crises when people surround us, encourage us, and minister to us—but the termites subtly eat away at a daily life of victory without our even being aware of them.

Does God know what's going to happen to us? I remind our missionaries that He knows all that is going to unfold when they reach the mission field, all the hardships and adjustments they are going to encounter. He knows what is going to happen to us this afternoon, tomorrow, next week, and the rest of our life. The psalmist tells us in Psalm 139, "For it was You who created my inward parts; You knit me together in my mother's womb. . . . Your eyes saw me when I was formless; all my days were written in Your book and planned before a single one of them began" (vv. 13, 16). "LORD, You have searched me and known me. You know when I sit down and when I stand up; You understand my thoughts from far away. You observe my travels and my rest; You are aware of all my ways. Before a word is on my tongue, You know all about it, LORD. You have encircled me; You have placed Your hand upon me" (vv. 1–5). God knows exactly what is going to happen in our life, including every trial and affliction.

If He knows it beforehand, why does He allow it to happen? After all, He is sovereign and all-powerful; why doesn't He intervene to prevent suffering, at least for a child of God who wants to live for Him? We would think He would especially protect missionaries from anything that would deter their witness and divert them from extending the kingdom of God among the nations. But He does allow us to experience adversity through illness, an accident, harm from war or violence, loss of possessions, or the death of a loved one. How do we react? Do we allow God to use adversity to draw us closer to Him, have the joy of finding His grace sufficient and experience a strength we had never known? Or do we allow Satan to fill our mind with doubts, causing us to be consumed with self-centered despair, and to forfeit the opportunity for God to work in our life? He explained this in Isaiah 48:10–11 when He said, "Look, I have refined you, but not as silver; I have tested you in the furnace of affliction. I will act for My own sake, indeed, My own, for how can I be defiled? I will not give My glory to another."

We have deprived ourselves of the fullness of God's blessings and knowing the reality of His power because of our unwillingness to deal with adversity appropriately. I am reminded of Elizabeth Hale, a former missionary to China, who had to leave in the early 1950s. She transferred to Malaysia, and I got to know Aunt Elizabeth when I became area director and began to relate to our personnel there. She had retired several years earlier but refused to leave the field. The mission board didn't know what to do with her because she would not come home. So she continued to receive her pension and stay there. Later her health began to fail. We convinced her that she needed to come back to America and that people would take care of her here. She didn't have any family and went to live at the Baptist Home in Culpeper, Virginia.

She has since passed away, but after she came back to the States, she would continue to write letters back to her missionary colleagues and her church friends in Malaysia. As she grew older, the letters became more and more incoherent and were difficult to understand. However, a statement in one of her later letters jumped off the page, grabbing my attention. I had no idea of the context, but in responding to Christian friends in Malaysia, she wrote, "Some of you are going through times of trial and hardship and therefore have the privilege of knowing our precious Lord in a deeper, more meaningful way." It reflected her intimate walk with the Lord over many years. It spoke of her loneliness and hardship in China and Malaysia. She had learned that suffering and self-denial were a way of identifying with Christ, and it was simply an opportunity to know Him in a deeper, more meaningful way.

Some people on the mission field give in to discouragement and feel forsaken. There was no response to our witness, the tropical heat was debilitating, the children were sick, we were lonely and felt no one cared. In pouring out my heart, I complained and blamed God. Why was

> *"Trials and hardship give us the privilege of knowing our precious Lord in a deeper, more meaningful way."*

He allowing this to happen? How easy it is for Satan to twist our thinking so that we blame God for not putting that hedge of protection around us as if He is obligated to protect us at all times, and we should be exempt from suffering. But that is not the way God works.

Recently I attended the funeral of Jan Moses who served as a missionary in the Philippines with her husband, Mark, for twenty years. Jan had battled cancer for three years prior to her death. Knowing it was terminal, she had an opportunity to use her illness as a powerful testimony and witness. Like so many, when she was first diagnosed with cancer, she asked, "Why? Why me, Lord?" But she gradually came to the perspective of "Why not me?" A significant percentage of people get cancer every year, so why should she deserve to be exempt? She was confident God could have prevented it, but He chose not to do so because, in Jan's words, "God said to me, 'I can entrust this to you, knowing you will be faithful and I will be glorified in your suffering.'"

God does not bring on suffering and adversity, but He allows it as an opportunity to be glorified in our life. God is most glorified when He finds us faithful, trusting in Him and drawing upon His grace in times of weakness and trial. We often talk about the providence of God. Providence comes from two Latin words, *pro* and *video*. *Video* means "to see"; with the prefix *pro*, it means "to see beforehand." The providence of God means that He has designed and foreordained a plan through which He can be glorified, no matter what happens, because He is able to see beforehand everything that is going to occur.

Why did God allow Job to be afflicted so severely? First, we need to be reminded that God was in control of this situation. Satan was chiding God because He had put a hedge of protection around Job; Satan suspected that was the only reason Job praised God and served Him faithfully. God said, "OK, I'll let down the hedge. But don't touch his life." Notice who is calling the shots here; God is. God did not bring all the suffering and adversity into Job's life, but neither did He relinquish His throne and authority. Why does He let down the hedge and allow Satan to afflict us with adversity, a thorn in the flesh, or disasters that are common to life? God, in His providence, knows the end from the beginning. God reminds us in Isaiah 46:9–10, "I am God, and there is no other; . . . I declare the end from the beginning, . . . saying, My plan will take place, and I will do all My will." Verse 11 continues, "Yes, I have spoken; so I will also bring it about. I have planned it; I will also do it."

God knew Job was going to lose his family, his children, all of his crops; be afflicted with sores; and go through all this suffering. But He saw the outcome and knew He would be glorified in the end when Job would be blessed and prospered more than he had been in the beginning. Job was blessed, and God was glorified because Job remained faithful through his adversity and stayed focused on God.

This is similar to the experience of Joseph, though his adversity came as a result of the evil intent and abuse of his brothers rather than through natural disasters and circumstances. When his brothers came to Egypt and Joseph revealed himself to them, they remembered all the evil they had done in mistreating him and selling him into slavery. Some of them had wanted to kill him; they put him in a pit, then sold him to slave traders to get rid of him. He had spent years in prison, unjustly accused. When his brothers realized they were confronting Joseph, who had been elevated to a position of authority, they had no doubt that he would exact justifiable revenge in dealing harshly with them.

But in Genesis 45:5, 7–8, Joseph says, "And now don't be worried or angry with yourselves for selling me here, because God sent me ahead of you to preserve life. . . . God sent me ahead of you to establish you as a remnant within the land. . . . Therefore it was not you who sent me here, but God." Three times in these verses he said that it was not them but God who brought him to Egypt. Yes, they were responsible for the circumstances, and they were experiences no one would desire—thrown in a pit, sold into slavery, spending years in prison. They were years of adversity, but Joseph recognized that God, in His providence, used them for a higher purpose, that of preserving the lives of His chosen people.

When Jacob died, Joseph's brothers thought that he had been nice for the sake of their father, but now they would experience the full force of his vengeance. But Joseph said to them, "Don't be afraid. Am I in the place of God? You planned evil against me; God planned it for good to bring about the present result" (Gen. 50:19–20). People are going to be mean toward us, treat us unjustly, abuse us, and take advantage of us with evil intent. It may bring suffering, but God is on His throne and sees how it can all result in our blessing and benefit and His glory. Whether or not that happens, like Job and Joseph, depends on our faithfulness to believe God, to keep our eyes on Him, and to be confident the victory is assured. Don't allow Satan to use suffering and adversity to defeat you and deprive God of an opportunity to work in your life.

A few years ago I participated in a retirement recognition service for Tom and Gloria Thurman who served in Bangladesh for thirty-two years. I had known the Thurmans from our common background in Mississippi as well as having had the privilege of working with them during our tenure in South and Southeast Asia. During the service Tom gave a testimony of their experiences. He related, "We've experienced many circumstances we would not have chosen these thirty-two years in Bangladesh. Earthquakes, floods, cyclones, famines, droughts, tidal waves that took hundreds of thousands of lives, three robberies, four broken bones, 291 countryside strikes, 186 flat tires,"—he was counting—"struggle with a difficult language, electrical blackouts, Gloria contracting leprosy, going through bouts of hepatitis, and one stabbing." Then he said, "But we have nothing but gratitude and praise that one day God tapped us on the shoulder and said, 'I've got a place for you.' We came because of the lost millions of this land. We walked with Him, and our joy has been full." I continue to reflect on that with amazement. In spite of hardships and adverse circumstances for thirty-two years in Bangladesh, they walked with God and could say, "Our joy has been full!" Suffering and adversity could not take away the joy they had in serving Christ.

Shortly after Genessa Wells's death, someone shared with me her last newsletter, written just a few weeks before as she anticipated finishing her term and coming home. She wrote:

This summer has definitely been the busiest summer of my life. I came to France for the Northern Lights Project. I knew little about it until I actually arrived. And looking back, it has been tougher physically, spiritually, and mentally than I had expected. I also grew more, learned more, and my eyes were opened to more than I had expected.

She continued describing the demanding nature of that summer assignment. Then she concluded,

I wouldn't change a thing if I could. She said, One of my favorite songs is "Open the Eyes of My Heart, Lord." Open the eyes of my heart, Lord, open the eyes of my heart; I want to see you. I want to see You high and lifted up, shining in the light of Your glory. Pour out Your power and love as we sing holy, holy, holy.[1]

Genessa explained,

It doesn't have too many words, but my mind and imagination go all over the place every time I sing it. Especially after I have seen what I have this summer. It seems that everything we do all comes down to one thing, His glory. I pray that my life will always reflect that—His glory. I've spent these two years in five different countries. This summer in

France was the first place I've been where I could
share my faith freely. I had a passion for it that
I never knew God had given me. And He has given
it to me for His glory.

We never expect our life to be ended prematurely. But
should not our desire be, whenever that time comes, that
we can say, "I wouldn't change a thing because I've done it
all for His glory"?

People commonly feel abandoned and forsaken by God
when they experience unexpected troubles and adversity.
They may walk away from their faith and allow a root of
bitterness to gain control of their life. All peace and joy are
gone, and they have forfeited their only source of strength
to persevere and gain victory over grief and pain. But often
the consequence is to have denied ourselves the opportunity, as expressed by Elizabeth Hale, of knowing God and
His grace in a deeper more meaningful way.

Once again we have to ask, couldn't God protect us from
all of this? Isn't He all-powerful? Doesn't He love us? The
problem is that our attitudes are shaped by a narrow and
distorted concept of blessings. We tend to think of blessings
as providing comfort, well-being, and joy in having what we
want in life. Blessing is seen as the opposite of suffering,
but to the contrary, anything that draws us closer to God is a
blessing. We are richly blessed by an experience that allows
us to know the depth of His grace and the faithfulness of
His love and compassion. We know Him more intimately
when we are given the privilege of identifying with the sufferings of Christ. How shallow is Satan's deception to make
us believe that health and prosperity are worth more than
knowing God.

One of the house church pastors in China, Samuel Lamb, was quoted in *Bold as a Lamb* by Ken Anderson about his experiences of persecution and harassment as a Christian who spent ten years in a labor camp. He said:

> Perhaps we're fortunate. We suffered so much and have so little. If we were secure and well supplied as we hear of Christians in other places, we might be much less sincere in our discipleship. The Christian faith is most precious when we experience it under testing. The primary purpose of prayer is not for gaining wealth or comfort or earthly security. Faith and prayer are to make us true followers of our Lord, who suffered as the greatest example of purpose in life. A Christian who has not suffered is as a child without training. Such Christians cannot receive or understand the fullness of God's blessing.[2]

When I travel, my wife often prays Psalm 125:2 as a prayer of protection, "As the mountains surround Jerusalem, so the LORD surrounds His people" (NASB). Why doesn't He surround us with His protective covering as the mountains surround Jerusalem? The fact is that He does, faithfully and consistently. We could not imagine the disastrous circumstances of life—tragedies and failures that never occur—because God is with us, guiding us, protecting us from harm's way. So why does He occasionally let down that hedge of protection and allow us to be subjected to adversity and trials? God's desire is to be glorified. He desires us to walk in victory more than we could ever imagine. But we don't get that victory by being isolated and protected from the battle.

When we complain about the difficult people we have to live and work with, blame circumstances for all the inconveniences that make life miserable, or become bitter due to a season of adversity, we are accusing God of mismanagement. When we fail to respond with Christlikeness and allow God's Spirit to take control and lead, we are just requiring more of the same until we quit trying to cope with it ourselves and learn to appropriate the victory in Christ. But once we do, it no longer bothers us when we encounter hard-to-love people, situations that try our patience or go through personal trials because we have found them to be an opportunity to experience God's grace and strength. When you are walking in the Spirit, trials and hardships no longer matter because you are experiencing His love, His joy, His peace, His patience, and His strength being poured into your life in a way you would not otherwise experience. And that brings glory to God.

Praising the Lord makes us aware of His presence and enables us to focus on His promises instead of our circumstances.

There is a practical key to claiming victory over adversity. When we lived in Indonesia, our place of assignment was five hours from any other missionary family, and we felt isolated. After two or three months, if we didn't have an occasion to be with other colleagues for a mission meeting or retreat, we would begin to feel the need to get away for a few days. We would usually drive to Kediri or Surabaya, the nearest locations where other missionary families lived; our kids could play with other MKs, and we could go to a nice restaurant, do some shopping, and be rejuvenated by fellowship with others. We would always try to leave early in the morning because the little narrow, broken-pavement highway would soon get congested with trucks, oxcarts, and pedicabs; if we didn't leave early in the morning, it would sometimes take two hours longer, and the trip would be miserably hot and dusty.

This particular morning we planned to drive to Surabaya and got up early so we could get on our way well before daylight. But all our plans and preparations began to unravel. The man we had hired to guard our house while we were gone didn't show up. We learned that he was sick, so we had to take time to find someone else we knew and trusted who was available. After considerable delay we were ready to leave when someone came from the church to tell us the pastor's child was sick and had been taken to the hospital. We would have to go check on him and minister to the family. Other interruptions followed from the neighbors, and with each delay I was becoming more and more irritated and impatient but glad to finally to be on our way.

We had to drive through town to get to the main highway, and right in the middle of town we had a flat tire. My patience had already worn pretty thin, and we had not even gotten out of town. I would have to change the tire, take time to get it repaired, and go home to clean up after getting dirty and greasy. The market was across the street from where I was changing the tire, and people began to gather around to watch. A big semicircle of people developed. No one offered to help, and I could hear them laughing and joking, amused at the inconvenience of this foreigner who had a flat tire. I wasn't feeling a lot of love toward those people among whom God had called us to live and witness.

Just as I was putting the last lug bolts on, Russell, our son, who had been leaning out the front window of the car watching me, said, "Praise the Lord, we had a flat tire!" The last thing I felt like doing was praising the Lord. Why did he say that? He was only four years old. We had developed a pattern in our family to praise the Lord in all things. When things go wrong, plans don't work out, one of the children falls and skins a knee, or a toy is broken, we just praise the Lord. Notice what happens when we praise the Lord. Instead of our focus being on the circumstances, it is redirected to the Lord. Once praise enables us to focus on the Lord, we are reminded that He is present with us. The Bible says that God inhabits the praises of His people: "But You are holy, enthroned on the praises of Israel" (Ps. 22:3). Praise makes us aware of His presence, and once we become mindful of His presence, He is able to take control of our emotions, our attitudes, and our demeanor. We don't react with anger and get upset because Jesus gives us patience and self-control. He puts adversity in perspective. What is a little inconvenience, a personal setback, going through a time of illness, compared to what we have in Jesus Christ? Reacting in the flesh, lashing out and blaming others, or feeling bitter that God has let us down certainly doesn't glorify the Lord. It doesn't edify and minister to anyone, and it allows Satan to deprive us of victory.

Our family discovered this simple practical key to walking in victory. No, we are not thankful for sickness, the death of a loved one, or a tragic accident that brings suffering; but we do praise God for who He is and thank Him in those circumstances. He is worthy of all praise and honor and glory, and that supersedes our problems and pain. Praise restores us to a proper relationship with God and puts our circumstances in perspective. God dwells in our praise and makes His presence real, and we do need that sense of His presence more in times of adversity.

First Thessalonians 5:18 admonishes us, "Give thanks in everything, for this is God's will for you in Christ Jesus." Colossians 3:17 adds this exhortation: "And whatever you do, in word or in deed, do everything in the name of the Lord Jesus, giving thanks to God the Father through Him." A few years ago one of our missionaries who went to Indonesia illustrated this principle of victory in the following excerpts from her newsletter.

She said, "The best advice given to me before we came to Indonesia was be grateful and praise the Lord in all things. I have been discouraged recently as we have gone through challenging cultural adjustments; I have been struggling with doubts and have lost the joy I used to have. So the Lord impressed me this morning that I should write down some of the things that He impressed me to be thankful for.

- I praise the Lord for the courage God gave my husband as I practiced driving for the first time in Indonesia.
- I praise God for the days I feel worthless because I am reminded of God's strength during my weakness.
- I'm grateful for the strong stomach and bravery God gave me one day at my neighbor's house to eat meat with fur on it.
- I'm thankful for the lessons of servanthood I've learned from my household helper.
- I praise the Lord for the congested crowds of people, for they are a reminder of the multitudes that live in darkness, and it keeps me on my knees.

- I praise the Lord for the times the Holy Spirit convicted me of my pride and my pitiful attitude and other sins that separated me from the Father so I could ask forgiveness and once again enjoy being in His holy presence.
- I'm grateful for the times our son has been sick so that I could teach him to pray for healing and trust God to meet his needs.
- I praise God for the struggle of knowing His will because through the struggle I listen more carefully and seek more diligently.
- I praise the Lord for the smog in Jakarta because I'm overwhelmed at the blessings and beauty of a bright blue sky on other days.
- I praise the Lord for the sometimes gagging smells of the open sewage in front of our house because it's a reminder to me of how my sins and the sins of all of Indonesia are such a stench to our Lord.
- I'm grateful for my nosy neighbor and how she is a reminder that I must live the kind of life to which I testify.
- I'm grateful for the peace and confidence of my calling, even in times when my unbelieving father's words of disapproval and discouragement were hurtful.
- I praise God for the time I was ugly with my kids, and the Holy Spirit said, "Out of the fullness of the heart speaks the mouth." And I was able to confess my anger and my ugliness to my children so that they could see me model humility and forgiveness.

- And one thing I'm most grateful for is my husband, and how God has kept him strong when I was weak and kept me strong when he was weak, and how God has grown our love even during the struggle.

Hebrews 13:15 says, "Therefore, through Him let us continually offer up to God a sacrifice of praise, that is, the fruit of lips that confess His name."

First Peter 4:12–13 reminds us, "Dear friends, when the fiery ordeal arises among you to test you, don't be surprised by it, as if something unusual were happening to you. Instead, as you share the sufferings of the Messiah rejoice, so that you may also rejoice with great joy at the revelation of His glory." Don't be surprised when you suffer, as if God has let you down. It is a common experience for us in this world just as it was with Christ.

Paul never made it to Spain, but he wrote in Philippians 1:12–14, "Now I want you to know, brothers, that what has happened to me has actually resulted in the advancement of the gospel, so that it has become known throughout the whole imperial guard, and to everyone else, that my imprisonment is for Christ. Most of the brothers in the Lord have gained confidence from my imprisonment and dare even more to speak the message fearlessly." Is that not what Paul wanted to see happen—people to trust the Lord and know Him? Believers emboldened to share their faith? Missionaries are often disillusioned when plans go awry and suffering infringes on their ministry. Satan would not want us to realize that the effectiveness of our witness may be enhanced by how we respond to adversity.

When you go through times of adversity, and Satan would discourage you, make you feel forsaken, bring doubt into your life and destroy your confidence and faith in God, remember that God is on His throne. When you feel sorry for yourself and are ready to give up, praise the Lord and realize how He is seeking to use your circumstances to advance the gospel and bring glory to Him. Suffering gives us an opportunity to experience God's grace and may be the greatest opportunity to reflect the victory that we have in Jesus Christ.

CHAPTER 9

FOUNDATIONS FOR VICTORY

*For although we are walking in the flesh, we do not wage
war in a fleshly way, since the weapons of our warfare
are not fleshly, but are powerful through God for the
demolition of strongholds. We demolish arguments
and every high-minded thing that is raised up against
the knowledge of God, taking every thought captive
to the obedience of Christ.*
—2 Corinthians 10:3–5

W e don't hear a lot of talk about the Spirit-filled
life in our churches these days. That was a more
prominent subject of preachers and classical
Christian writers in the past, but today's Christians seem to
have little interest in holiness and a ministry characterized
by spiritual anointing. Contemporary expressions of our
faith seem to focus on finding a minimal level of commitment in which we can have the benefit of salvation but live
as we desire. Perhaps we think it presumptuous to desire
to be filled with the Spirit or to assume there is more to

the Christian life than we are already experiencing. Many scholars and speakers emphasize that we receive all that we will ever have when we are born again, and there is nothing more to be desired. In a sense that is true. When Jesus comes to live within us, He has given us a new life that is now declared righteous not because of our own goodness but because Christ became sin for us "that we might become the righteousness of God in Him" (2 Cor. 5:21).

However, it is sad, indeed, that many have accepted a mediocre level of Christian living, convinced nothing more is to be experienced. The typical Christian knows his salvation is secure but continues to struggle with a sinful lifestyle, lustful thoughts, living for self and carnal values. The Bible doesn't teach a second blessing and a subsequent experience of receiving the Holy Spirit after we have received Jesus Christ as Lord and Savior. But we should experience a yearning to appropriate the power over sin and a desire for a victorious life that God has already provided through His Spirit's presence within us.

Occasionally we come under conviction, rededicate our life, and get serious about living a Spirit-filled life, but it is usually short-lived as we get tired of the struggle and find the victory elusive. Throughout my life I have been dealing with the problem of a leaky bucket. I have had wonderful times of blessing and the joy of an intimate walk with the Lord, sensing His touch on my life, and then it just seems to evaporate. I have also experienced seasons of spiritual dryness and struggle. I always have known the Bible taught a level of spiritual maturity, empowered witness, and holy living beyond that reflected in my life, but how does one reach that and then consistently maintain the deeper walk with the Lord?

From time to time we desire to experience the power of the Holy Spirit. We sing about wonder-working power, but the threat of charismatic labels often intimidates us, causing us to shy away from simply appropriating what the Bible describes as normative for one walking in the Spirit. In every position and role of ministry, I have been confronted with my own inadequacy and longed to see evidence of something that had no explanation other than the work of God's Spirit. While I am aware of God's blessings, too much of my success could be explained by hard work, personality, and clever implementation of church programs. Each time I read Acts 1:8, "You will receive power when the Holy Spirit has come upon you," I wondered why there was no evidence of this power in my life. I have always known beyond a doubt that God's Holy Spirit dwelt within me, but I so wanted Him to have total control of my life. I would read in Revelation 3:8, "Behold, I have put before you an open door which no one can shut, because you have a little power, and have kept My word, and have not denied My name" (NASB). I pleaded, "Lord, I have followed Your Word and not denied You. Could there be just a little power in my life? I'm not looking for great, miraculous manifestations of signs and wonders but just the evidence of Your power in my life, reflected in consistent holy living, power over sin and temptation—genuine victorious living that would bring glory to You."

Well, this is what spiritual warfare is all about. The battle is real because we have an enemy, an adversary, that is seeking to deprive God of His glory in our lives. He is seeking to rob us of the power and fullness of blessing God has provided to us in Christ. He deceives us into embracing the struggle and accepting defeat in our battle for victory over sin. He deludes us into engaging in a futile strategy of trying to obey God's law and live a holy life by our own efforts and then flaunts our failure to embarrass God and discredit our witness.

Any athletic coach will tell you that the best defense is a good offense. A team can have a good defense and keep the other team from scoring a lot of points, but if they don't have an offense that can put points on the scoreboard, they are not going to win. As we discuss the steps to appropriate victory, it's not about finding a formula to defend against Satan and his devious tactics. Our focus needs to stay on the offense—to claim and walk in the victory that has already been provided. Much that we read on spiritual warfare creates paranoia and fear of Satan as if he were an all-powerful, omnipresent enemy against which our passive, halfhearted efforts are no match. Others try to teach us formulas that are no more than verbal fetishes lacking any substance of faith. We have been given the victory, but it becomes a reality in our life only when we believe God and walk with Him, consistently appropriating the power of His Spirit every day.

Some say, "Just claim the blood of Jesus," or, "In the name of Jesus, defy Satan and he will flee." Others advocate quoting 1 John 4:4, "The One who is in you is greater than the one who is in the world," and that takes care of any problem with Satan. There is some validity to this as such confessions affirm our faith and give strength to what we believe. Paul quoted Psalm 116:10 in saying, "I believed, therefore I spoke" (2 Cor. 4:13). Confession with the mouth reflects a strong conviction of what is in the heart, and speaking a truth strengthens our faith to believe that truth and make it a reality.

However, claiming the victory in spiritual warfare is not simply learning the words to say; it is about our relationship with the Lord, because it is His power and presence in our lives that provide the victory. That victory has already been won and provided to us. It is not about still needing to receive the Holy Spirit; He has already come to dwell within us when we received Jesus Christ into our life as Savior. We just need to learn how to appropriate what we have been given. We can't expect to stand firm against a devious, clever, unseen enemy that works in anonymity and secrecy. We will always fail. God is our refuge and our strength; by His power we can claim the victory because God never fails!

As some of our illustrations emphasized, the disciplines of walking with Christ and being led of the Spirit come from truly desiring Him and all that He has made available to us. As we encounter external manifestations of evil and Satan's activity in the world, God gives us wisdom and discernment regarding our response, but only if we are claiming the victory in our own life. We may encounter manifestations of demon possession. We may find ourselves, like many of our missionaries, in places where there is a real fore-boding spiritual oppression. People throughout the world are in bondage to powers of darkness. Satan has deluded them to believe and follow that which is false, and we encounter it every day in America as well as on the mission field. If something is not of God and does not bring glory to our Lord Jesus Christ—whether philosophies, religious forms, lifestyles, civil policies, attitudes, or behavior—it is of Satan, who is opposed to God and all that He represents. One of Satan's most effective deceptions is to persuade us there is a neutral moral ground in which something may not be of God, but it is neither evil nor wrong.

Around the world I have seen manifestations of the powers of darkness I could not explain, such as Brahmin priests in India walking over white-hot coals without any visible effect on their feet. In the Middle East I observed a dervish worship in which men danced themselves into a trance and then ate glass and cut themselves with knives without any evidence of blood or injury. When one encounters a person who is apparently demon possessed, it's not important to determine if they are possessed or mentally ill. It is obvious that they are afflicted and need to be made whole. Is God going to refuse to work in response to our sincere prayer because we are not able to identify the symptom or the name of the demon? I don't think He imposes legalistic approaches to faith-based power encounters. But neither should we just throw up our hands in helplessness when we have been given access to the power of Almighty God. God is able to give discernment and wisdom in how to confront such situations. However, we dare not presume to confront external manifestations of Satan's power if we have not claimed the victory in our personal walk with the Lord. Otherwise we become like the sons of Sceva in Ephesus; when the seven sons of Sceva tried to imitate Paul in casting out demons, the demons jumped all over them and replied, "Jesus I know, and Paul I recognize—but who are you?" (Acts 19:15). I have thought about that a number of times. When I encounter the enemy in spiritual warfare, does he see me, or does he see Jesus

> *We dare not presume to confront external manifestations of Satan's attacks if we have not claimed the victory within our own life.*

Christ in my life? That is why we must claim the victory personally and live day to day in that victory.

The presence of Jesus in our lives protects us and is a deterrent to personal attacks. It is not possible for believers to be demon possessed as Satan would have to displace the Holy Spirit to gain control over our lives. However, by the choices we make—yielding to temptation, rejecting God's will, ignoring His Word—we can become involved in a lifestyle that reflects all the wickedness and evil of the enemy. In contrast, being conscious of God's Spirit within us and choosing to yield to His control allows Him to manifest His power and presence.

I was once traveling from village to village with one of my Indonesian coworkers, witnessing and preaching as we had opportunity. We were in a little market town where a man had gathered a crowd. A showman, magician, and hypnotist, he was clearly invoking spiritual powers in his performance. We watched as he manipulated the people with strange psycho-phenomenal tricks. He was selling little amulets and charms, convincing the people that these trinkets would give them health, safety, and security. Here were poor, destitute people giving him money and being totally duped. As we stood on the edge of the crowd, I began to pray silently against the spiritual darkness and falsehood that was being propagated. We didn't create a scene or say anything openly. After a moment the man's associate came to us and said, "I respectfully ask you please to leave; you are Christians, and your presence is interfering with the power."

We have received the power of the Holy Spirit. There should be a recognizable contrast between us and the self-serving worldliness and godless powers of darkness. We are

God's servants, His instruments, to represent His kingdom, His goodness, and His power in the battle that is raging in the world. Walking in victory is not just for the sake of being blessed personally, but it is so we can be equipped to represent our Lord Jesus Christ in the world.

The matter of artifacts and objects associated with the demonic and pagan worship should not go without mention. These things are inanimate objects of wood, stone, or metal and cannot possess spirits. Whereas our Western rationalism would dismiss any meaning to such items, their association with evil spirits is not treated lightly by Scripture. We would have to acknowledge our relative ignorance regarding the realm of spirits—the communication, power, and influence that go on in what the Bible identifies as "the heavenlies." There doesn't seem to be any reasoning that would warrant Christians associating with these things. I have heard too many testimonies of people having nightmares and psychological disturbances until they disposed of an African prayer mask used in spirit-possession ceremonies, a Buddhist prayer wheel, or a Hindu idol. I cringe when I see such things in missionary homes and on display tables. Usually the intention is to portray something of the culture. But even if there is no demonic effect, it still is not a good witness, especially among the people who revere such things.

In the Old Testament God made it clear that He had called His people to be a holy people, which meant they were to be separated from everything related to the false religions and Baal worship of their neighbors. He said that graven images and idols of the pagan tribes were an abomination that were to be destroyed. They were not to be brought into their homes lest they be "snared by it." He used strong language in saying they should detest it and utterly abhor it (Deut. 7:25–26). He said that anyone using divination, practicing witchcraft, a sorcerer, medium, or spiritist was detestable. His people were to have no association with them. In response to Paul's ministry, those practicing magic in Ephesus came under conviction and burned their magic books and artifacts (Acts 19:18–19). God calls us to be holy. I am not going to be superstitious and cannot understand or explain such cause-and-effect relationships. But I believe associating even with inanimate objects related to the demonic makes us vulnerable to Satan's powers and influence.

Victory Is Built on a Foundation of Faith

The world is around us, the flesh is within us, the devil is against us—all conspiring to defeat us in our Christian walk and show spite toward God by our failure. How can we appropriate the victory and make all that Jesus has given us a practical reality? We have clearly seen that the foundation is faith. First Peter 5:9 says regarding our enemy, "Resist him, firm in the faith." John explains why faith, our believing God, is the source of victory: "Because whatever has been born of God conquers the world. This is the victory that conquers the world: our faith" (1 John 5:4–5).

What is faith? Hebrews 11:1 gives us a good definition: "Now faith is the reality of what is hoped for, the proof of what is not seen." It's not what you feel and experience. It's not what you see as the visible circumstances in the world. Faith is believing God and what He has said rather than what we may perceive and understand to the contrary. We received Jesus Christ as our Savior by faith, that is, we believe what God's Word has said about His death on the cross and resurrection as effectual in paying the penalty for our sins. In the same way faith is believing what God has said in every regard concerning the practical victory we have been given over sin and the devil, even when all evidence is to the contrary. An empowering comes from claiming God's promises by faith.

For many Christians the only application of faith is believing in Jesus Christ and trusting Him as Savior. But God tells us so much more in His Word. Do we believe that? Are we claiming the truth of all He has told us? If so, it will be difficult for Satan to convince us otherwise. If not, it will be easy for Satan to defeat us. Satan speaks to our mind to create doubts and make us believe that God's promises are not true or do not apply to our situation. He causes us to engage in lofty speculations, rationalizing away God's truth, filtering our perceptions through the values of the world. When the Bible instructs us otherwise, he subtly persuades us to focus on our rights and to justify our entitlement to worldly behavior.

For example, Jesus said, "Peace I leave with you. My peace I give to you. I do not give to you as the world gives. Your heart must not be troubled or fearful" (John 14:27). Can we accept that in every situation? Or do we allow Satan to make us fearful and accept the anxiety he would create in our hearts? Worry and anxiety characterize many Christians. We may not doubt the promises and truths of God's Word, but worrying reflects our lack of confidence in God's goodness and providence. Worry means we are no longer resting in Him, trusting submissively in His leadership and allowing Him to lead us through our problems and trials.

Many of our missionaries live in places similar to a family in northern Uganda where there is no electricity, running water, or nearby medical facilities. They are located in the midst of warring Muslim tribes that do not welcome their Christian witness. They sometimes have to spend the night on the floor of their house when a battle breaks out across their yard. In fact, when I was visiting with them, their son came to the breakfast table with a plastic sack of AK-47 shells and said, "Look what I found in the front yard," after the last battle. Can you have peace in that kind of situation? Well, what did Jesus say?

Several years ago we got a call from one of our single ladies in Gaza. She had totally panicked, explaining that the Israeli soldiers had just destroyed the house next door and their tanks were surrounding her house. "Do they know Americans are here in the house?" she cried. We immediately got in touch with our contact at the State Department. They obviously have a hotline to the Israeli military. After awhile they got back with us to confirm their intelligence knew Americans lived in the house and there was no danger. But if you are in the house and the tanks and mortars are pointed your direction, you don't know that. In that situation can one be expected to have the peace that He gives to the point of our heart not being troubled or afraid?

Peace that passes all understanding—the Bible is full of such amazing promises. Do we believe them and accept them as valid and applicable to our situation? The only way we can do that is by faith—absolute confidence in God's Word and His faithfulness. When He says that our old, fleshly nature is dead and has no power over us, are we going to believe Him or not? When He says that He has given us authority over the evil one, are we going to believe Him and claim that authority? The difference faith makes it apparent. If we believe something, not only will we act on it, but it permeates our mind, determines our attitude, and shapes our perspective on a situation. If we don't believe the truth of what we are told, where does that leave us?

Isaiah 65:2 says, "I spread out My hands all day long to a rebellious people who walk in the wrong path, following their own thoughts." We are so vulnerable to Satan's lies and deception because we not only tend to follow our own thoughts and reasoning, we arrogantly insist on it! Proverbs 3:5 says, "Trust in the LORD with all your heart." Note the exhortation that follows: "And do not rely on your own understanding." Don't let Satan tempt you to rely on your own understanding. You may be wise and educated, but you do not have the capacity to see and understand things from God's perspective. He has given us His inspired Word, which 2 Timothy 3:16–17 tells us, is "profitable for teaching, for rebuking, for correcting, for training in righteousness, so that the man of God may be complete, equipped for every good work."

Paul began his instructions to Timothy, saying, "Now the goal of our instruction is love from a pure heart, a good conscience and a sincere faith" (1 Tim. 1:5). Success in the Christian life is not just a matter of behavior but also of genuine faith that believes and follows God. He concludes the chapter by pointing out those who had rejected the word and "suffered the shipwreck of their faith." The result was to deliver "them to Satan" (1 Tim. 1:19–20). This should be a strong admonition to remind us of the consequences of rejecting the truth of God's Word. If we don't believe, where does that leave us? Satan gains free reign over our thoughts and mind if we are not countering him by faith in what God says.

Many Christians want to grow and become more effective in their Christian life; they spend a lifetime trying every formula and program without success. We read self-help books by the dozen without attaining the Spirit-filled life and victory over sin when believing and following God's Word is all we need for righteousness and to be adequately equipped for the battle. The simplicity of believing the Bible is foolishness to a rationalistic, postmodern world. But that's exactly what faith is all about—accepting as reality what God has said. This is why 2 Corinthians 10:4–5 is so important: "We demolish arguments and every high-minded thing that is raised up against the knowledge of God, taking every thought captive to the obedience of Christ."

This is why Timothy was encouraged to preach the Word of God. There is a devious tendency for us to believe contrary to the Bible in order to appeal to our own desires and justify concepts that are consistent with the conventional wisdom of the world.

> Proclaim the message; persist in it whether
> convenient or not; rebuke, correct, and encourage
> with great patience and teaching. For the time will
> come when they will not tolerate sound doctrine,
> but according to their own desires, will accumulate
> teachers for themselves because they have an itch
> to hear something new. They will turn away from
> hearing the truth and will turn aside to myths.
> (2 Tim. 4:2–4)

If faith is the key to victory in spiritual warfare and the Christian life, how do we get it? How do we grow and strengthen our faith to the point of claiming the victorious life? Romans 10:17 gives us the answer. "So faith comes from what is heard, and what is heard comes through the message about Christ." Other translations refer to this as hearing the Word of God. This compels us to ask the question, How much time do you spend in the Word of God? How much time do you spend reading, studying, and meditating on what God has said relative to the time you spend reading secular material and watching and listening to the messages that come from the world via television or to time on your computer? Our behavior and what we believe are shaped by our values; and our values are shaped, to a great extent, by what feeds our mind. Why would we expect to have a strong faith when the Bible, the source of faith, occupies such a miniscule portion of the information flowing into our brain?

Certainly the major portion of our time is spent at work or school and carrying out our responsibility related to those tasks. There is also the need to use our leisure time conscientiously in a way that would honor God. We cannot expect to believe what God says and apply it to our lives, to claim His power and victory in times of temptation if we don't know what He says. How can we have faith to resist the devil if we are not

> *Faith to live a consistent victorious life comes from spending time in prayer and in God's Word.*

even mindful of the warnings given us in God's Word? Most Christians typically read a few verses each day for devotional inspiration, if at all, rather than feeding on the Word as if it were absolutely essential for our survival and sustenance each day. Reading the Bible consistently feeds our faith. The truths are there, and the more we read them and become familiar with them, the more they become a part of our life and thinking.

I was discipled as a young person and have always had the discipline of "daily Bible readings." I have to admit that it was often perfunctory rather than something approached for spiritual nurture. In busier days I would resort to a little formula I found in a pamphlet titled, "Seven Minutes with God." One is instructed to read a few verses of Scripture for three minutes and then pray for a minute on each aspect of the ACTS acrostic—Adoration, Confession, Thanksgiving, and finally Supplications. Then you can get on with the agenda for the day. Well, seven minutes with God doesn't build a lot of faith.

God got my attention back in the 1980s. I had been asked to lead a church-growth strategy study for Japan. Southern Baptists had been in Japan for years with a large missionary force but had never seen significant church growth. The culture was resistant to the gospel, and the high-cost economy created other challenges for a highly subsidized strategy. We engaged in an in-depth study, two years of research and interviews, trying to find the key to effective outreach and growth. The experience was discouraging. We interviewed pastors and missionaries. Everyone was reconciled to the fact that the Japanese were hard to reach. They reflected, "Japanese men are not open to Christianity. We just don't have the budget to do what needs to be done." Some had spent a lifetime planting a church, a struggling congregation with a handful of members. Optimism and vision were practically nonexistent.

In this context we were surprised as we interviewed one of our young, first-term missionaries who related how he had started a new church. They had baptized more than

120 new believers, including many men, and had already started another mission without any subsidy. We got out our notebooks and said, "OK, now step by step tell us how you did this." We felt that maybe we had finally found a key to the strategic dilemma of church growth in Japan. Before he could answer, his wife interrupted and said, referring to her husband, "First, you need to know that he gets up at 5:00 o'clock and spends an hour in prayer each morning."

We put our notebooks away. I had read books on prayer. I knew that spending time with the Lord and in His Word was essential to being used beyond our own ability and means. As I look back on that impressionable moment, I felt like it was more about God getting my attention than it was the Japan strategy study. I came under conviction that I had to spend time with God and in His Word if I wanted to have a significant role in what God was doing. If I really wanted God to empower and bless my work and witness, I must be willing to pay the cost of commitment. I needed constantly to practice being conscious of His presence in my life throughout each day and have a faith that allowed Him to work in my life.

I wasn't a morning person, but I realized that Jesus is! If I wanted to meet Him before the distractions of a busy day began to infringe on that opportunity, I needed to get up earlier. Throughout the Gospels we read that Jesus got up while it was still dark in order to stay in touch with the Father, to know His will, and to be empowered for His ministry. How can we think that we can neglect what our Savior considered essential and have the power to live for God and resist the attacks of our devious enemy?

I began to get up at 6:00 a.m. and spend a half hour in Bible study and prayer. I could not even get through my prayer list in that amount of time, so I began to get up at 5:30. As I took more time to get into the Word, God began to reveal Himself, and the time seemed to go by so quickly. It was such a blessing, I began to feel deprived when the hour was up, so I began to get up at 5:00 and then 4:30. His Word became alive. Each morning became a time of intimate fellowship with the Father that gave me a sense of His presence through-out the day. My testimony is not necessarily what anyone else should emulate, but one cannot expect to have the spiri-tual sensitivity to recognize the attacks of the enemy and the strength of faith to repel the doubts and distractions he brings into our minds if we neglect the Word of God. It is the source of faith, and faith is the victory. Jesus said, "Those who hear the Word of God and keep it are blessed" (Luke 11:28).

The book of Hebrews recounts the experience of the faithless Israelites who forfeited entering into the promised land and "the rest of God," a life of blessing and prosperity. Hebrews 4:2 explains they had clearly heard the Word of God, but it "did not benefit them, since they were not united with those who heard it in faith." "They were unable to enter [into the land] because of unbelief" (Heb. 3:19). In the same way we are not able to enter into the victory that God has provided for us if we do not have faith to believe His Word and what He has told us. Earlier in this account the warning is applied to us: "Watch out, brothers, so that there won't be in any of you an evil, unbelieving heart that departs from the living God. But encourage each other daily . . . so that none of you is hardened by sin's deception. For we have become companions of the Messiah if we hold firmly until the end the reality that we had at the start" (Heb. 3:12–14). And we hold on to that reality of all we have in Christ only through faith and a believing heart.

Paul attributed evangelistic success to the fact that "the Lord's message [the Word of God] flourished and prevailed" (Acts 19:20). The problem in our society, and one of the reasons Satan's influence is so pervasive, could be a situation described by the prophet Amos: "The days are coming—this is the declaration of the Lord GOD—when I will send a famine through the land: not a famine for bread or a thirst for water, but of hearing the words of the LORD" (Amos 8:11). Our society is not hearing or heeding the words of the Lord, but what about our own lives? Is there a famine and neglect of hearing the Word of God? How much time do we spend with God and in His Word? Do we find reading the Bible boring and uninteresting? Do we find it irrelevant to our life and contemporary needs? That should alert us to the reason we may be so weak in resisting sin and walking in victory.

Faith is the foundation for resisting Satan's temptation and the allure of the world's values, and it comes from God and His Word. John writes to the believers and commends the "young men," observing, "You are strong, God's Word remains in you, and you have had victory over the evil one" (1 John 2:14). That, too, is how we are to remain strong and overcome the evil one, by the Word of God abiding in us.

Renewing the Mind

Having a foundation of faith and believing God, the next step is renewing the mind. The Bible has several references to this. "Therefore, brothers, by the mercies of God, I urge you to present your bodies as a living sacrifice, holy and pleasing to God; this is your spiritual worship. Do not be conformed to this age, but be transformed by the renewing of your mind, so that you may discern what is the good, pleasing, and perfect will of God" (Rom. 12:1–2). Satan tries to get us to conform to the world. It's all around us. We are inundated with pressures to embrace worldly values. How can we avoid conforming to the world, yielding to the subtle temptations and tendencies to embrace its values and attractions? The enticement and subtle allure of sin can be overwhelming. Gideon's three hundred pales in comparison to the minority we represent in standing against this massive juggernaut of the world.

The only way to avoid being conformed to a sinful world is to be transformed. Such a transformation takes place through a constant process of renewing the mind. Our mind represents our thought process, our perceptions, how we view reality. It's where we make choices. Renewal of the mind is a constant process of consciously choosing to believe God, choosing to stand on the principles and values of what He has said rather than embracing the things of the world.

We have already pointed out the important role of the mind in the battle between the flesh and Spirit. Throughout Scripture we are told that in the heart of a person one is defiled. The seed of sin is planted in the heart; lust and sinful desires originate in the mind and thoughts. This was true in the days of Noah, "When the LORD saw that man's wickedness was widespread on the earth and that every scheme his mind thought of was nothing but evil all the time" (Gen. 6:5). That's why victory must begin with a renewal of the mind and the choices we make.

This reality was reflected in David's confession in Psalm 51. He had committed adultery, an obvious sin of the flesh; but his prayer was, "God, create a clean heart for me and renew a steadfast spirit within me" (Ps. 51:10). David realized that was his problem. The sinful action and behavior came from a heart that was unclean. He experienced defeat because of the lack of steadfastness in his relationship with God and the holiness and obedience in which he was to live. He lost the joy of his salvation; he felt separated from God and was no longer able to give spiritual leadership to his people because of a heart problem.

If we are renewing the mind, it has got to be a process of renewal to something. It is not just a one-time decision to resist sin but an intentional choice daily to believe God and seek to follow the leadership of His Spirit. Do you remember the story Jesus told in the Gospel of Luke about the house that was swept clean of unclean spirits? The evil spirits came back and occupied it, stronger than ever, because it was still empty. "When an unclean spirit comes out of a man, it roams through waterless places looking for rest, and not finding rest, it then says, 'I'll go back to my house where I came from.' And returning, it finds the house swept and put in order. Then it goes and brings seven other spirits more evil than itself, and they enter and settle down there. As a result, that man's last condition is worse than the first" (Luke 11:24–26).

Commitment to God

Even when we readily recognize Satan's attacks and consciously reject indulging in deeds of the flesh, we will continue to be vulnerable if the mind is not being constantly renewed in a recommitment to God and His lordship in our lives. We can never stand against the onslaught of spiritual warfare apart from a continual yielding to the reality of the Holy Spirit within us and trusting Him to guide, to lead, and to empower us. Instead of conforming and readily going along with the world, we must choose to focus our thoughts on God's Word; believing the truth of what He says is the foundation of victory. That is what ought to be feeding our minds.

James 4:7 says, "Therefore, submit to God. But resist the Devil, and he will flee from you." This is the sequence in spiritual warfare. We dare not think we can resist the devil and his subtle temptations and influences if we are not submitted to God—committed to Him and to His presence and power in our life. In learning to claim the victory in spiritual warfare, it is essential to acknowledge that we cannot do it ourselves. We are not able even to recognize the subtle attacks of the enemy, much less the power and ability to resist them. That is why we must be constantly yielding to Christ. We are in Christ, and in Him Satan has no power to make us do anything that we do not choose to do.

> *Renewing the mind in submission to God and the truth of His Word is essential because it is in our minds that Satan deceives us.*

In commitment to Christ, we train our minds constantly to put every decision impacting our attitude and pattern of life in the context of that which glorifies Him. It is not unlike that popular cliché, "What would Jesus do?" What fits the image of Christ? Renewing our minds makes us aware that Jesus would not behave in certain ways. Jesus would not speak in a harsh and hurtful way to those He loves. Jesus would not be entertaining lustful thoughts and fantasizing about self-gratifying things. Jesus would not abuse and betray others. What in your life doesn't look like Jesus or act like Jesus? Renew your mind to conform to His character by yielding to God. There is a victorious empowering that comes from a simple, conscious decision to be led by His Spirit.

Satan deals with us in our mind, leading us to think of ourselves, our needs, our comforts, and the things of the world. But when we are renewing the mind—a conscious choice and process of submitting to God and focusing on Him—God is able to take control. Being in Christ becomes a practical reality. When we are not renewing the mind, we become vulnerable. Satan is deceptive, working in secret; we don't readily recognize when our thoughts, our attitudes, and our affections are under attack. If we knew it, we would resist. But instead of throwing up arguments we would easily recognize, Satan just diverts our attention, distracting us from Christ and enticing us in the wrong direction.

C. S. Lewis said in his introduction to *The Screwtape Letters*, "There is no neutral ground in the universe. Every square inch and every split second are claimed by God and counterclaimed by Satan."[1] I shared this with a group of missionaries, and one of the ladies in the group spontaneously exclaimed, "That's it!" She was embarrassed with the disruptive nature of her comment, but I recognized who had spoken and asked her, "What is it?" She said, "That's my problem. Most of the time I'm in neutral. I don't choose the things of Satan. I don't want to follow the ways of the world. But neither am I consciously choosing and submitting to God, to follow Him." She had realized that when our minds are in neutral we are vulnerable. We have to fill them with God's thoughts, God's truth, and a conscious commitment to Him.

Scott Peck was a psychiatrist who was saved later in life and wrote several books, including *The Road Less Traveled*. I don't endorse all of his premises, but he has some unique insights from the perspective of one who was constantly dealing with human problems and disturbed people. In his book *The People of the Lie*, he observed, "There are only two states of being: submission to God and refusal to submit to anything beyond one's own will. The latter of which enslaves one to the forces of evil."[2] I think he is absolutely right in this regard. It is a deception to think that a massive number of good people in our society are morally neutral. Many non-Christians appear to be good people when judged by the norms and mores of society. But if a person is not living in submission to the lordship of Christ, the only alternative is living for self. Choosing to be Lord of one's own life, even if that decision is passive, enslaves one to evil. That is not to say one is evil in terms of an immoral lifestyle, but submission to Christ and to His truth is the only fortification against evil.

Scripture makes clear that renewing the mind is something we do. "You took off your former way of life, the old man that is corrupted by deceitful desires; you are being renewed in the spirit of your minds; you put on the new man, the one created according to God's likeness in righteousness and purity of the truth" (Eph. 4:22–24). We are constantly putting aside that old nature, the flesh, rejecting it and denying it. We refuse to acknowledge it and give place to it. But how do we put on the new self that is in the likeness of God, that is, a Christlike life? We do that by renewing our minds, making the conscious decision to reject the old, sin nature and choosing to view our life as in Christ. Realize how this aspect of claiming the victory fits with the sequence we have discussed. We don't readily do this unless every day we are feeding on His Word and building up our faith in an awareness of God's truth. Only then can we discern and recognize when something is contrary to God's truth and Christlikeness.

Someone once pointed out to me an interesting fact as I was emphasizing that living in the flesh is not necessarily blatant sinful living as much as it is having a self-centered life. They said they had just realized, if we cross out the "h" in the word *flesh* and spell it backwards, we get "self." That is a good reminder for us that whenever we see a reference to the flesh in the Bible. Anything that is focused on self, living for self, exalting self, and gratifying selfish desires instead of glorifying Christ is the nature of the flesh.

As mentioned earlier, the best defense is a good offense. Submission to God, feeding on His Word, and appropriating His truth builds up our faith and leads us consciously to be able to renew our commitment to things that glorify Him on a consistent basis. Colossians 3:2 says, "Set your mind on what is above, not on what is on the earth." "Finally brothers, whatever is true, whatever is honorable, whatever is just, whatever is pure, whatever is lovely, whatever is commendable—if there is any moral excellence and if there is any praise—dwell on these things" (Phil. 4:8). The best way to resist the thoughts that Satan places in our minds is to think God's thoughts. That is what it means to renew the mind.

CHAPTER 10

GAINING THE ULTIMATE
VICTORY FOR GOD'S GLORY

*The salvation and the power and the kingdom of our
God and the authority of His Messiah have now come,
because the accuser of our brothers has been thrown
out: the one who accuses them before our God day
and night. They conquered him by the blood of the
Lamb and by the word of their testimony, for they
did not love their lives in the face of death.*
—**Revelation 12:10–11**

S teps for appropriating the victory in spiritual warfare are not necessarily progressive or sequential.
Each one stands on its own as a valid principle and
an essential element in a life that glorifies God. However,
it does help to see how they are related and build on one
another as a foundation for victory. If we are grounded on
a foundation of faith, believing God and whatever His Word
tells us, constantly renewing our minds in commitment

and submission to the Lord, the result will be obedience, or what the Scripture often refers to as righteousness. This is what glorifies God—living in a right relationship with Him, doing His will, conforming to a righteous, holy lifestyle. It is a life that fulfills the law of God but not because of our own efforts and ability; it is because we are in submission to God, appropriating the life of Christ and being led of His Spirit.

We need to come back to 1 John 3:7–8 to reinforce the importance of how we attain a righteous life and live in obedience. "Let no one deceive you! The one who does what is right is righteous, just as He [God] is righteous. The one who commits sin is of the Devil, for the Devil has sinned from the beginning. The Son of God was revealed for this purpose: to destroy the Devil's works." There is no excuse for continuing to live in sin by indulging in self-centered gratifications that are contrary to the holiness and will of God when we are renewing the mind and have come into a position of submission to Him that makes us righteous.

First John 5:18 is an awesome promise, assuring us we have been given victory over the devil. We can recognize and resist his deception that would lead us to yield to lusts of the flesh and to embrace the ways of the world. "We know that everyone who has been born of God does not sin, but the One who is born of God keeps him, and the evil one does not touch him." We have learned about Satan's nature and character, his deviousness, and the way he works to defeat us. But God's Word says that if we're born of God he cannot touch us. He has no claim, no power, no right to our lives whatsoever. For him to do so means we are accepting his lies and giving him a power he doesn't have.

We know the difference between what is of God and is pleasing to Him and what is not. We should readily recognize that those things that do not honor and glorify Him come from our enemy. The Holy Spirit lives within us; He leads us and convicts us. It is not simply a matter of doing what is right or wrong. It's a matter of being led of the Spirit. The problem is that many believers want to start with obedience. We know what God expects of us and constantly struggle to do what is right and avoid doing what is wrong. That is where many of our discipleship efforts begin—training, learning, studying how to be an obedient Christian and to live a righteous life. But seeking to be obedient in our own effort will be futile. Obedience must begin with a foundation of faith, believing and accepting the truth and promises of the Word of God. Then there must be a continuing commitment to renew our minds and bring our perceptions into alignment with that truth. Such renewal will remind us of our own helplessness and inadequacy. The victory comes in submission to the lordship of Jesus Christ.

Many find the victory elusive and efforts to live an obedient Christian life a failure because they have not built their efforts on a foundation of faith, renewal of the mind, and commitment to be led of the Spirit. Paul observed this problem in the lives of the believers in Galatia. "You foolish Galatians! Who has hypnotized you?" (Some translations use the word "bewitched." Does that sound like something Satan might do?) "I only want to learn this from you: Did you receive the Spirit by the works of the law or by hearing with faith" (Gal. 3:1–2)? The answer is obvious. They had received the Spirit—a new life in Christ—by faith, not by their own works or the law. He goes on in verse 3, "Are you so foolish? After beginning with the Spirit, are you now going to be made complete by the flesh?"

This is one of Satan's most effective deceptions. Yes, we are saved. We have been born again by faith alone, trusting the grace of God in receiving Jesus Christ. But now we try to live the Christian life through our own efforts and in the flesh, rather than realizing an obedient and righteous life is also one that comes through faith by the grace of God. Like the Galatians we are foolish to strive to gain the victory in our own ability. Has Satan not bewitched us to believe becoming a Christian is by faith, but living a Christian life is by our own works? We resist the devil and his deceptive thoughts only by submitting to God. God-glorifying obedience comes from Him, not through our own efforts.

Obedience
Commitment
Renewing the Mind
Faith

Perhaps it has occurred to someone that throughout this material we have yet to make other than a passing reference to Ephesians 6:10 and following. Most students of the Bible would identify this passage, which speaks of putting on the armor of God, as the one with which they are most familiar on spiritual warfare. It tells us to claim the victory by standing firm, resisting the devil, and putting on the protective armor that God has provided us. It has been used prominently in teaching and preaching on the subject.

"Finally be strengthened by the Lord and by His vast strength. Put on the full armor of God so that you can stand against the tactics of the Devil. For our battle is not against flesh and blood, but against the rulers, against the authorities, against the world powers of this darkness, against the spiritual forces of evil in the heavens. This is why you must take up the full armor of God, so that you may be able to resist in the evil day, and having prepared everything, to take your stand" (Eph. 6:10–13).

When we lived in Singapore, the little church where we were members was planning a church retreat and asked if I would be available to lead the Bible studies. This was at a time when God was revealing to me many of these insights from Scripture. I suggested that I would like to focus the Bible study on a series of lessons on spiritual warfare. The committee agreed that would be a good topic and picked up on the idea. The discussion developed around having an artist in the church paint a backdrop with a Roman soldier in armor and then organizing the theme of each session around a part of the armor. I became uneasy because I had not planned to use this passage as the focus of my presentations.

This incident stimulated a desire to discover why I did not find this passage particularly helpful or the key to claiming the victory in the spiritual warfare that constantly rages in our lives. I had preached on the armor of God; it makes a natural outline. I think I fully understood the rationale for these specific implements of protection against Satan's attacks. Why had it not given me any answers or satisfactorily enabled me to claim the victory? I prayed about it and devoted myself to studying the passage more intensely. I came to the conclusion that the reason it did not represent the key to victory for me was because putting on that armor, and each aspect of it, was something I had to do. I had to put on the belt of truth. I had to put on the breastplate of righteousness. I had to take the sword of the Spirit and so forth. Yes, God had made the elements of victory available, but it was back to my own efforts, my own struggle—the struggle to keep the armor on and consciously to put it on every day. I just wasn't adequate for that, so this passage did not give me a real key to the help I needed.

I continued to study the passage, believing there was something about it that I was missing. A unique insight emerged as I was attempting to analyze the grammar. When we are told to put on the armor of God, it is in the genitive case, which commonly is used for the possessive form of a noun. We understand it as saying we are to put on the armor that belongs to God. It is God's armor, something that He possesses but has made available to us. That is an appropriate translation and the way we have traditionally understood "the armor of God."

However, grammatically there is one other use of the genitive case; it is also used in apposition. For example, if this verse had said, "Put on the armor of steel," steel doesn't possess the armor, but steel and armor are in apposition. They are one and the same. Could the Scriptures imply that God Himself is the armor? We are encouraged to put on something that is alien to our nature; it belongs to God, and we've got to figure out how to put on each implement in order to be protected from our enemy. It seemed that being protected by the armor was back to my own effort. But God Himself is the armor. We are to put Him on as our protection. Throughout the New Testament we are told to "put on the Lord Jesus Christ," "to be clothed in Christ";

time and time again the Bible refers to Christians as "being in Christ."

Yes, the belt of truth, the breastplate of righteousness, and other aspects of the armor are God's; and they are made available to us by God. They assure us of victory in standing firm, armed for defense against our enemy, if we heed the admonition to put them on. God does make available all the implements and weapons of warfare we need for overcoming Satan's tactics, but the ability and will to put on the full armor of God is contingent on our position in Christ.

The Victory Is Our Position in Christ

Christ was the One who defeated Satan on the cross and rendered him powerless. We can appropriate the victory, not in our own strength and efforts but because we are in Him. We put on the armor, which is God, and we're clothed in Christ when we die to self. He is always with us. I don't put on the implements of the armor each day through my own efforts lest I become vulnerable to Satan's attacks. Yes, we need salvation, righteousness, truth, peace, and the Word of God; but when we put on Jesus Christ by faith, God becomes our refuge, our shield, our strong tower to enable us to stand secure in victory.

Note what we have if God is our armor:

- We have the belt of truth that quenches all the lies of Satan. Jesus said in John 8:32, "You will know the truth, and the truth will set you free."
- In God, we have the breastplate of righteousness; that's not our righteousness but His. "He made the One who did not know sin to be sin for us, so that we

might become the righteousness of God in Him"
(2 Cor. 5:21).

- Our feet are shod with the preparation of the gospel
of peace. "How welcome are the feet of those who
announce the gospel of good things" (Rom. 10:15). The
power of God's Spirit compels us to be His witnesses
proclaiming the gospel even to the ends of the earth.
That good news is that man can have peace with God.

- We have the shield of faith when we put on God. He's
the One who gives the faith to quench Satan's darts.
"This is the victory that has conquered the world: our
faith" (1 John 5:4). But that faith comes from God; it
is His faith. Ephesians 2:8 says, "For by grace you are
saved through faith, and this is not from yourselves; it
is God's gift."

- Only in God do we have the helmet of salvation, which
is our security. We cannot put on salvation and be
saved apart from Him. But in Him and His salvation,
Satan cannot create doubts and speculations in our
minds that discount the truth of God's Word and
threaten the security of our salvation.

- God is feeding our mind with His Word—the sword
of the Spirit—when we are in Him. He leads us to
claim His promises, following the example of Jesus in
appropriately using and claiming the truth of God's
Word rather than Satan's twisted distortions that would
confuse and defeat us.

The victory begins with a foundation of faith. It proceeds
to a renewing of the mind to see reality through the truth
of God's Word and choosing to believe what God says and
has promised. That process is a constant renewing of one's

commitment to God, the truth of His Word, and submission to the lordship of Christ, resulting in a life of obedience or righteousness in word and deed—being led of the Spirit. However, the ultimate victory that follows is actually our position of being in Christ. He is the One who conquered Satan and has given us all authority over him and his wickedness. Christ is our armor and protection; He is our security against Satan's temptation and deceit. It's not what we do to resist temptation, to walk in obedience, to be empowered by the Holy Spirit and overcome Satan. I cannot be expected to stand firm against an unseen enemy who works in darkness and anonymity, but in Christ I can claim the victory.

In Christ

Obedience

Commitment

Renewing the Mind

Faith

The only way we can avoid stumbling and yielding to sin is to be in Christ. The only way we can be considered righteous and can stand blameless before God is for our life to be hidden in Him each day. The only way God will be glorified and we can experience all the blessings and joy intended for us is through Him. Jude expressed it clearly in verses 24 and 25 of his little one-chapter book, "Now to Him who is able to protect you from stumbling and to make you stand in the presence of His glory, blameless and with great joy, to the only God our Savior, through Jesus Christ our Lord, be glory, majesty, power, and authority, before all time, now, and forever. Amen."

The diagram and relationship between the various components of victory may provide some helpful insight, but how do we appropriate it and make it a practical reality in our lives? A helpful clue is given at the conclusion of the passage on the armor of God: "With every prayer and request, pray at all times in the Spirit, and stay alert in this, with all perseverance and intercession for all saints" (Eph. 6:18). Prayer is communion and fellowship with God. This may be more important than all the elements of the armor collectively. The key to maintaining an awareness of His presence is prayer. "Pray constantly" (1 Thess. 5:17) is not vocalizing and chanting prayers nonstop. Neither is it expecting a morning devotional time to sustain us through the day in the spiritual battles of life. It is a relationship in which we are able to yield to Him the temptations and challenges we encounter, confident He will bear them. But more than that, it is a heart receptive to His guidance and sensitive to convicting reminders when we tend to go astray.

> *Praying at all times in the Spirit assures the armor is in place and the victory is secure.*

When we arrived as missionaries in Indonesia, one of our colleagues told us about a practice that we soon adopted as well. He said: "I have always had a regular time of prayer in the morning. Our family always prays at mealtime. There are other times of prayer as well, such as when I'm sharing with someone and there is something we need to pray about. But I realized that I needed something that would more consistently turn my thoughts to God; I sensed most of my activities and interests, even in my missionary role, distracted me from a conscious awareness of God." He didn't use the terminology, but what he was expressing was the need for a pattern of prayer that would facilitate renewing his mind to focus on God's presence, His will, and resubmitting to Him. This was in Indonesia, a Muslim country, and he went on to explain, "It occurred to me that every time Muslims hear the call to prayer they stop and pray. Why couldn't I do that? Why isn't my devotion equal to theirs? Now it is just a routine or a ritual for them; they don't know God or really gain anything by it. But every time I hear the call to prayer, whatever I'm doing, I just stop for a few moments and pray." When we first arrived in the country, the call to prayer from the Muslim minarets that echoed throughout the city was an irritation, especially at 4:30 a.m.! But it began to remind us to turn to the Lord, to appropriate His presence, to pray for the Muslims and the people of the world, and praise Him that we could know Him personally.

I was impressed by the example of another missionary colleague, almost to the point of amusement. Nothing happened in his life that did not become a focus of prayer. When he met us at the airport, he welcomed us and immediately suggested we bow our heads to thank God for our safe flight. As we were driving to his house, he wanted to drop by a church that had just been started. We got out at this little house and stood on the porch as he led us in prayer, praising God for the congregation and this place of worship. When we got to his house, we had no more set down our suitcases in the foyer when he grabbed our hands and said, "We want to pray and just thank God for your being with us and for how He is going to bless your visit." Later as we were driving down the highway, he pulled over to the side of the road and stopped in the middle of nowhere. I asked, "What's wrong? Why are we stopping here?" He replied, "The odometer just turned over another ten thousand miles. And every time that happens, it reminds me to stop and thank God for our automobile and for the Lottie Moon Christmas Offering and people who give to make our car available to us." Everything in his life and daily routine seemed to be a trigger to pray.

I once heard a friend who ran marathons say that he had radically improved his performance by stopping and walking periodically. Every five miles he would interrupt his pace to walk for five minutes rather than pushing himself to run and keep the pace for the entire race. That respite gave rest and new energy to his legs and fresh wind in his lungs, and he could press forward at a faster, more consistent pace than he would have been able to do had he not rested, especially in the latter stages of the race. I met a young missionary who seemed to have a high level of confidence and vibrant spirit in spite of living and working in a challenging environment. He explained that during college and seminary, he normally had fifty-minute classes with a ten-minute break in between. He had developed a habit of stopping his work wherever he was and whatever he was doing ten minutes before each hour to talk to the Lord, seek His guidance, and perhaps practice a verse of Scripture he was memorizing. He explained that it helped him to have a constant sense of God's presence and, whether or not it increased his productivity, it definitely gave him a positive attitude and joyful demeanor throughout the day.

The Scripture says, "Pray at all times in the Spirit" (Eph. 6:18). Some extrapolate this to conform to their doctrinal presupposition to believe that praying in the spirit is praying in unknown tongues as a sign of the baptism of the Spirit. However, we have seen the critical importance of being led of the Spirit, walking in the Spirit, being filled or controlled by the Spirit in all our actions, attitudes, and behavior. Does not the Holy Spirit also desire to lead our praying as well? How else can we assuredly pray according to God's will? First Corinthians 2:11 tells us, "No one knows the concerns of God except the Spirit of God." And when our words are not adequate, and we "do not know what to pray for as we should," Romans 8:26 goes on to explain, "the Spirit Himself intercedes for us with unspoken groanings." Walking in the Spirit would obviously be the key to praying at all times; our daily walk would be constant communion with the Father through the ministry of His Holy Spirit within us.

All over the world phenomenal growth is taking place in many churches and mission organizations. They tend to be independent rather than denominational and would often be identified as charismatic or Pentecostal, though there also are Baptists and traditional denominational churches that are blessed with an outpouring of God's Spirit, even in some resistant cultures. Just about everywhere, there is a group or church drawing in massive crowds and reaching people in a life-changing experience. It is typical on the part of other churches to disregard it as something that is charismatic. The implication is that it is a shallow appeal based on the perversion of biblical truth, an overemphasis on spiritual gifts and emotionalism without substance. But one has to be impressed that these churches include people out of pagan, non-Christian backgrounds, whom others are not successfully reaching with the gospel. These new believers have turned their backs on their culture and religious traditions and are devotedly worshipping and praising the Lord Jesus Christ. That cannot be ignored and brushed off as mere emotionalism.

I began to engage in an informal survey of these groups wherever I observed something happening and excited growth taking place in areas where I served overseas. I visited with the pastor or the missionary and occasionally attended a worship service. Not all of them were charismatic; in fact, some were Baptists. While some did practice spiritual gifts in a way that did not appear to be scriptural, that was not a prominent emphasis in most of these groups. I found three common threads in every situation where significant growth was taking place, even in unlikely resistant cultures.

First, I found these were people who had a passion and zeal for sharing Jesus Christ. Discretion wasn't in their vocabulary. They had a life-changing experience in coming to know Jesus Christ; they realized people around them were lost, and there was a zeal and passion about Jesus and sharing Him with others.

Second, they had a faith that really expected God to work. There were occasional reports of healing. But if someone needed a job or deliverance from oppression—whatever the need—they prayed and fully believed and expected God would work in response to their prayers. They exhibited a bold faith that was evident in practical ways, even what some might identify as signs and wonders.

The third common factor was a devotion to prayer. There was a pattern of early morning prayer meetings and times of all-night prayer and fasting. The worship service would be characterized by frequent and extended times of praying. My thoughts in response to this, admittedly, subjective survey were that none of these common elements were contrary to who we are and what we believe. Yet how often do we see such a passion for prayer, such a bold faith and zealous witness?

We have highlighted some practical disciplines that are helpful in claiming the victory in spiritual warfare. Devotion to Bible study is what builds our faith as a foundation for victory. Prayer keeps us connected to Christ and allows the Holy Spirit to lead us. Praising the Lord in all things renews our mind and changes our perspective, especially in times of adversity, and deters Satan from using these situations to discourage and defeat us. Fasting is the intentional denial of the flesh out of desire to know God in His fullness and experience His blessings and power that help us overcome the subtle, self-centered nature of the flesh. Body life within a Christian fellowship strengthens us through mutual accountability and provides the support and encouragement we all need to remain faithful and avoid succumbing to worldly influences.

Yet another practical element from God's Word is often neglected and needs to be brought to our awareness before we bring closure to the matter of gaining the ultimate victory.

When I was serving as area director for South and Southeast Asia, I often had extended times of travel. I was coordinating our work in India while living in Bangkok as well as relating to almost five hundred missionaries in fifteen countries. I would try to limit travel circuits to ten days or two weeks as a maximum time to be away from my family.

But often other situations would arise, and I would find the need to add additional stops to my itinerary, expanding the trip. As Bobbye looked over my itinerary, she would often ask the question, "Jerry, where is your Sabbath?" There wasn't a gap in my scheduled meetings and visits with our personnel as I tried to cover as much territory in as short a time frame as possible. Sundays were certainly not a restful Sabbath, even though I engaged in numerous worship experiences, as they were usually the busiest day of the week. My wife had traveled with me frequently and knew me well enough to know that if I didn't have some alone time for refreshing, my productivity, sensitivity, patience, and wisdom in dealing with problems and advising missionaries quickly diminished. So she would ask, "When is your Sabbath?"

The command to the children of Israel to observe the Sabbath was prominent in the Old Testament. Look at what the Bible says about this in Exodus 31, beginning in verse 12:

> The LORD said to Moses, "Tell the Israelites:
> You must observe My Sabbaths, for it is a sign
> between Me and you throughout your generations,
> so that you will know that I am the LORD who sets
> you apart. Observe the Sabbath, for it is holy to
> you. Whoever profanes it must be put to death. If
> anyone does work on it, that person must be cut off
> from his people. For six days work may be done,
> but on the seventh day there must be a Sabbath
> of complete rest, dedicated to the LORD. Anyone
> who does work on the Sabbath day must be put to
> death. The Israelites must observe the Sabbath,

celebrating it throughout their generations as a perpetual covenant. It is a sign forever between Me and the Israelites." (Exod. 31:12–17)

What does God say is the purpose of the Sabbath? The issue has been totally diverted in our society to focus on what is considered appropriate or inappropriate activity on Sunday. Can one go to ball games, eat out in restaurants, do shopping on the Lord's Day? I wonder if Satan has had anything to do with distorting what it's all about in order to contribute to our defeat in the Christian life. The Old Testament law defined what one could do on the Sabbath, but it was embellished and distorted by pharisaical legalism. What we can and cannot do is really not the point. God set aside the Sabbath as a sign of a relationship with Him. It is to signify a covenant relationship in which we recognize that He is the one who sanctifies us! We want to live a holy life and walk in victory, but we can't do it ourselves. The Sabbath is to be a reminder that God is the one who makes us holy. In fact, God said that acknowledging this covenant relationship was so important to Him that it was better for a person to die rather than profane the Sabbath. Who do you think has distorted our whole perspective and understanding about that Sabbath covenant

> *Obedience in observing a Sabbath is a key to living a holy, sanctified life.*

and our need for it? Our enemy doesn't want us to appropriate the sanctification God provides and to walk in victory.

When I first came into my current position, I had been overseas for twenty-three years and had little preparation and training for leading a global mission organization like the International Mission Board. Reports and other reading accumulated until it overflowed my desk, and I had to stack it on the floor. E-mail messages multiplied as I processed them to the point it was impossible to clear out my in-box between meetings and other responsibilities. Meetings and staff consultation filled every day; the phone messages, letters needing response, and writing assignments were prolific. I had not consistently preached in my role on the field but found myself having to prepare messages for up to a dozen speaking engagements, internally and externally, each week. My workday, including constant travel, was typically fifteen hours long, seven days a week. I was totally overwhelmed by the time-consuming demands of all the responsibilities and tasks. Maintaining my consistent time with the Lord each morning apparently provided the grace to survive, but my schedule definitely deprived me of an opportunity for spiritual refreshing that was desperately needed. There was absolutely no margin, no time to prepare messages and get all the tasks done.

God brought to my mind an experience that occurred years ago when we were in Indonesia. We had found a significant response among the Chinese. They were the storekeepers, the commercial segment of society, and represented a significant population group. They weren't generally characterized by fervent religious devotion like the Muslim majority. We found a spiritual openness and response to our witness among them. But I did not have much success in convincing them to close their store or business on Sunday in order to go to church. Now that was another issue. I told them, and sincerely believed, that if they would close their store on Sunday to worship and honor the Lord, God would bless and prosper them more in six days than He would in keeping their business going seven days.

It was interesting that God would bring that to my mind as I struggled with a demanding 24-7 schedule of work and responsibilities, wondering where I could find the time to meet the Lord and to prepare messages for inspiration and challenge. God convicted me that if I would set aside a Sabbath to spend with Him and in His Word, in which I would put my normal work aside, that He would be my sufficiency. I'm often with other people, traveling on Sunday, filling speaking engagements, but I put aside the things that are normal to my six-day workweek that didn't fit with a focus on the Lord. The Jewish Sabbath started on sundown the day before, and I discovered a day of meaningful worship on Sunday begins with preparing one's focus on the Lord on Saturday evening. One cannot get up on Sunday morning suddenly conscious of God's presence if the previous evening has been filled with worldly entertainment.

Coming back from a weekend engagement on Sunday afternoon, I often think of all the e-mails that have accumulated, my schedule and obligations for the next week, and am tempted to get out my computer and get a head start on Monday morning. Invariably the Lord checks my spirit and directs me to get my Bible or focus on a message that needs to be prepared. In fact, I have told my staff to confront me and hold me accountable if they get an e-mail from me dated on Sunday. It's amazing how God blesses our devotion to obey Him and acknowledge our need of Him because He is the One who sanctifies us. He knows what we need. He knows the stress that we are going to encounter. He knows the pressure and demands of our job. He created us and knows the fatigue and the struggles we face, how they make us vulnerable to temptations and anxieties and defeat. And He has provided a solution if we would just recognize it, honor it, and practice it.

God said, "You and I have a covenant relationship that I expect you to acknowledge by setting aside a day when you cease from other activities to focus on Me and our relationship; it is essential if I am to provide you with a sanctified life." It wasn't just relevant in the Old Testament or for the Jews, but it was to be a perpetual covenant forever with His people. We are, spiritually, the children of Abraham, God's people. And that's what the Sabbath is all about. It's not a legalistic requirement about what we do or don't do on Sunday. It is a key that He has given us for walking in victory, constantly aware that we are in Christ and walking with God. Our Sabbath may not be on a Saturday or Sunday due to work schedules and other factors; it may not even be once in every seven days that we can observe a Sabbath. But how can we expect Him to empower us and bless us and manifest His presence in constantly providing all that we need to overcome Satan when we care so little about our relationship with Him that we don't even observe the Sabbath as He has told us to do. We have repeatedly mentioned that the key to victory in spiritual warfare is for God to be the desire of our heart and to know God in all His fullness. Observing a Sabbath rest is another practical, biblical discipline that reflects one's heart for God.

As we move toward a conclusion in claiming the ultimate victory in the daily battle of spiritual warfare, there is one other element that we need to understand and add to our diagram. The victory begins with a foundation of faith in believing God and renewing our mind in submission to God and His truth, which changes our perception and diminishes our

Practical Disciplines in Claiming the Victory

- *Feeding on God's Word*
- *Praying at all times*
- *Praising the Lord in all things*
- *Denying the flesh in fasting*
- *Being accountable to others*
- *Observing a Sabbath*

vulnerability to Satan's deception and influence. Commitment to God and the lordship of Jesus Christ brings our lives into obedience to God's righteousness because we are then led and empowered by His Spirit. This affirms our position in Christ and allows Him to provide all that He has promised in blessing, power, and victory rather than in our futilely trying to claim the victory through our own efforts.

Finally, how does the Bible sum up obedience, righteousness, and fulfilling the law? It's in one word, as we saw in Galatians 5:13, *love*. Love is others centered. It's an antidote to Satan's attacks because it is the antithesis of the self-centered nature of the flesh. Satan uses that self-centered flesh of our old nature so effectively to entice us to respond to temptation that leads to sin. Love is also the ultimate step of victory because it emanates from God Himself. "Dear friends, let us love one another, because love is from God, and everyone who loves has been born of God and knows God" (1 John 4:7). We do not have the capacity to love and focus on others rather than ourselves apart from a commitment to God and knowing Him. Walking in the Spirit will be manifested in giving of ourselves in self-denial, or love for others, and devotion to God.

Paul speaks of spiritual warfare in 1 Corinthians 16:13–14, saying, "Be alert, stand firm in the faith, be brave and strong. Your every action must be done with love."

While the diagram below does not imply sequential steps as a formula to victory, it reflects the relationship between the elements of victory. Love is the ultimate expression of victory in spiritual warfare because Satan does not understand love. He is not capable of comprehending those who would give themselves to another and be more concerned for someone else than for themselves. The weapons of his warfare—unforgiveness, anger, pride, temptation to self-serving motives, and sinful gratification—all come from focusing on self. The strength of his strategies to defeat us all comes from his own self-centered nature. He cannot comprehend why anyone would give of himself. He is so self-centered and limited in his understanding that the concept of love is foreign to him. Satan thought he had won when Jesus was nailed to the cross, but he was totally deluded and defeated. He, and all his strategies, are completely disarmed by someone who is not self-centered but is willing to give of his or her life in love for others. One reason for this is the fact that love makes possible the phenomenon of sacrifice, rather than living for self, giving of one's life for others and for a lost world.

LOVE/Sacrifice

In Christ

Obedience

Commitment

Renewing the Mind

Faith

You may remember a few years ago when Dana Curry and Heather Mercer were imprisoned by the Taliban in Afghanistan; they were arrested for showing the *Jesus* film and threatened with the death penalty for proselytizing. The prospects for a resolution and their release were not looking hopeful as they went to trial. These young ladies had been in prison for several months, and they knew the severity of what they were facing. During this time their church issued a press release, excerpting a letter from them. Heather wrote of living in total abandonment for the Lord. She said, "I'm learning every day what it means to love the Lord your God with all your heart, mind, soul, and strength. It is my desire that I would lay down whatever is to my profit and consider it loss for the sake of Christ. I'm learning what it means to be satisfied in the presence of Jesus Christ alone and to offer my life as a living sacrifice for Him." What can Satan do with that? When one comes to the point of total abandonment of one's own life, what does Satan have to get hold of? He can't appeal to our selfish instincts. There is no love of the flesh and carnal appetites with which he can entice us.

No fiery dart of Satan counters the kind of commitment and personal abandonment that comes from a love for Jesus. Romans 12:1 speaks of the kind of selfless love expected of believers: "Therefore, brothers, by the mercies of God, I urge you to present your bodies [your lives] as a living sacrifice." Jesus said, "If anyone wants to come with Me, he must deny himself, take up his cross, and follow Me" (Matt. 16:24). The outcome and expression of love is sacrifice. Is there anything that we are not willing to give up, that we haven't yielded and placed on the altar? Is there anything we are holding on to for our own pleasure, comfort, enjoyment, and gratification that we would not be willing to sacrifice? Are any conditions placed on our love for Christ and for a lost world? I think most Christians realize that God calls us to total commitment and would affirm that they are willing to die for Christ. But we are unwilling to die for Him each day through self-denial. Most would glibly affirm that they would not intentionally deny Christ and would even die for Him because it is not likely we would ever be confronted with the real possibility of martyrdom. But love compels us to a life of self-denial. Revelation 2:10 says, "Be faithful until death, and I will give you the crown of life."

Look at how Revelation 12:10–11 identifies this ultimate weapon in spiritual warfare. It describes that future day when Satan, the accuser, will be finally defeated. "The salvation and the power and the kingdom of our God and the authority of His Messiah have now come, because the accuser of our brothers has been thrown out: the one who accuses them before our God day and night. They conquered him by the blood of the Lamb and by the word of their testimony, for they did not love their lives in the face of death."

In the last days these are those who claimed the victory. It did not come by their struggle and efforts but by the blood of the Lamb. The victory was provided when Jesus Christ died on the cross, defeated Satan, and gave us all authority over the evil one. But it also came by the word of their testimony—the confession of their faith, believing God and His Word. They did not waver even in the midst of persecution, trials, and adversity, but staked their life on what God had said. The word of their testimony proved that faith was the victory. But finally, they did not love their life, even unto death. There was no way for Satan to get to them. How could he tempt them? How could he distract them and create doubt when they were not living for self? How could the things of the world have any attraction to them when they were willing to sacrifice everything, even their lives? Only God's love in Christ makes that possible—loving God with all our heart, mind, strength, and soul enables us to love others, a lost world, and to give ourselves completely.

Only love will give us a desire to go all the way in a life of sacrifice. If we draw a line anywhere short of a willingness to die, Satan will take our limited commitment and play havoc with our lives by appealing to those affections, emotions, and self-centered will. We can claim the victory and be set free from any fear, from conflict and dissension, and from any selfish gratification that would lead us to sin, but only when we take up our cross and die. We have been called to present our bodies a living sacrifice. God has given us the privilege of living and serving Him, but the victorious, holy life that glorifies Him will not come without dying.

What we are saying is the theme of a song by Steve Green—"Enter In." The lyrics graphically portray the victory that comes only through sacrifice and dying to self.

Nothing chills the heart of man like passing through death's gates.
But to him who enters daily, death is a glorious fate.
Dear beloved we are gathered here to be His Holy Bride,
To daily cross death's threshold to the holy life inside.

Enter in, enter in, surrender to the Spirit's call to die and enter in.
Enter in, find peace within, the holy life awaits you, enter in.

The battle still continues, raging deep within my soul.
The spirit wars against my flesh in a struggle for control.

My only hope is full surrender, so with each borrowed breath
I inhale the Spirit's will for me to die a deeper death.

If mourners should lament, then let them weep for those alive.
For only when self-will is killed can my soul survive.
Enter in, enter in, surrender to the Spirit's call to die and enter in.

Enter in, find peace within;
The holy life awaits you, abundant life is waiting for you, enter in.[1]

In February 2003, I was speaking at the annual meeting of all of our IMB personnel serving in East Asia. This was right after the tragic murder of three of our missionaries in Yemen. Following memorial services in the States, I had gone to Yemen to be with our personnel and international staff there. It had been one of the most difficult times I had ever experienced as we sought to minister to families and colleagues and explain to a skeptical public why missionaries would go to dangerous places. After walking through the clinic and reliving every detail of that fateful morning, seeing the bullet marks and blood stains that were still there, we then walked up the hill behind the hospital to the grave where two of the victims, Bill Koehn and Martha Myers, had been buried. I was overcome with emotion and knelt there weeping uncontrollably.

Now at the gathering in East Asia, I had been hearing testimonies of how God was moving in a powerful way throughout China. House-church networks were exploding with growth in spite of persecution, restrictions, and harassment. I heard testimonies of pastors who had been imprisoned, beaten, and martyred, yet masses of people continued to respond to the gospel and come to Christ. I was

also impressed with the dedication and passionate commitment of these young families to reach the peoples of East
Asia for Christ. I related the recent incident of the death of
their colleagues in Yemen and the confidence that through
the testimony of their life and death that the church would
be planted. It had been said several times that they didn't
die when that gunman took their lives in the Jibla Baptist
Hospital clinic, for he could not take from them what they
had already given. They had already died to self when they
gave their lives to go to Yemen as missionaries. Every time
they got up in the morning and gave their lives to minister
to the people, they had to lay their lives on the altar and
die.

I addressed those in East Asia and had not planned to
say what followed. Spontaneously, out of emotions still
fragile, I said, "I've heard you tell how Chinese believers
and house-church pastors have given their lives for the sake
of Christ. You have given testimonies of how the church is
being planted among people groups and cities because of
the sacrifice and suffering of believers. I've heard the passion of your testimony and your call. What if God should
choose for your people group and city to come to the Lord,
but the cost would be, not a local pastor or believer, but
like those in Yemen, the gospel would take root and God's
kingdom extended because of your blood and at the cost of
your life. Are you willing for that to happen in order for
your people, a lost world, to know Him?" I continued, "If
you're willing to give your life, even to the point of death,
for the sake of the salvation of the multitudes in this region
of the world, I want you to stand."

I expected a handful of people to stand; and, once they
had done so, a few others would follow their example and

join them. I was overwhelmed as most of the people in that massive auditorium instantly stood. They understood. They had already dealt with the cost of following Christ in obedience. They knew the risk and danger, but the love of Christ for a lost world compelled them to give their lives. That's the victory. When one does not love his own life, even unto death, Satan is disarmed and rendered powerless. He cannot entice us to indulge the selfish gratifications of the world and the flesh. They overcame him because they loved not their life even unto death.

> *"My call is to obedience. Suffering is expected; His glory is my reward!"*

Others have lost their lives serving the Lord overseas. One of those martyred among four personnel killed in Iraq on March 15, 2004, was Karen Watson from Bakersfield, California. Karen had seen the destruction and warfare we all watched on television newscasts; but as she saw the despair, chaos, and hopelessness, she realized the real answer was Jesus Christ. Her heart was burdened and stirred to realize these people would never know Jesus unless someone was willing to go to love them, minister to their needs, and share with them the hope that could only be found in Jesus.

A year earlier she had resigned her job, sold her house and car, and given away most of her belongings. She packed what was left in a duffel bag and left for Iraq to be a part of a team seeking channels of ministry in that war-torn country. Knowing the risk and danger, she had written a letter and left it in a sealed envelope to be read if something happened to her and she did not return. When the church received news of Karen's tragic death, the pastor recalled having put her letter in a file. He retrieved it, opened it, and read a two-page, handwritten letter that began, "If you are reading this letter, it means I won't be coming home to Bakersfield, for I am with Jesus!" Then in large, capital letters she wrote across the page, "THERE ARE NO REGRETS!" She proceeded to say, "My call is to obedience. Suffering is expected; His glory is my reward." And she wrote again, "His glory is my reward."

God's desire and purpose are to be glorified in each of our lives. Satan is doing all that he can to deprive God of His glory. He tempts us to sin and live for self. He creates doubts and defeats us with deceptive truths that contradict the promises of God's Word. He leads us to live compromised lives, influenced by the materialism and the carnal values of the world around us. But God has given us the victory. Our call is to walk in obedience to His holiness, being led of His Spirit. We are to recognize that conflict with the world and self-interest will entail suffering. But to die to self and give our lives, sacrificing everything in terms of comfort and self-serving gratification out of the love Christ brings to our heart, results in a life of victory in which God will be glorified.

Notes

Chapter 1

1. Jack R. Taylor, *Victory over the Devil* (Nashville, TN: Broadman Press, 1973), 5.

Chapter 2

1. Beth Moore, *When Godly People Do Ungodly Things* (Nashville, TN: B&H Publishing Group, 2002), 20.

Chapter 7

1. C. S. Lewis, *The Screwtape Letters* (Uhrichsville, OH: Barbour Publishing, 1990), 29.

2. Ibid.,58.

Chapter 8

1. "Open the Eyes of My Heart, Lord," Words and music by Paul Baloche, © 1997 Integrity's Hosanna! Music/ASCAP, c/o Integrity Media, Inc., 1000 Cody Road, Mobile, AL 36695. All Rights Reserved. International Copyright Secured. Used by Permission.

2. Ken Anderson, *Bold as a Lamb* (Grand Rapids, MI: Zondervan, 1991), 16

Chapter 9

1. C. S. Lewis, *The Screwtape Letters* (Uhrichsville, OH: Barbour Publishing, 1990), n.p.

2. M. Scott Peck, *The People of the Lie* (Clearwater, FL: Touchstone Books, 1998), 83.

Chapter 10

1. "Enter In" by Greg Nelson, Jon Mohr, and Steve Green. Copyright © 1986 Birdwing Music/Careers BMG Music/Greg Nelson Music/Jonathan Mark Music. All Rights Reserved.

SCRIPTURE INDEX